WITHDRAWN

Current Trends
for the
Developmentally
Disabled

Current Trends for the Developmentally Disabled

Edited by

Margo S. Berkler, Ph.D.

Gary H. Bible, Ph.D.

Shawn M. Boles, Ph.D.

Diane E. D. Deitz, M.Ed.

and

Alan C. Repp, Ph.D.

University Park Press

Baltimore

UNIVERSITY PARK PRESS
233 East Redwood Street
Baltimore, Maryland 21202

Typeset by Action Comp Co., Inc. Manufactured in the United States of America by The Maple Press Company.

This text represents the proceedings of the Atlanta Conference on Current and Future Behavioral Trends for the Developmentally Disabled, held in the spring of 1976. This work was supported by a grant (G00-73-06070) from the Bureau of Education for the Handicapped, U.S. Office of Education, Department of Health, Education, and Welfare, to the Georgia Retardation Center, Atlanta, Georgia. However, the content does not necessarily reflect the position or policy of that agency, and no official endorsement of these materials should be inferred.

Library of Congress Cataloging in Publication Data

Atlanta Conference on Current and Future Behavioral
Trends for the Developmentally Disabled, 1976.
Current trends for the developmentally
disabled.

Bibliography: p.
Includes index.
1. Developmentally disabled—United States—
Congresses.   2.   Developmentally disabled services—
United States—Congresses.   I.   Berkler, Margo S.
II. Title.
HV3006.A3A85   1976   363.2   77-28066

ISBN 0-8391-1215-7

CONTENTS

EDITORS AND CONTRIBUTORS

David A. Begelman, Ph.D.
Department of Psychology
Kirkland College
Clinton, New York 13323

Margo S. Berkler, Ph.D.
Department of Special Education
University of Louisville
Louisville, Kentucky 40208

Gary H. Bible, Ph.D.
Georgia Retardation Center
4770 N. Peachtree Road
Atlanta, Georgia 30341;
and The University of Georgia
Athens, Georgia 30602

Shawn M. Boles, Ph.D.
Center for Social Structure
P.O. Box 5036
Eugene, Oregon 97405

William A. Bricker, Ph.D.
Department of Special Education
Kent State University
Kent, Ohio 44240

Diane E. D. Deitz, M. Ed.
Department of Special Education
Northern Illinois University
DeKalb, Illinois 60115

John H. Hollis, Ed. D.
Bureau of Child Research
10 Bailey Hall
The University of Kansas
Lawrence, Kansas 66045;
and Kansas Neurological Institute
Topeka, Kansas 66604

R. Don Horner, M.S.
Bureau of Child Research
10 Bailey Hall
The University of Kansas
Lawrence, Kansas 66045

Louise R. Kent, Ph.D.
Department of Speech and Theatre
Arts
The University of Pittsburgh
Pittsburgh, Pennsylvania 15261

James R. Lent, Ph.D.
Project MORE & Project CHANGE
George Peabody College for Teachers
Nashville, Tennessee 37203

Reed Martin, J. D.
Project on Law and Behavior
2437-A University Blvd.
Houston, Texas 77005

Alan C. Repp, Ph.D.
Department of Special Education
Northern Illinois University
DeKalb, Illinois 60115

Dennis J. Tucker, M.S.
Bureau of Child Research
10 Bailey Hall
The University of Kansas
Lawrence, Kansas 66045;
and Kansas Neurological Institute
Topeka, Kansas 66604

David B. Wexler, J. D.
College of Law
University of Arizona
Tucson, Arizona 85721

FOREWORD

The past decade has produced so many remarkable changes in the field of developmental disabilities that it is often difficult to keep abreast of all the current developments. Recent court decisions, instructional innovations, and concern about accountability of services have placed new demands on teachers and program administrators that ensure that the status quo will never be the same. There is a need for a publication that undertakes to critically review recent developments in this expanding field. The present book, a collection of essays written by distinguished specialists, is an attempt to meet this need.

The chapters are intended to address the gaps in knowledge facing professionals and students who are or will be involved in implementing programs with this population. Contributors were selected for their expertise in "applied behavior analysis" or empirically based behavioral enhancement approaches. The problem areas that are discussed deal with contemporary legal-ethical and service delivery requirements for developmentally disabled citizens. Accordingly, Section I reviews current legal and ethical challenges, provides a serious critique of the major rights won by the developmentally disabled, and discusses the obstacles to the realization of these rights. Recognizing not only a right to treatment but also a right to effective treatment, Section II presents trends in effective programming and service delivery.

Section I

Legal and Ethical Challenges

EDITORIAL INTRODUCTION

Legal and ethical issues, for example, those raised by the right to treatment and by informed consent, are appearing more and more frequently in the consideration of developmentally disabled individuals. No longer is it sufficient for an individual providing services to the developmentally disabled to be only adequately prepared in programmatic areas (such as those discussed in Section II). The service provider must now be both knowledgeable about the law and aware of the accompanying ethical issues. It is to these ends that the following chapters are directed—to help prepare the service deliverers in all essential legal areas and to stimulate further thought and discussion about the numerous unresolved ethical questions.

In the first chapter, Martin argues for knowledge of the law by all those serving the developmentally disabled. He presents a clear and concise statement of the current rights afforded by the courts and/or legislation and discusses ways in which those delivering services may comply with these rights, including the right to education/treatment, the right to notice, the right to a hearing, the right to the least restrictive alternative, the right to freedom from abuse, and personal and community rights. Martin very adeptly summarizes some of the past, current, and future problems raised by compliance with the full requirements of the law, and he suggests the use of effectiveness measures for all programs as one means of accomplishing our goals of both providing appropriate services to the developmentally disabled *and* protecting and providing them with all of their rights.

RIGHT TO EDUCATION/TREATMENT

Wexler discusses some of the recent court decisions concerning the rights of patients and prisoners. However, his arguments are centered on the recent question of the right to resist treatment. Within this question lies the large issue of legal regulation of behavior modification techniques, both the positive and the potentially offensive means (e.g., token economies and tier systems). Wexler skillfully argues for legal regulation of behavior modification and provides guidelines, such as the Florida Guidelines, for so doing.

Access to Services

Consideration of the legal regulations that relate to the developmentally disabled that are presented by Martin and Wexler has made it apparent that ethical issues are even more numerous than a few years ago. Or, at least, according to Begelman, our awareness of the issues is greater. Begelman breaks down some of the current ethical issues into easily understandable categories, such as determinable versus indeterminable, and raises the issues of preventive and remedial techniques, such as genetic counseling, prenatal screening, abortion, and euthanasia. His discussion of behavior modification, its definition, its regulation, and the ethical issues associated with it, is both enlightening and thought-provoking.

Finally, ethical issues relating specifically to institutional settings are discussed by Repp and Deitz. They emphasize four major ethical issues associated with programs aimed at reducing the responding of institutionalized persons: 1) restrictions produced by institutional life itself, 2) objectives of specific reductive programs, 3) protection of residents subjected to intervention programs, and 4) protection of the rights of persons other than the subject of the reductive program. Repp and Deitz provide insight into the realities of how the legal and ethical challenges presented in this section have been, are, and should be met.

LEGAL REGULATION OF SERVICES TO THE DEVELOPMENTALLY DISABLED

Reed Martin

Recently we have seen a judicial activism in services to the developmentally disabled that is unparalleled in other branches of the law. In the past, most courts simply would not look into the area of mental health care or the treatment of the developmentally disabled. If a client had a problem, if he felt he was not getting adequate services or was being excluded from services altogether, he had to find a solution inside the institution. The courts did not offer a forum and stuck to a judicial policy known as "hands off."

It is important, for two reasons, to know why a change has taken place. First, everyone should understand the substance of the law that now exists and why it is definitely the courts' job to be involved. Second, the arguments that were made to justify hands off, and which have now been rejected, are often made by some professionals to explain why they will never have to answer to a court. If any reader sees his own justifications in this chapter, perhaps he will realize he is on thin ice.

At first, the courts simply would not inquire into the workings of institutions or public programs. Once they did begin to inquire, they still refused to change things because they accepted the argument that mental health decisions were akin to medical decisions, and that they had best be left up to the experts. Courts felt they could not quibble with or second guess "expert" administrators. As they did begin to question the wisdom of some decisions, the courts still deferred because they decided that, even if the decision were poor, it was within the prerogative of the executive branch to make those decisions. Courts felt that if they superimposed their own decisions they would trample over the line that separated the executive branch from the judicial branch. Furthermore, carrying out a judicial decree would mean money would have to be spent differently, but allocation of funds is presumably a legislative function. Worst of all, to intrude into the decision-making sphere in mental health care or in treatment of developmental disabilities would place the courts in the position they have found themselves in with education and desegregation—the courts appear to be taking over the institution and running it on a day-to-day basis. No court appeared ready to go that far.

An important underlying reason that the courts did not act was the assumption that the clients of these services did not have rights of their own. Someone else might come into court on their behalf and argue who should take care of these second-class citizens, but the administrator, the institution, the physician, and all others involved in their care had rights superior to the rights of the clients.

However, suddenly, in a series of cases tied to the Federal Constitution[1], these clients, whether they are mentally ill, developmentally disabled, students, or juveniles, are now finding rights equal to all others. This means that courts have to hear their complaints and act on them. It is to be hoped that things will never be the same again.

In the past few months, the federal government has contributed another important source of law for the developmentally disabled that will ensure that the isolated rights won in hard-fought court battles will be woven together. In 37 states, individual actions had been brought to win rights to education for handicapped children. Now, the Education for All Handicapped Children Act of 1975[2] establishes virtually all the rights won in the landmark cases, starting with *Pennsylvania Association for Retarded Citizens* v. *Commonwealth of Pennsylvania*.[3] The Developmental Disabilities Bill of Rights

---

[1] See *Pennsylvania Association for Retarded Citizens* v. *Pennsylvania*, 334 F. Supp. 1257 (E.D.Pa. 1971); *Mills* v. *Board of Education*, 348 F. Supp. 866 (D.D.C. 1972); *Wyatt* v. *Stickney*, 334 F. Supp. 373, 344 F. Supp. 387 (M.D. ALA. 1972) aff'd *sub nom. Wyatt* v. *Aderholt*, 503 F. 2d. 1305 (5th Cir. 1974); *Morales* v. *Turman*, 383 F. Supp. 53 (E.D. Tex. 1974).

[2] Public Law 94-142.

[3] See footnote 1.

Act of 1975[4] and the Community Mental Health Center Act of 1975[5] extend many of the same substantive as well as procedural rights to the general disabled population.

So the law has changed. However, as I talk to people across the country I still get the reaction, "I don't have legal problems. I don't need to hear what you are saying." What that means, I assume, is that those speaking have not yet been sued. However, professionals do have legal responsibilities to their clients right now, if they are in a position of responsibility in the care of the developmentally disabled, and they have rights as a client or friend of a client, if that is their perspective.

Those professionals in positions of responsibility must know what these rights are. The recent Supreme Court case of *Wood* v. *Strickland*[6] dealt with a school board's failure to observe the constitutional rights of some students. Their defense, as always, was, "We didn't know we were not following the law, and we are immune from prosecution because we were acting in good faith." The Court stated that operating in a position of responsibility in ignorance of the constitutional rights of those in your care is the same as acting with malice, and you therefore lose your immunity. So everyone must know what the rights are of those for whom he cares or else he may find himself open to attack.

The usual response by professionals to this gloomy news is that the courts would never dare look over their shoulders. Wrong. Well, even if they did, the argument goes, they would not understand what is being done in terms of treatment so they would simply have to take the expert's word and accept his judgment. Besides, the argument continues, there is no reason to introduce the law into this relationship; it is not an adversary relationship; the professional is on the same side as the client; they are working together. And, the argument usually concludes, there should be no regulation from an outside agency like the court because the profession regulates itself.

All these arguments have recently proved to be of no avail if a serious complaint is made to a court about the adequacy of services. Clients have rights, and the court is the proper forum for determining what an institution must do to fulfill those rights.

---

[4] Public Law 94-103.

[5] Public Law 94-63.

[6] 95 S. Ct. 992 (1975).

RIGHT TO EDUCATION/TREATMENT
Access to Services

The most basic right, now established in court cases and federal legislation, is the right to receive education or treatment, depending on the need. Clients have a right not to be arbitrarily excluded from public facilities and programs, as the developmentally disabled have been in years past. If the offering of services is a hollow one—i.e., the service is too far from your home, too expensive, impossible to utilize because of architectural barriers—then clients have a valid complaint that the services are not in reality being offered at all.

Fairness in Diagnosis

When clients accept services, they have a further right to adequate and accurate diagnosis and classification and to placement in a program that will help them. Diagnoses have been the subject of much litigation recently. Where there is a physical disability, what is the cause? Is it organic, or a chemical imbalance, or a psychic trauma? The diagnosis must be accurate in order to make sure that services meet the legally mandated standards of adequacy. If there is a mental or emotional disability, how do the professionals diagnose it and determine a likely cause and a likely cure? Often, psychological tests are used that do no good at all. They are often biased against one culture, race, or sex. The conditions under which they are administered are often intolerable, and the interpretation of results is often subject to challenge. By now, everyone knows of the weaknesses of using standardized I.Q. tests to diagnose a mental disability and place a child in a program. Equally troublesome are the projective tests, which often give more information about the tester's interpretations than they do about the client. The law is quite clear—no one diagnostic instrument alone, and certainly not an I.Q. or a projective test alone, will be considered adequate for diagnosis.

Some professionals rely on records in their files. But how valid and reliable are these subjective comments tucked away in file folders? Do they gain credence only because of their cumulative weight? In schools, the recently enacted Family Privacy Act[7] restricts what can be kept in a child's file, and other legislation has forced open files in other types of institutions. The result is that subjective comments cannot be relied upon to diagnose and classify an individual as different from the general class of people and thus in need of

---

[7] Public Law 93-380, action 438.

special services. In addition, they cannot be the source of a diagnosis and prescription of treatment for a client. There must be much more.

The best source for diagnosis and classification is observation by a trained professional. If an individual cannot function adequately while doing something he needs to be able to do, then he should be considered for a program that will help him acquire that needed behavior—no more, no less.

Equal Protection

Once diagnosed as in need of special attention, an individual has a right to equal protection of the law in treatment. In some programs, all the children are Black or Chicano or male. There is a need for a good justification for that situation in case a court inquires about it. A typical problem in schools[8] is that White children with problems are likely to be labeled "learning disabled" (LD) while Black children are more likely to be labeled "educable mentally retarded" (EMR). Worse, the LD child is more likely to get back into the regular classroom some day, while we all know that the EMR child may get placed on a one-way track that takes him out of society's view forever. Therefore, we must take a look at the classification of our programs. Does one class of clients seem to be labeled one way and another class get a different designation? We must pay attention to what happens when a placement is made. Clients have a right, which will be elaborated later, to be in the most normal environment. In school, "normal" means in the mainstream. If the placement is in a program that temporarily takes the client out of the mainstream, remediates some problem, and returns him to the normal environment, that is permissible. However, if all the educationally disabled children are tracked off to alternative schools that are a dead-end and from which they will never return, then the law may well be violated.

Therefore, the right to services means the right to be properly diagnosed, properly placed, and helped. The law has begun to recognize that the only possibility for help is individual treatment. The Developmental Disability Bill of Rights Act,[9] and recent judicial decisions indicate the specificity that must now govern the plan for each individual's treatment.

---

[8] *Exceptional Children,* 1971, 37:537–538.
[9] See footnote 4.

Individual Educational Plans

First, an individual educational (development) plan must be developed and presented in writing. The plan should be developed in a joint conference among a representative of the program responsible for delivering the services, the client, if that is possible and appropriate, and the client's parent, guardian, or other representative.

Second, the plan should include a detailed description of the individual's conditions and needs. These should be concrete, behavioral descriptions and should involve an assessment of physical condition, physical development and motor coordination, self-care competence, language skills, social skills, academic skills, and vocational skills where such assessment is appropriate.

Third, the plan must state long-term treatment goals as well as intermediate treatment objectives. These must be stated specifically, in sequence, and expressed in behavioral terms that provide measurable indices of progress.

Fourth, the plan must state a timetable for the attainment of the overall goals and all the interim goals. The plan must specify the date for the initiation of each step of the program and the anticipated duration of each service.

Fifth, the plan must detail all the services that will be provided, and it must relate each element of the treatment plan to a specific element of the goals statement. This means not only that no goal must be left unmet but also that there should not be overtreatment. If there is medication or some other form of restraint and it is not directly related, in proper sequence, to treatment goals, then it should not be allowed.

Sixth, the plan must detail each agency that will provide each specific step of the treatment services. Within each agency, the actual personnel to be used should be described, along with the qualifications necessary to accomplish the task. We are all familiar with overcrowded facilities either putting individuals in the care of staff who are simply not able to care for them or stating that a person will receive speech therapy when in fact there is not a staff member available with qualifications in speech therapy. This specificity should be a real aid to accountability.

Seventh, the plan should detail how the services can be provided in the normal environment or in that setting which is the least possible deviation from normal.

Eighth, the plan must state objective criteria that will be used for evaluation, an evaluation procedure, and a schedule for determining whether interim objectives and long-term goals are being reached.

Ninth, the entire plan must be periodically reviewed to see if it is working. The client, if appropriate, or his guardian, parent, or other representative, must be given an opportunity to participate in this review.

RIGHT TO NOTICE

When the service provider becomes involved with the client, notice must be given in several steps. First, there should be written notice of what behaviors or conditions will qualify someone to be considered for being placed in a special program. This is helpful to the person trying to get into the program and to avail himself of the special services — he will know exactly what he is entitled to, and, if the services are not forthcoming, he will have something definite to turn to. Equally important to the person whose child is about to be classified as disabled and placed in a special program against his will, the written notice gives the framework for considering who can be placed in such a program.

Second, notice must be given *before* the professional begins to collect data on a person. If an individual wants to get into a program, the notice will allow him to get his information to the right person at the right time. If the individual doesn't want in, he will know to be on the alert that data are being gathered. One case[10] recently suggested that psychological data gathering is similar to a police investigation, because in both cases the individual can end up being deprived of liberty. Thus, this case suggests both that the state must warn you that data are being gathered and that it must give you the fifth amendment right to remain silent. As is often seen in police shows on television, the police must give what is called a "Miranda warning," and perhaps state agencies should begin doing the same thing before gathering data to place someone in a special program. Persons who oppose inclusion in a program should be able to refuse to take tests and to refuse to cooperate without that information being used against them.

Notice must also be given when some action is contemplated with regard to the individual. The action may be a meeting to decide to include him in a special program or to decide to remove him from

---

[10] *McNeil* v. *Director, Patuxent Institution,* 407 U.S. 245 (1972).

a special program and send him back to the normal environment. Either way, the individual has due process rights and must be informed that a decision is about to be made that will affect him.

CONSENT

Once notice is given, consent ought to be forthcoming from all concerned, but there are several potential problems with consent.

First, the person consenting must be competent to do so. In general, it is all right to get the consent of someone who has not been adjudged incompetent by a court, but since they are dealing with the area of developmental disability, and often with children, professionals will be getting consent from others, such as parents or guardians. In that case the law is shifting. A recent case[11] indicated that a parent cannot simply commit a child to a program for the mentally retarded against the wishes of the child when there is no indication that the best interests of the child have been considered. If the child objects, but the parent consents, you should probably proceed to a full hearing on the matter, as detailed later.

If the client is of age or is a "mature minor," his consent should be sought. If diminished competence is assumed, this should be discussed in full with others legitimately concerned, and a note should be present in his file that such a discussion took place.

When the client is incompetent, and consent cannot be secured from anyone else, and the professional feels compelled to proceed, some jurisdictions allow this, if a full hearing is held in which it is determined that the proposed treatment is in the best interests of the individual and is the least restrictive approach available.

Assuming competence, consent must also be voluntarily given in order to be adequate. The problem often confronted here is the institutional coercion built into many contacts between state agencies and individual clients. The client wants help; the practitioner says he strongly recommends that the child be placed in this particular program; the parents are afraid that if they do not agree it will irritate the staff and their child may get less treatment than otherwise, so they agree. It is hard to draw the line between the subtle coercion that will always follow a professional's strong advice and more obvious coercion, such as a school's saying, "If you don't agree to place your child in this program we will expel him." However, if there is a

---

[11] *Bartley* v. *Kremens*, 402 F. Supp. 1039 (E. D. Pa. 1975).

complaint later, the law may attempt to draw a line, and professionals must make sure their programs are on the right side.

The third element of consent is information. It doesn't matter that a client is competent and that consent is voluntary if the client does not know what he is consenting to. He must be informed of his right not to consent, or, if he does consent, his right to withdraw at any time. Next, he must be informed of the benefits and risks inherent in the treatment approach or program that is recommended. If possible, some easily obtained publications that are intelligible to laymen and that will explain the same points should be cited. Furthermore, it is good policy to recommend others who have been through the proposed treatment so that the prospective client can talk to them as well. This avoids the problem of deception, which may arise when one persuasive professional talks about the program and later the client claims that the full story was not told. It is also important for the professional to estimate the risk inherent in not undergoing the type of treatment or program recommended.

For a person to be truly informed he should be addressed in his native language, and he should have the opportunity to read, in his native language, as well as hear, the information. The disabled, handicapped, retarded, and disturbed often come from families of sufficiently different culture or even language that it is difficult to talk to parents and get them to understand, but the program must make the effort.

Hearings

If consent is not forthcoming, or if there is some other dispute, a hearing may be ordered. The potential client or his parent or guardian has a right to be accompanied by counsel.

At the hearing, the parent or client can present evidence, can confront and cross-examine any witnesses offered by the state agency, and can compel the attendance of witnesses. If mental health professionals make a written recommendation that a child be treated some special way, they can be compelled to attend a hearing and be cross-examined by the lawyer for the parent opposing that treatment.

The client has a right to both a written, verbatim transcript of the hearing and a written statement of the decision and the reason for it. He can then appeal up through the state hierarchy or go into state or federal court to oppose an adverse decision.

Access to Records

The general due process rights that we have been discussing also extend in most circumstances to a client's records. The client must have access to the data on which decisions about him would be based, so that if he sees what he considers to be erroneous information he can either attempt to have it removed or have competing information entered by his own experts. If, for example, a parent sees in the child's record a test with a very low I.Q. score, he could either have the school throw it out, or retest the child, or have the child retested himself by a private psychologist and insist that those results be placed in the record alongside the other I.Q. results. This is important because, if there is something in the record that might eventually precipitate the child's assignment to a special program, it is like a time bomb ticking away, and the parent should have an opportunity to defuse it before anyone is hurt. Also, part of the record will comprise the individual development plan and the record of progress. Some recent court action indicates that staff conferences about the client must be reduced to minutes and placed in a record available to the client.

LEAST RESTRICTIVE ALTERNATIVE

When treatment is begun, the client has the right to receive it in his normal environment, or, if the normal environment is unsuitable for the clients needs, he has a right to treatment in the next least restrictive environment. For many years the law seemed to favor placing the disabled in total care institutions. This step was assumed to be needed for good care and for the safety of the community, but that notion has changed drastically. The harmful effects of long-term institutionalization are now apparent. After a few years of institutionalization, clients lose functional behavior or may acquire dysfunctional behavior. Courts and legislatures have realized this and reflect that realization in stringent requirements about deinstitutionalization. The Developmental Disability Bill of Rights Act requires effort both to provide alternatives to institutionalization to anyone being considered for care and to re-examine those already institutionalized to determine who could be appropriately cared for or treated in a less restrictive environment.

This move to deinstitutionalization, and the full enjoyment of the right to treatment in the least restrictive alternative, will succeed only if there are adequate alternative facilities. Without them, the move to deinstitutionalization becomes a cynical dumping of persons out onto the streets. That has already happened in some states, but in the District of Columbia there was a recent court victory in *Dixon* v. *Weinberger*[12] that suggests that alternatives must be created even if funds are to be taken away from the institutions and reallocated to community care facilities.

The notion that the environment must be the least restrictive one suitable for one's needs raises, in the issue of suitability, a type of effectiveness measurement rare in treatment of the mentally disabled. Ordinarily, professionals in the mental health field practice their trade claiming to do the best they can, but seldom are they evaluated for their effectiveness and even less seldom is their effectiveness contrasted with another therapeutic approach. However, we must now look to the outcomes of various treatment approaches and move toward those that prove themselves most suitable. The concept of the least restrictive alternative also raises, in the issue of "least," further support for the requirement that therapies be contrasted and compared along some continuum.

As the doctrine is developing, it means that when you begin to offer treatment to an individual, treatment must first be attempted in the most normal environment. Only after evidence that the approach will not work has been documented and duly recorded in files can the next least restrictive environment be tried. After gaining some experience with types of individuals and with outcome measurement on types of approaches, a professional can begin to place clients on the continuum with less trial and error. Obviously, a profoundly handicapped child would not be started out in the mainstream in an average classroom, but he had better start out in a program as close to normal as possible, and the placement should always err in the direction of normal.

This concept will obviously require a tremendous re-allocation of resources in the years to come. One would certainly expect no new institutions to be built. Not only will there be a problem in transfering funds from already existing and costly institutions whose operation, even with lessening numbers of clients, will continue to soak up funds, but also there will be a problem with continuity of services across institutional lines. The *Dixon* case suggests that the right to the least restrictive environment is a continuing right that must be constantly exercised. At any given moment that a client qualifies for

---

[12] 405 F. Supp. 974 (D.D.C. 1975).

a less restrictive environment within an institution he must get it, and, as soon as he qualifies for care outside, he should get it. This means that federal, state, county, and local governmental entities must cooperate in some way as clients are transferred from facility to facility in order to maintain adequate care.

FREEDOM FROM ABUSE

An Affirmative Standard of Care

Possibly the most important recent development in the legal regulation of treatment for the disabled came in the so-called Willowbrook case, *New York State Association for Retarded Citizens* v. *Carey.*[13] The Eighth Amendment's prohibition against cruel and unusual punishment had been used sparingly by courts to strike down certain bizarre practices, but it had never been used to establish an affirmative that there is no such thing as a static condition—that people either get better or they begin to get worse; and that, therefore, in order to keep someone in the state's care from regressing into a worsening condition the state must take affirmative action to prevent that harm.

This judgment provides possibly broader relief than the right to treatment cases because it certainly applies to voluntary admissions to treatment. It raises important questions about a durational limit on institutionalization, because, after a certain point, no matter how good the treatment, the client will inevitably begin to worsen in other ways. This protection should not be misunderstood to mean that, if someone worsens, the professional will be liable. It simply means that if the approach is not working, another one with more promise must be tried. It also means that administrators must set up systems to monitor progress and discontinue programs that are not producing positive results.

The Right to Refuse Therapies

This right to protection from harm lends support to another right, the right to refuse certain therapies. Certain hazardous or intrusive therapies, particularly aversive ones, are now restricted in some jurisdictions by the requirement for consent. Without consent, the professional cannot proceed. But where does the law draw the line? Is there a right to refuse medication? Is there a right to refuse one type of therapy and to insist on another more appealing to the client? This

---

[13] 357 F. Supp. 752 (E.D.N.Y. 1973).

will be governed by the specific facts of a given situation. For now, there is no easy rule that can be stated for application to all situations.

Evidence is beginning to mount on the damage caused by the types of psychotropic medication inflicted on populations like the developmentally disabled. A typical management tool of the large institution, and even the school, is chemical restraint through the use of the phenothiazines. Courts, and some legislatures, have now stated that such medication cannot be used as a substitute for a program, which is the case in many large institutions, where the "treatment" for the disabled child is to keep him drugged. Second, the courts have said, drugs cannot be used simply to aid the staff in custodial management, which is the case in some institutions and schools. In far too many schools, children needing treatment are managed, rather than helped, by the liberal use of tranquilizers. Drug salesmen appear at P. T. A. meetings; parents are browbeaten into consenting to use of the drugs and threatened with their child's expulsion if drugs are not administered; in one instance, a school developed a private fund to pay for medication if the parents would not, or could not pay for it.

Third, the courts are saying that drugs cannot be used for discipline or punishment. Administrators must monitor the dispensing of drugs, often prescribed on an "as needed" or "as requested" basis. Are drugs pushed by ward staff when patients begin to act up? In one school I know of, the students who used to be sent to the principal for troublesome behavior are now told to go to the school nurse for medication. Fourth, the courts have said that medication cannot be used if it hampers other programs. But how many times do we see children who are unable to speak clearly or to work with the speech therapist because their tongues are swollen from tranquilizers; who are unable to take part in physical recreation; who are unable to stay awake during academic classes because of drugs? That kind of abuse in treatment programs is clearly against the law today. The kind of long-range harm caused by excessive use of these drugs, which have now been shown to cause symptoms of Parkinsonism and to drastically increase the chances of Hodgkins disease, runs directly into this new right to protection from harm. I expect there will be, and I look forward to, large money judgments against doctors and institutions that allow this to go on.

One of the results of the long inattention to the rights of the disabled, particularly those in institutions, has been that others with more power in our society have been allowed to experiment on them. Drug companies and others have been fairly free in their access to this population. I am not by any means condemning research, but those persons who have in the past set up projects by talking to administrators must now realize that each individual client has a right not to be experimented on without his full knowledge and consent.

Other kinds of experimentation—experimental therapies directly related to the condition afflicting a particular client—provide a different case. A client has rights with regard to those experiments, too, but the problem is, what is an experiment? If the approach has been tried often before and described in professional literature, if the benefits far outweigh the potential risks, and if the results are not irreversible, then probably no extra safeguards need to be developed. However, for approaches that do appear to be experimental, most institutions now function with two types of committees. The first is a human rights committee, which reviews any suggestion for research or the use of an experimental therapy and monitors the process by which consent is obtained. The human rights committee would also review any complaints about abuses in treatment programs, experimental or not. The second type of committee is a peer review committee composed of professionals who review research designs, experimental safeguards, treatment outcomes, and so forth, and who shut down any experiment that does produce harm.

Peonage

Another area in which the disabled have been abused in the past, and which is now tightly regulated by law, is peonage, or institutional work over long periods of time at very low wages. The federal Fair Labor Standards Act has now been applied to workers in institutions,[14] and the Department of Labor is actually collecting back wages from institutions not paying a fair wage to clients performing work. If a client performs work that the institution would otherwise pay an outside employee to perform, then that client cannot be forced to do that work as part of occupational therapy or otherwise, and, if he voluntarily performs work, then he must be compensated at the minimum wage. An institution can apply to the Department of Labor for certification that the client's performance is less than full productivity and thereby receive permission to pay as little as 25% of the minimum wage.

---

[14] *Souder* v. *Brennan*, 367 F. Supp. 808 (D.D.C. 1973). NOTE: The amendments relied on in *Souder* were overruled in *National League of Cities* v. *Usery*, 44USLW4974, June 24, 1976, but 29 U.S. Code 794 appears to give the same statutory support.

This condition should correct the abuses that have existed, e.g., retarded citizens worked long hours seven days a week for very little pay. They became slaves to an institution that did not treat them because it was assumed they would never get better. Because the clients would be there for life, the institutions assumed, they might as well be kept busy. Now we know that treatment must proceed with actual programs geared to specific needs. No program of legitimate treatment could conceivably include work "therapy" for twelve hours a day, seven days a week.

The danger is that institutions will attempt to do nothing, under the guise of discontinuing illegal work situations. Many state institutions have shut down work programs rather than pay the wages to the clients; but clients cannot be allowed to languish. Enforcement of the right to individual treatment plans should ensure that clients are not left without some program. The argument has been made that this new development is tragic, in that it takes away from the client the job that he had held, and that, like anyone else, he will feel a psychological blow by being unemployed. The fact is that the new requirements for individual treatment mean that clients would be leaving one environment after another as they progressed toward more normal settings, so the previously held jobs would be lost anyway.

Regulation of Punishment

The last element of this right to protection from abuse includes protection from the mistreatment that often comes in the guise of discipline, which is really corporal punishment. Corporal punishment is still allowed in many programs, unfortunately, although it is coming under much closer regulation. Although the courts have not finally outlawed it, that does not mean that professional organizations and administrative bodies could not move faster than courts and strike it down. No mentally disabled client should ever be subject to physical abuse for any reason. Eradicating the thought that something could be taught, that discipline could be instilled in someone, though the use of physical abuse is certainly as much within the province of professional ethics as legal regulation.

One type of therapy that does pose an unintended problem is the token economy. Typically, in a token economy an individual earns points by exhibiting certain behaviors and then is able to trade those points, or tokens, for tangible rewards of his own choice. The problem comes when a person in a token economy program is deprived of certain necessary items, which are then to be earned back and purchased with the tokens. For example, freedom of association might be severely limited, personal effects might be taken away, and even meals might be restricted. One issue is whether or not a client has a constitutional right to those things without having to earn them. Another problem is the state of deprivation to which the individual is subjected if he fails to earn, and until he earns, enough tokens to buy the elements of a better environment. In some settings, the token economies, which can offer great promise for an individual to participate in his own treatment program, go wrong and turn into states of deprivation that are abusive.

Finally, a problem occurs when aversive contingencies used to manage behavior turn into abusive events. Incidents in a Florida setting a few years ago, which gave rise to the Florida Guidelines for Behavior Management, indicated how shame therapy could become an absolutely uncontrollable and abusive approach that could hardly be called therapeutic. Certain behavioral therapies, which can work well with individual consenting patients who have full mental faculties, can become quite twisted when used with mentally disabled groups. Therapists, administrators, and professional organizations must keep alert to any use of aversive contingencies to manage the behavior of populations of the mentally disabled.

PERSONAL RIGHTS

Along with vast increases in judicial activity in the area of legal regulation of services to the developmentally disabled, the law has progressed in recognizing the personal rights of the disabled. These are interwoven with services, because the service offered must not trample on these personal rights.

Courts are now recognizing the right of individuals to marry and to bear children. Some social planners might argue that the developmentally disabled are not competent to make such a choice, that they will probably have disabled offspring that society will have to take care of, and that they should therefore not have that right. However, the emerging right to privacy, coupled with notions of due process and equal protection of the laws, means that no governmental activity or publicly funded program can deprive a person of a right given to any other citizen.

Once children are born to disabled parents, there are some social welfare agencies that would take the children away "for their own good." We are beginning to learn enough now to know that the love of natural parents, even in a not-normal home environment, far outweighs any presumed good that comes from the state's taking over the child's life. We also know the realities of foster care placement. It is more likely that the child taken away "for his own good" will spend the first 18 years of his life in a poorly run institution. Some recent cases have successfully challenged the right of the state to break up families just because the parents are presumed to be less than normally capable of caring for their children.

At one time, disabled girls in public programs were likely to be sterilized, possibly without their full comprehension, by some doctor willing to play God. It was more convenient for the institutions not to have to worry about pregnancies and extra children to care for. However, federal courts and administrative bodies are now outlining rules for sterilization: in general, no one under 21 may be sterilized except for medical necessity; other less drastic methods of birth control must have first been considered; there must be written consent of the client; and, if the client is not competent to give consent, there must be a review committee and a court decision that the sterilization is in the best interests of the woman.

COMMUNITY RIGHTS

For the thrust of legal regulation of services to the disabled to work — for there to be treatment in the normal environment and access to services and so forth — the disabled must be able to enjoy the normal rights of anyone else in the community.

The disabled have often been prevented from voting, but several court cases and legislative changes indicate a trend toward restoring this right. Important cases have also been won that establish the right to access to public buildings that offer public services. Architectural barriers are being removed in some instances. In my own city of Washington, D.C., the new accessible subway station recently opened. Thus, access to transportation is being established, along with the right to access to services and the buildings in which they are housed.

One important right is the right to live a normal life in a residential community. Often, the disabled must live in some type of group home, for a variety of reasons, but finding a suitable location for the group home is often frustrated by zoning restrictions. However, there have been some hopeful signs in recent cases. Zoning should best be attacked at the community level by informing and educating the public. A zoning variance can be allowed in a community that understands what the program is all about. A community that has a group home forced on it by virtue of a lawsuit is unlikely to be a normal environment ideally suited for a group of disabled citizens.

A final right is the right to employment without discrimination about mental or physical conditions that do not interfere with the job. The Vocational Rehabilitation Act of 1973[15] contains an affirmative action requirement binding upon government contractors to employ and to advance in employment physically and mentally handicapped individuals. It further provides that no handicapped individual may be denied the benefits of, be excluded from participation in, or be subjected to discrimination under any program or activity receiving federal financial assistance, solely by reason of his handicap. Practically every activity in our bureaucratically swollen society receives some federal financial assistance these days, so this affirmative action requirement should furnish the basis for securing better opportunities in employment for the developmentally disabled.

PROBLEMS IN COMPLIANCE

The law is now actively regulating services for the developmentally disabled, but there are many failures of our programs to comply with the full requirements of the law. Institutionalization still exists too often. Punishment is used to control populations, as is over-medication. Many citizens entitled to services are excluded from them on some pretext and forced to receive nothing or to go to court. Sterilizations are still performed, and jobs are still being denied.

The best hope for effecting compliance is through adequate performance measures of services for the developmentally disabled. It is not true that services cannot be measured, that professionals cannot be evaluated, that the system is not responsible if the client does not get better. We have minimum standards in institutions and in many programs, but that is not enough. We have process evaluation beginning in many situations so that we know that individual treatment plans are being drawn up and that periodic reviews of progress will be made, but these will not be enough. We need effectiveness

---

[15] Public Law 93-112.

measures—every step in the process must be evaluated solely on its effectiveness in remediating a behavioral deficit of a disabled client. Eventually we should move toward funding for services on the basis of performance. Programs that do not perform should be terminated. Programs that do perform should get more funds. Funding often goes in a counter-productive way to reinforce nonperformance—by sending money repeatedly to places where the worst problems are, we think we are meeting the problem head on, but we may simply be rewarding the poorest programs. Why not send more money to the programs that work?

The newest legal rights of the developmentally disabled give us a structure for accountability—we will be able to determine when a program is not working or when a therapy is ineffective—but, until we tie funding into performance, accountability will just be a word laughed at by institutions, rather than a reality. The developmentally disabled deserve the reality.

BEHAVIOR MODIFICATION AND OTHER BEHAVIOR CHANGE PROCEDURES
The Emerging Law and the Proposed Florida Guidelines

David B. Wexler

As is to be expected in areas of rapidly changing social attitudes and scientific and technological advances, the law—particularly as embodied in Supreme Court pronouncements—lags appreciably behind the heated controversies of the moment. At present, the legal lag is clearly evident in the field of mental health law. Thus, while the Supreme Court is pondering for the first time whether confined mental patients have a constitutionally recognized right *to* treatment—an issue already considered somewhat jaded by law journal standards—public attention across the country is shifting sharply to the question whether patients and prisoners ought to have a right *against* being subjected to some of the frightening therapies now being popularized by congressional investigations and by the press.

LAW ON RIGHT TO RESIST TREATMENT

Mackey v. *Procunier*

The law regarding the right to resist treatment, when measured by judicial decisions, rather than by articles in legal journals, is virtually

Reprinted by permission from *Criminal Law Bulletin* 11(5):600-616, September-October, 1975.

nonexistent. Only a handful of cases have addressed the issue, and not surprisingly, those cases have involved particularly bizarre incidents. One such instance is *Mackey* v. *Procunier,*[1] which challenged "anectine therapy" in the California correctional system. Anectine is a relaxant which induces paralysis and respiratory arrest. It is ordinarily used, together with anesthesia, as an adjunct to electroconvulsive therapy in order to minimize the possibility of bone fracture. Mackey, the plaintiff, was a California prisoner-patient who claimed that, with his consent, he had been transferred from Folsom to Vacaville for the purpose of receiving electroconvulsive therapy. Once at Vacaville, however, he was apparently administered anectine, not in conjunction with electroconvulsive therapy, but instead in connection with a program of "aversive treatment"—without his consent and while he was fully awake. In other words, Mackey claimed that, at Vacaville, anectine was administered to him contingent upon his engaging in inappropriate behavior. Persons who have experienced the effects of anectine while fully conscious describe the sensation as one of suffocating, drowning, or of dying. The Ninth Circuit ruled that proof of Mackey's allegations could raise "serious Constitutional questions respecting cruel and unusual punishment" under the Eighth Amendment or of "impermissible tinkering with the mental processes," presumably in violation of the First Amendment.

Knecht v. Gillman

An opportunity to take more decisive action was offered to—and accepted by—the Eighth Circuit in *Knecht* v. *Gillman,*[2] a December 1973 decision which sharply curtailed a so-called aversive treatment program at the Iowa Security Medical Facility. *Knecht,* like *Mackey,* dealt with the use of a drug for conditioning purposes. The drug in *Knecht,* however, was not the "suffocation" drug anectine but was instead the vomit-inducing drug apomorphine. Armed with blanket orders from physicians, nurses at the Iowa Security Medical Facility (an institution for the "criminally insane") apparently administered the drug whenever they determined—either first-hand or through hearsay remarks of other inmates—that institutional rules had been transgressed. Under the Iowa scheme, an incident of swearing could trigger an injection of apomorphine.

On those facts, the Eighth Circuit ruled squarely that the

---

[1] 477 F. 2d 877 (9th Cir. 1973).
[2] 488 F. 2d 1136 (8th Cir. 1973).

administration of apomorphine without the informed consent of a patient contravenes the constitutional proscription against cruel and unusual punishment. The *Knecht* court held, however, that the drug could be constitutionally administered to *consenting* patients, so long as each injection was authorized by a physician and, to increase the integrity of the fact-finding mechanism, so long as the rule violation was witnessed personally by a staff member.[3]

Kaimowitz

Perhaps the best known of the behavior control cases is *Kaimowitz v. Department of Mental Health*, a 1973 unreported decision by a three-judge Michigan trial court which disallowed the performance of experimental psychosurgery on involuntarily confined patients. The *Kaimowitz* court began with the premise that psychosurgery that was *coercive* or that was otherwise accomplished without a patient's informed consent would contravene constitutional commands relating to the First Amendment freedom of expression and to the constitutional right to privacy. The court ultimately concluded that psychosurgery would similarly offend the Constitution, even if performed on a committed patient who ostensibly *consented* to the procedure. This result was made possible by the court's holding that involuntarily confined patients could not, as a matter of law, give legally adequate consent to experimental psychosurgery.

Legally adequate consent consists of three conjunctive elements: competency, knowledge, and voluntariness. The *Kaimowitz* court found none of them to be satisfied. Competency was missing because the court viewed confined patients as being too affected by the "institutionalization syndrome" to competently make the serious and complex decision to undergo psychosurgery. Knowledge — the "informed" portion of the informed consent formula — was wanting because the outcome of the proposed operation was profoundly uncertain. And voluntariness was absent because the court viewed the lure of possible release from the institution to be so powerful that it would coerce patients into consenting. Elsewhere, I have been severely critical of the court's reasoning on each of those points (a matter to which I shall return briefly later), though not of the result reached.[4]

---

[3] The present discussion of *Mackey* and *Knecht* is drawn largely from Wexler, *Behavior Modification and Legal Developments*, a paper read to the Law and Society Research Group, Florida State University, Tallahasse, Florida, May 1974.

[4] Wexler, "Foreword: Mental Health Law and the Movement Toward Voluntary Treatment," 62 Cal. L. Rev. 671 (1974) (hereinafter cited as "Foreword").

LEGAL REGULATION OF BEHAVIOR MODIFICATION

Certainly, few would quarrel with the proposition that drastic, punitive, and sometimes irreversible therapies are worthy of legal attention and regulation. Some may argue, however, that the above incidents, though serious, are mere therapeutic aberrations, and that, moreover, the gist of behavior change and behavior modification today consists of *positive* control—of rewarding appropriate behavior, rather than of punishing inappropriate behavior. Thus, some would question the necessity of stringent legal regulation of such seemingly benign therapeutic efforts.

Scrutiny of Behavior-Shaping Goals

Such a noninterventionist argument can, however, be easily answered. First, even assuming arguendo that positive reinforcement schemes do not involve offensive *means* in their attempt to shape behavior, scrutiny is, nonetheless, essential to ensure that their behavior-shaping *goals* comport with satisfactory legal and ethical standards. Just as one can properly question the propriety of eliminating adult swearing behavior at the above-described Iowa facility, one can similarly question the propriety of shaping—even by the benign means of dispensing refreshments—exceedingly docile classroom behavior in schoolchildren and of encouraging the performance of institutional labor by mental patients, alcoholics, and juvenile delinquents.

Offensive Means: Token Economies and Tier Systems

Second, clinical endeavors in applying positive reinforcement to build desired behavior have often involved, in practice, *means* as alarming as some of the aversive techniques. Thus, "token economies"—where patients earn tokens for appropriate behavior and are then permitted to cash the tokens in to purchase desired items or events—and "tier systems"—where privileges increase hierarchically and patients are promoted or elevated to higher tiers upon engaging in appropriate behavior—often involve severe states of *deprivation*, which, in effect, force patients to earn their way to improved living conditions. Thus, many very basic items and events are employed in institutional settings as reinforcers: meals, beds, ground privileges, privacy, attendance at religious services, etc.

No cases have yet squarely condemned token economies and tier systems for their fast-and-loose reliance on severe states of deprivation, but such a constitutional condemnation is only around the corner. Judicial decisions not involving behavior modification, but extending to patients certain rights as part-and-parcel of a constitutionally required "humane environment" (according patients a right to nutritious meals, a comfortable bed, privacy, the right to attend religious services, etc.) may be interpreted as removing certain basic items and events from the arsenal of legally available reinforcers or as at least greatly restricting their legal availability.[5]

Recently, a U.S. Bureau of Prisons "tier" program at the Medical Center for Federal Prisoners at Springfield, Missouri, known as the START program (an acronym for Special Treatment and Rehabilitive Training), was subject to challenge in a federal lawsuit. Among other claims, the inmate plaintiffs contended that the deprivations which they were involuntarily required to endure at the first level of the program—in terms of visitation rights, exercise opportunities, and reading materials—amounted to a constitutional violation. In response, the government argued that it was necessary, at the initial stage, to deprive the inmates of those rights so that they might be used as reinforcers. Moreover, the government continued, the fact that the inmates deemed the denial of the rights significant enough to challenge actually established the psychological effectiveness of those reinforcers as behavioral motivators. Note that the government's argument comes close to creating a legal Catch 22: "If you complain of the denial of certain rights, you are not entitled to them: you are entitled only to those rights the denial of which you do not challenge."[6]

While the lawsuit was pending, the Bureau of Prisons decided to terminate the START program, though the Bureau's director testified in congressional hearings that such "positive-reinforcement" approaches would in all likelihood be employed in future correctional efforts. Because of the START termination, however, the federal court found the suit to be moot, except with respect to certain procedural aspects, and accordingly did not address the merits of the deprivation issue.

RIGHT TO TREATMENT AND PERSONAL AUTONOMY

In light of the foregoing examples, the case for the legal regulation of behavior modification—both positive and aversive—and of other

---

[5] Wexler, "Token and Taboo: Behavior Modification, Token Economies, and the Law," 61 Cal. L. Rev. 81 (1973).

[6] Wexler, "Of Rights and Reinforcers," 11 San Diego L. Rev. 957, 964 (1974).

behavior-change technologies seems to be clear. When I speak of regulation, however, I do not mean outright prohibition. Blanket prohibition would, under the label of paternalism, infringe on notions of personal autonomy and privacy as much as would practices endorsing unscrutinized therapeutic techniques carte blanche. Thus, "it may be constitutionally impermissible" — on First Amendment freedom of mentation or on right to privacy grounds — "for a court or legislature to deny a [willing] patient access to a drastic therapeutic technique and in effect mandate continued confinement if the technique, while possibly injurious, offers a likelihood of freedom."[7] Elsewhere, I have argued that:

[T]he Supreme Court abortion cases — which found the physician-patient decision regarding abortion to be constitutionally protected against non-compelling state interference — could well be extended to *other* physician-patient decisions, including agreed-to therapeutic procedures. As with abortion, the courts could find state interference with such procedures unwarranted if interference or prohibition of the procedures could lead to 'the taxing of mental ... health' and to a 'distressful life and future.' (*Roe* v. *Wade*, 410 U.S. 113, 153 (1973)[8])

Informed Consent

To preserve the above-mentioned notion of autonomy while simultaneously hoping to prevent therapeutic excesses, the courts and commentators have relied on the concept of informed consent. The emerging view, at least with respect to intrusive procedures, seems to be that if a person is capable of giving informed consent to a proposed therapeutic procedure (and most prisoners and many mental patients are so capable), and such person in fact consents to it, the institution ought to be permitted to proceed with it, but that if consent is refused, "the state lacks a sufficient interest to thrust an intrusive behavioral procedure upon an unwilling competent person."[9]

The matter is somewhat more complex with respect to persons incapable of giving informed consent (such as certain mental patients and many residents of mental retardation facilities), but the prevailing view seems to be that the patient's supposed desire is not conclusive. He may be subjected to certain procedures if it is determined — and the means of determination is now a matter of great dispute —

---

[7] *Foreword,* note 4 *supra,* at 681.

[8] Wexler, *Reflections on the Legal Regulation of Behavior Modification in Institutional Settings* 4 (paper submitted to Behavioral Law Center, Oct. 1974) (hereinafter cited as "*BLC* paper"). See generally Foreword, note 4 *supra,* at 681–684.

[9] *BLC* paper, note 8 *supra,* at 1.

that less onerous alternative therapies are or have been unsuitable and that, in an anticipated cost-benefit sense, the proposed procedure is in the best interest of the patient or client.[10]

California Model—Organic Therapies

A recently enacted California statute[11] generally follows the above model. The statute seeks to regulate, in institutional settings, what it refers to as "organic" therapies, which exclude psychotherapy and, apparently, chemotherapy, but include psychosurgery, electronic stimulation of the brain, electroconvulsive and insulin shock therapy, and aversive therapy involving shocks, physical pain, and drugs as part of a conditioning effort. The California scheme (1) permits the use of all those therapies when consent is obtained from competent patients; (2) disallows them if refused by competent patients; and (3) with the exception of psychosurgery, permits their use with incompetent patients if the "best interest" and "least restrictive alternative" tests are satisfied. The crucial facts regarding questions of competence, cost-benefit analysis, and less drastic therapeutic alternatives are found by a superior court. In other words, under the California model, the organic therapies are permissible only in accordance with a court order, which is obtainable only after a judicial hearing at which the patient is entitled to appointed counsel and to an independent medical expert.

"Inherent Coercion"

In order for regulatory schemes that hinge on the notion of informed consent to work—and in order, under the abortion case analogue, to preserve as best we can the value of autonomy—it is necessary to pierce through the rhetoric, fueled by the *Kaimowitz* case, that institutions are inherently coercive and that voluntary consent is unobtainable in an institutional setting because the lure of release is so overpowering. If the "inherent coercion" formula is accepted, "the logical result would be that *all* therapy on involuntarily institutionalized persons would, despite their expressed desires to submit to therapy, be deemed coerced and therefore either prohibited altogether or referred for approval to a surrogate decision-maker (guardian, etc.) who in this situation would surely be no better equipped (and who

---

[10] See generally Shapiro, "Legislating the Control of Behavior Control: Autonomy and the Coercive Use of Organic Therapies," 47 So. Cal. L. Rev. 237 (1974).

[11] AB 2296.

would indeed probably be far *less* equipped) than the resident to decide whether the procedure should be agreed to."[12]

The lure of institutional release *per se* ought not to be deemed legal coercion. The law does not generally view

"the simple pressure to select a particular option, by itself, to constitute coercion. In law, for example, conditions of probation or parole must be voluntarily assumed in order to be enforceable, and pleas of guilty must be given voluntarily if they are to be upheld. Yet, the law upholds reasonable probation and parole conditions as voluntary, and similarly upholds plea bargains, even though, in all those instances, the avoidance or reduction of incarceration is the supreme motivating force underlying the agreement. Thus, the law, though it has not been terribly explicit about it, actually employs the concept of coercion not to condemn pressure *per se*, but rather employs it as a normative concept to condemn choices regarded as *unfair* or *unreasonable*."[13]

The normative notion of coercion is in obvious need of further refinement (to which some philosophers are now addressing their attention), but its mere recognition as such is an important assistance to the development of the law.

REFORM EFFORTS: FLORIDA GUIDELINES

Largely because of the public outcry over behavior control technologies and because that outcry is beginning to find its way into legislative and judicial forums, many mental health professionals are now scurrying to draft guidelines and to put their therapeutic houses in order. By far the greatest effort seems to be coming from professionals in behavior modification—principally persons who apply clinically the psychological theories of learning—rather than from persons who practice other forms of behavior change or behavior control. A task force commissioned by the Florida Division of Retardation has already drafted proposed standards for the use of behavioral procedures in state programs for the retarded. Also, the American Psychological Association has established a Commision on Behavior Modification to address pertinent questions in an extensive range of settings, and the Association for the Advancement of Behavior Therapy has set a similar goal. In addition, the Behavioral Law Center has engaged lawyers, behavioral psychologists, consumer advocates, and consumers to prepare papers to serve as springboards for discussion

---

[12] *BLC* paper, note 8 *supra*, at 3. See generally Foreword, note 4 *supra*.

[13] *BLC* paper, note 8 *supra*, at 2. See generally Foreword, note 4 *supra*.

at an anticipated national conference designed to formulate standards for the use of behavioral procedures in institutional settings.

The concentration of reform efforts among behavior modifiers, rather than among other behavior change professionals, seems partly explainable by the greater organizational cohesion of the former group. However, it may be also partly attributable to an accident of semantics: The public and the press do not employ the term "behavior modification" in its limited scientific "conditioning" sense; instead, they employ it nontechnically to refer to *all* forms of behavior control and behavior influence. The public's outcry, then, against such procedures as psychosurgery is expected as a concern about "behavior modification," which has, in turn, put the pure-bred behavior modifiers on the defensive and encouraged them to review and explain their techniques and safeguards with the hope of gaining public support or of at least avoiding the wrath inflicted on the psychosurgeons. [14]

Florida Retardation Scandal

The effort of the Florida Task Force (on which I was privileged to serve) was sparked not only by the above factors, but also by a full-blown scandal—extensively aired by the local press—at one of the state's retardation training centers. The problem arose at a training-center cottage which operated under a token economy and tier system and which housed retarded boys who were also delinquent or emotionally disturbed.

The abuses reported by the press (and confirmed by a blue-ribbon Resident Abuse Investigating Committee) included, among many other things, forced public masturbation and forced public homosexual acts as punishment for engaging in proscribed sexual behavior; beatings with a wooden paddle for running away; and washing the mouth with soap for lying, for abusive or vulgar language, or sometimes for speaking at all. Further, food, sleep, and visitation privi-

---

[14] An excellent example of the semantic confusion is in the Law Enforcement Assistance Administration's (LEAA) termination of funding of so-called behavior modification programs. After the ban, LEAA received an inquiry about the funding of a token economy and tier program at a penal institution. LEAA officials responded that the questioned program did not involve drugs or electric shock—the sort of procedures that sparked its behavior modification guidelines—and that the prohibition was not clearly directed at token systems and systems involving the graduated acquisition of privileges (APA Monitor, Aug. 1974 p. 7, col. 1.). In other words, the clarification illustrates that the LEAA behavior modification funding prohibition was directed at programs which fall without or on the periphery of behavior modification, properly defined, but not at programs which constitute its core.

leges were withheld as punishment; incontinence was punished by requiring residents to lie in soiled sheets and to hold soiled underwear to
their noses; a resident accused of theft was addressed by staff and residents as "The Thief" and was required to wear a sign so designating
him; and one boy was required to walk around publicly clothed only
in female underpants. [15]

Even more remarkable, perhaps, is that these abuses were not
isolated incidents but were parading under the banner of behavior
modification as part of what the Investigating Committee found to
be a system of "programmed abuse." The incidents were carried out
by staff members, who recorded them in great detail in well-kept
records with the encouragement, or at least the acquiesence, of the
chief psychologist (who held a Ph.D. degree, though not in psychology). Moreover, the Committee believed the participants to be generally well-meaning and hard-working and attributed the problem
generally to an unscrutinized and unsupervised system run by poorly
trained personnel.

The principal pitfall, according to the Committee, was the
structure of the token economy and tier system, which made the system highly vulnerable to rampant abuse. At Phase 1 of the structure,
the boys were able to earn tokens for appropriate behavior but were
not allowed to exchange them for primary reinforcers (refreshments,
etc.) until they had accumulated a sufficient number of tokens to be
elevated to Phase II. To deal with disruptive and problem behavior,
the staff members were instructed to emphasize the natural consequences of behavior, to devise their own remedies to fit the situation,
and to follow through on every promise or threat.

According to the Committee's psychological evaluation of the
program, the structure was faulty in two respects. The token and tier
system was "upside-down." During Phase I, when behavior problems
should typically be more difficult to control, and where strong and
immediate reinforcement is apparently essential in order to bring behavior under control, tokens were not redeemable and the token reinforcers were accordingly not meaningful. (Curiously, tokens were
redeemable only in Phase II, where ideally the reinforcement schedule should be thinned out and should be replaced by such natural reinforcers as social praise.) The system, therefore, was bound to result
in a high incidence of disruptive behavior. With positive reinforcement being unavailable, the staff members were left to devise their

---

[15] *Report of Resident Abuse Investigating Committee* 10–11 (unpublished, undated);
May, *Ethical and Legal Contingencies in and Upon Behavior Modification Programs*
(unpublished 1974).

own responses. Being untrained, they relied on familiar "home remedies," such as washing mouths with soap. As their control efforts became frustrated, they simply resorted, out of frustration, to increasingly punitive methods.

As a result of the Investigating Committee's report, many of the institution's employees were discharged. But in the wake of the incident, behavior modification was itself indicted as a responsible agent. A staff morale problem developed statewide. Staff members, fearful of losing their jobs, refused to become involved in even well-recognized behavior-modification procedures, often leaving highly inappropriate resident behavior to proceed without intervention. Put another way, a highly abusive program was replaced by a virtual therapeutic paralysis.

FLORIDA TASK FORCE

These crises of polar extremes led to the formation of the Florida Task Force. A group of behavioral psychologists and lawyers were called to Tallahassee and were virtually sequestered in a hotel for a four-day period to draft a set of psychological and legal principles for the appropriate use of behavioral procedures in state facilities for the retarded. The psychologists prepared a manual of recognized techniques, emphasizing throughout that if "milder" procedures are ineffective, more intrusive ones should not be resorted to before ascertaining whether the milder procedures failed because of an insufficiently stimulating environment, because of improper staff training, etc. The legal members of the Task Force drafted procedures of advice, review, and consent for the use of intrusive procedures.

Though the proposed legal guidelines were strict, officials and staff members of the Division of Retardation indicated that they could live with them. (From their perspective of paralysis, perhaps even strict guidelines were viewed as a freeing agent, informing the staff that they *could*, with a sense of security, employ at least *some* procedures under *some* circumstances.)

Proposed Guidelines

Constitutionally, the proposed Florida guidelines conform to the analysis addressed earlier. Concepts of competence, informed consent, and the least restrictive alternative are built into the scheme. But the Florida approach relies heavily on an "administrative model" to resolve issues of efficacy, fact-finding, approval of therapeutic goals, and selection of therapeutic techniques.

The guidelines contemplate the creation of one statewide Peer Review Committee (PRC) composed of highly regarded professionals trained in applied behavior analysis. A lay review committee would be created for each region of the Division of Retardation. Designated as the Committee on Legal and Ethical Protection (CLEP), it would consist of, among others, a behavioral scientist, a lawyer with experience in representing the handicapped or versed in matters of civil liberties, and a parent of a retarded person. If the proposal of the legal members of the Task Force is included in the final draft of the guidelines, the members of PRC and the CLEP will be wholly unaffiliated with the Division and will be appointed by the governor from a list of names submitted by the Florida Association for Retarded Citizens, an active organization of concerned citizens.

PRC and CLEP have roles to play both when behavioral procedures are proposed for initial use in Division facilities and when certain intrusive procedures are sought to be employed in particular cases. With regard to the introduction of new techniques, PRC approval is also required, "based on its judgment regarding the appropriateness of the behavior proposed to be strengthened or weakened and on the ethical propriety of the means to be employed to achieve the behavior change."

Specified Behavioral Procedures

The heart of the Florida scheme, however, deals with the knotty questions of when particular procedures can be employed to modify particular behavior of particular patients—questions which, before the necessity of legal intervention was recognized, used to go by default to therapists and staff members. Here, the Florida Task Force, aware that these are largely ethical questions and desirous of avoiding accusations of elitism, engaged in arguably legitimate buck-passing. Rather than deciding those important public matters itself, the Task Force proposed instead a mechanism for fairly resolving those issues. The CLEPs, presumably meeting on a statewide basis, are to classify behavioral procedures and behaviors to be modified (strengthened or weakened) according to a three-tiered scheme of escalating safeguards:

1. **Specified Behavior to be Modified by Specified Behavioral Procedures Regarded as Standard, Reasonable, and Conventional** Examples of behavior that might be specified as appropriate for strengthening could include mobility, self-help, and language acquisition. Self-stimulation or temper tantrums might be examples of be-

havior deemed appropriate for weakening. Behavioral procedures that might be listed under this first tier could include extinctions as well as positive reinforcement employing non-basic reinforcers. Following initial CLEP specification of these behaviors and procedures,[16] this first-level activity can be carried out, in accordance with proper professional standards, in individual cases without CLEP notification or approval.

2. **Somewhat More   Intrusive Behavior Procedures Regarded as Sometimes Necessary and as Relatively Standard, Reasonable, and Conventional, Used to Modify Level-One Specified Behavior**   Examples might be brief time-out or the use of educational fines to weaken temper tantrums or assaultive behavior against other residents. Subject to initital CLEP approval, these procedures can be employed without case-by-case prior approval of CLEP, so long as CLEP and PRC are *notified* of the use of the procedures within a reasonable time—no longer than seven days—after their use. After-the-fact notification is required so that CLEP and PRC can *monitor* the reports for possible excessive, unnecessary, vindictive, or ineffective use of the tier-two procedures.

3. **Behavioral Procedures not Specified in Tier-one or Tier-two or the Strengthening or Weakening of Behavior not Specified as Being Reasonable and Conventional**   This third-tier residual category, providing for the greatest protective procedures, would include the most drastic techniques and the most controversial behavior. Procedures would probably include the use of electric shock to eliminate severe self-mutilating behavior and the use of basic reinforcers for the purpose of acquiring language skills. The modification of controversial behavior patterns—such as certain sexual activity— would similarly be subject to scrutiny under this section. The third-tier protections require *prior, case-by-case* CLEP approval, and require that CLEP find that PRC has approved the use of the procedure and that the client, if competent, has consented to the proposed modification of behavior and to the use of the procedure. If the client is found by CLEP to be incompetent, CLEP cannot approve the proposal unless it finds that less restrictive alternatives have been ex-

---

[16] Although the Task Force did not do so, perhaps it should have itself specified the *minimal* placement of behaviors and procedures in the three-tiered protective hierarchy. That would enable the CLEPS to *approve* the placement or to *elevate* the protection deemed necessary with regard to certain behaviors and techniques, but would prevent the CLEPS from *lowering* the required safeguards to levels where constitutional problems might arise. It is hoped, however, the CLEPS will be strict and responsible in their protective classification efforts.

hausted without success or that they would be clearly ineffective. It must also find that the proposed treatment would, in a cost-benefit sense geared to normal developmental and educational goals, be in the best interest of the client. Again, if the legal members of the Task Force have their way in the final version of the guidelines, clients will have the right to representation by appointed counsel (or perhaps by a legal paraprofessional) in three-tier proceedings before CLEP.

With respect to the least restrictive alternative notion, an interesting provision of the proposed legal guidelines specifies that "if, in rendering a decision under [the section relating to third-level procedures] the CLEP finds that a less restrictive alternative is insufficient only because of the lack of staff or funds, it shall in each such case immediately notify the Director of the division, the Governor, the Secretary of the Department of Health and Rehabilitive Services, the Attorney General, the Chairman of the House and Senate [Health and Rehabilitative Services] Legislative Committees, and the Chairman of the House and Senate Appropriations Committees."

"Administrative Model"

The Florida guidelines follow an "administrative model" both in their method of proposed promulgation and in their contemplated function of adjudicating and approving the use of certain behavioral procedures in particular cases. There are, in my view, several advantages to this administrative approach.

In terms of promulgation by administrative regulation, rather than by legislation, there is an obvious advantage in having the package prepared by specialists and in avoiding legislative "mark-up" and rewrite sessions. Administrative enactment will expectedly also be swifter than legislative enactment. Of course, some of the advantages of the administrative route can be abused. For example, although administrative rule-making power derives theoretically from legislative delegation, the legislature is in practice often totally unaware of administrative action taken pursuant to delegated authority. In Florida, for example, a statute has just taken effect which will bring the administrative rulemaking process out into the open. A recent *Miami Herald* article [17] quotes a state senator as stating that the origin of the new statute can be traced to the period after the 1973 legislative session. At that session, many controversial bills were defeated, "but

---

[17] Jan. 4. 1975, p. 18A, col. 1.

within 90 days we found that the laws that failed were put into effect by agencies as rules."

That sort of legislative circumvention is unwise, particularly if legislative budgetary action would be helpful or essential to support the activites created by administrative regulation. But the principal advantage of administrative promulgation (an advantage that ought to be understood in legislative halls) is that administrative rules and regulations can be enacted, modified, and superseded easier than can statutes and that, in a field as new and as rapidly changing as the regulation of behavior control, the ease and flexibility of administrative action, as opposed to the "freezing" effect of legislative action, cannot be overestimated.

Equally important is the adoption by the Florida guidelines of an administrative, rather than a judicial, approach to adjudicating the propriety of resorting in individual cases to intrusive behavioral procedures. In this respect, the Florida guidelines differ considerably from the previously discussed California scheme of court-approved behavior control. Again, there seem to be several advantages to the administrative model. If the analogue of the judicial handling of civil commitment hearings for the mentally ill is relevant, there is every indication that the courts will not be eager to involve themselves in the day-to-day business of behavior control. Empirical studies firmly conclude that courts have permitted — indeed encouraged — remarkably perfunctory procedures in civil commitment hearings and that they effortlessly and routinely rubber-stamp the recommendations of the testifying psychiatrists.[18]

A lay body such as a Committee on Legal and Ethical Protection, on the other hand, has at least a genuine potential[19] for bringing together a broad-based group of persons carefully selected on the basis of concern and other factors, and of giving them a chance to develop know-how so that they might perform with skill and vigor. The acquisition of know-how is greatly facilitated in the Florida guidelines by several techniques that could not appropriately be performed by courts: the CLEP is required to conduct periodic visitations to inspect Division facilities to ensure their continued familiarity with the operations. Also, the CLEP and PRC are required to moni-

---

[18] See generally Wexler, Scoville, et al., "The Administration of Psychiatric Justice: Theory and Practice in Arizona." 13 Ariz. L. Rev. 1 (1971).

[19] Unfortunately, the potential seems not to have been realized in the *Kaimowitz* context, where the proposed psychosurgical procedure condemned by the *Kaminowitz* court had been previously approved both by a scientific and by a lay review committee.

tor reports of second-level procedures for possible excessive, unnecessary, vindictive, or ineffective use of those procedures, and they are required to conduct periodic random-sampling of current cases to ensure that each client has an individual treatment plan and to ascertain whether CLEP notification and approval is in fact being observed in required instances.[20]

The Florida guidelines are, of course, far from perfect, and it is not yet certain whether their final form will fully satisfy the legal members of the Task Force. But they at least represent an important effort, and they promise to be somewhat influential, if for no other reasons than that four members of the Florida Task force now sit on the American Psychological Association's Commission on Behavior Modification and that Paul Friedman, managing attorney of the Mental Health Law Project and a member of the Florida group, is preparing a set of proposed guidelines for discussion at the forthcoming Behavioral Law Center conference and will expectedly draw upon the Florida experience in his draft. There should, then, be ample opportunity for the Florida guidelines to be seriously scrutinized in several settings.

---

[20] An additional advantage of the Florida guidelines, not present in the California statute, is the former's explicit dealing with the problem of therapeutic *goals*, rather than merely with the question of therapeutic *means*.

ETHICAL ISSUES FOR THE DEVELOPMENTALLY DISABLED

David A. Begelman

Ethical problems confronting the helping professions are among the most challenging they face. Avenues of approach to their resolution differ substantially from those in the purely scientific realm. Their solution need not be facilitated by augmentation of resources allocated for their examination. Indeed, it often seems that resolutions of ethical problems get postponed as the context of their discussion becomes increasingly interdisciplinary. Needless to say, mental health professionals find this working aspect of ethical issues bothersome. Katz (1969) has referenced the American Psychiatic Association's coolness on right to treatment rulings like *Rouse* v. *Cameron*,[1] and while psychiatry's 1967 *Position Statement on the Question of Adequacy of Treatment* may strike us in retrospect as a bold declaration of professional territoriality, the resentment is still very much alive. It is also not confined to psychiatry. A question frequently posed is: why should professionally qualified treatment specialists defer to those whose skills are in the conceptual, not scientific area: lawyers, philosophers, clergyman, and even community representatives? Such persons are regarded by segments of the scientific community as "outsiders," intruders into matters over which they have no rightful jurisdiction. One also gets the impression that occasional invitations

---

[1] 373 F. 2d 451 (D.C. Cir. 1966).

to them to comment on the ethical aspects of treatment programs are merely strategic concessions to groups that, if antagonized, will give us a worse press than the one we have already created by our own efforts. In spite of this, ethical issues will continue to be examined in mixed company. When the dust has settled, collaborators will probably agree this has been a good thing. Those of us who now bewail the trend must at any rate appreciate its ironic aspect. The indignation of some behavioral scientists over legal curtailment of their activities seems misplaced, considering that their own relentless efforts over the years to erode the concept of criminal responsibility are everywhere in evidence in the law (Begelman, 1975a). Among the noteworthy (even if experimentally unsubstantiated) contributions of behavioral science to the law is the inferential process, tailor-made for mediating between the accused and his alleged act, in order to define an excusing condition. The divestment of criminal law (Kittrie, 1971) is but one step ahead of its sympathy to an endless parade of explanatory fictions: e.g. the unconscious impulse, the hypnotic spell, the subliminally based act, and brainwashing. The production of madness (Szasz, 1961) in law purports to supply us with deeper insights into persons like Sadie, Squeaky, Charlie, and Tania. It only succeeds in blinding us to political realities and a perhaps shattering revelation: Evil cannot be understood by forever labeling its perpetrators as "crazy" or "different" (Arendt, 1963). The importance of the Patty Hearst case is what struck many as the plausibility of F. Lee Bailey's defense. However, even to suppose that we require a special psychological theory of why the rich get radicalized is, *inter alia*, only another variant on the ideological theme that there is no reason for this to happen—other than a "psychological" one. That is, the search for special psychological explanations (e.g., "possession," "mental illness," "brainwashing") for why a favored value system is overthrown or abandoned is itself ideologically tinged. The same is true for "compulsions," those dark forces psychoanalysts claim to observe everywhere. Yet the prevalence of "compulsions" also corresponds to the urgency of the need for exculpation in relation to such crimes as shoplifting. The youngster who filches trinkets from Woolworth's is a potential "psychopath," a diagnosis implying improper socialization. The affluent dowager caught red-handed by store detectives in the same act is only a helpless victim of unconscious urges resulting in kleptomania, diagnosis implying the influence of some esoteric process.[2] Psychological effects are "brainwashing," "conditioning," or "programming" when they are techniques used by the Rev. Moon, Hare Krishna, the North Koreans, B. F. Skinner, or L. Ron Hubbard. When inspired by Jesus Christ, as in the case of Charles Colson, Billy Graham, and Eldridge Cleaver, they become "being born again" or "reawakenings." Ominous psychological processes always seem to characterize those patterns representing a shift away from cherished values.

TAXONOMY OF ETHICAL ISSUES

Determinable versus Indeterminable Issues

In a complete taxonomy of ethical issues of the developmentally handicapped, a broad but somewhat fuzzy (and by no means ultimate) distinction might be drawn between "determinable" and "indeterminable" ones. The former category encompasses those over which pretty much of an ethical consensus prevails. Determinable issues are noncontroversial, in the sense that there are no significant problems arising over their actual status or classification. Public outrage may be the response to more glaring types of ethical abuse uncovered in institutional programs. Nevertheless, such revelations involve determinable violations of ethical principles. They prompt questions about how to explain, rectify, or prevent the violations, not about their ethical status as violations. The experiments conducted at Willowbrook State School in New York on retarded clients who were injected with hepatitus virus (Ramsey, 1970) fall into the determinable category, as do the practices uncovered by Risley (Risely, 1975) in the course of investigating a program at a Southern training school for retarded. Among the violations he observed were forced public masturbation, forced homosexual acts, public shaming rituals, and other drastically punitive measures. Determinable abuses, involving as they do a consensus about the ethical principle involved, give rise to the language of *excuse*, in contrast to the language of *justification*, on the part of

---

[2] It may be held that a *prima facie* case for psychological excusing conditions is suggested by the inconsistency between behavior and needs. Thus, "compulsivity" in the case of the dowager is said to be a plausible hypothesis, since she doesn't need to steal trinkets. This argument usually confounds: *a*, she doesn't need to *steal* because of her financial status, and, *b*, she doesn't need to steal *trinkets* in light of her tastes or standards If *a* is the significant element in a successful plea for an excusing condition, it follows that a *prima facie* case for "compulsivity" cannot be made in relation to stolen goods whose purchase would otherwise constitute a financial hardship on the dowager (e.g., Winston jewelry, yachts, stock or real estate). If *b* is the significant element, then on what plausible basis can a Black youth be said to *need* trinkets a dowager doesn't?

those held responsible. Thus, directors of agencies or program supervisors might plead ignorance of the abuses in question, or claim a lack of control over them due to any number of factors, including work overload, absence of administrative authority, or niggardly financial support.

Indeterminable issues are those defined by events whose ethical status remains in question. Their resolution depends upon complex legal or philosophical arguments not yet established as valid. Paradigm cases of indeterminable ethical issues would be those bearing on the settlement of a question of law by the courts (and perhaps involving a significant division of opinion). For example, it may be argued that meaningful consent is a necessary condition of ethical experimentation. If the element of coercion nullifies the possibility of meaningful consent, what bearing does an involuntary status have on the possibility of "coercion," hence meaningful consent? Some physicians, e.g. Lasagna (1969), have held that the element of coercion can be divorced from the institutional framework in which experimentation is undertaken. In spite of this, a state trial court in Michigan in 1973 declared otherwise, and held in *Kaimowitz* v. *Michigan Department of Mental Health* [3] that the plaintiff's consent to experimental psychosurgery cannot be regarded as truly "voluntary" in light of the institutional context in which it was obtained.

The language of justification, rather than excuse, characterizes positions taken on indeterminable ethical issues. Treatment specialists whose past practices are in violation of a recent legal precedent usually react very differently than the individual who figures prominently in a newspaper "exposé." The former may react indignantly to the way newer trends in the law hamper his professional activity; the latter individual is usually closer to contemplating a change of profession or a period of anonymity.

There is, of course, no hard and fast distinction to be made between determinable and indeterminable issues. The element of uncertainty or arguability in indeterminable ethical problems may yet characterize the approach you or I take to issues long since thought settled by most or ruled on by the courts. For example, Davison (1974) and I (Begelman, 1975a, 1975b), in contrast to a majority of our colleagues in behavior modification, think there is an ethical problem surrounding sex-reorientation procedures for *voluntary* homosexual clients. Our arguments are predicted on an analysis of voluntariness

---

[3] No. 73-1943-AW (Cir. Ct. Wayne County, Mich., 1973).

similar to the one playing a role in *Kaimowitz*. Likewise, there appear to be ethical issues that are not easily classified as determinable or indeterminable. For example, an issue that will prove to be of greater future significance of the developmentally disabled than we have yet imagined is the problem of abortion. Yet its controversial aspect is due less to the degree of uncertainty many feel about its ethical status, than to the fact that, on the contrary, abortion is controversial precisely because there is violent disagreement between pro- and anti-abortionists, who feel the problem is determinable, albeit in different directions. From the standpoint of a wide opinion split or the existence of controversy, the abortion issue seems indeterminable; whereas from the standpoint of the law, as in *Roe* v. *Wade*,[4] or individual conviction, it seems otherwise.

Inventories and Evolutionary Models

One way of approaching ethical issues of the developmentally disabled, or, for that matter, any disadvantaged client population, is simply to list them. Accordingly, it is possible to establish an inventory of concerns arising from whatever dimension of the problem we wish to consider. Any such listing would consist of problems whose very formulation presupposes a network of prior ethical assumptions we tend to take for granted. Yet the latter may have figured as indeterminable issues in the distant past, before they were brought over into the realm of "moral knowledge" requisite for furthering present inquiry. What at first blush appears to be a straightforward inventory of problems calling for ethical commentary may have been transformed as such only at the tail end of a meandering history of interwoven issues played out before it. Accordingly, while the most abstract ethical principles appear unchanging,[5] the category of events to which we feel they apply constantly shifts. It is the failure to grasp the evolutionary character of the development of ethical issues that has us puzzling over why, for example, everyone seemed to be en-

---

[4] 410 U.S. 113 (1973).

[5] There might be wide consensus on the Nuremberg Code first principle that voluntary consent of human subjects to experiments in which they participate is essential. Yet there may also be substantial disagreement about whether or not what was obtained in the course of conducting a particular experiment constitutes "voluntary consent." In addition, an issue may arise about whether or not what was conducted constitutes an "experiment" (Martin, 1975). It was perhaps in reference to the consensus on abstract principles that London (1975) asserted there are no "new" ethical issues arising over behavior modification practices. With respect to ethical and legal issues of the application of those principles, there are, of course, many new dilemmas.

gaged in such unethical professional practices twenty years ago. However, the benefit of historical hindsight is the advantage of a perspective on concepts like individual rights, which have been appreciably expanded over what they were held to cover in the past. This expansion is an evolutionary one, based upon perceived connections among issues that are made in layers or stages. The historical process cannot be conceived as a discovery of new facts or data that demand realignments in our notion of determinable ethical problems. On the contrary, what we tend to construe as an ethical problem, determinable or otherwise, will be largely influenced by what evolutionary stage of the process we are at, and what it, not merely the "data," permits us to see.

Recently the Supreme Court agreed to hear arguments about whether or not retarded children have the legal right to a lawyer in commitment proceedings initiated by their parents. The evolutionary background of issues influencing such a decision is complex. One is tempted to suppose that the Supreme Court's decision was predictable solely on the basis of legal acknowledgment of the possibility of child abuse and the public record. That something more is needed to explain it is suggested by the fact that child abuse was appreciably greater during the nineteenth century, when parental jurisdictional rights went unquestioned. The legal and moral emphasis on the rights children have independent of parental definition is a legacy of recent origin. It also happens to coincide historically with the increased dissolution of the family as a social unit (Novak, 1976). The family is no longer perceived as that structure in terms of which a child's welfare can be meaningfully assessed. Because of this, what is now viewed as being in the interest of a child is even more ungummed from what is "good" for the family than it has been in the past. Consequently, it becomes easier to "see" ethical abuses of children in acts which in the past seemed to fall far short of this.

The effect of such momentous developments as dissolution of family ties on the perceived ethics or legality of issues ostensibly remote from it is sweeping. The proposal several years ago by a leading journalist of opinion that addicted New York City youths be detained in "camps" upstate as a rehabilitative measure, was attacked on the grounds of its perceived connection with "concentration camps." What would have been the fate of the proposal if the Nazi regime had never come to power? The question is far from academic, since before the horrors of World War II were publicized widely enough to become an inescapable part of our national consciousness, detention camps on the west coast for innocent Japanese-American citizens were very much a political reality.

Preventive Issues

Along similar lines, Williams (1957) has pointed out that it was the sterilization programs of World War II Germany, particularly their racial and political character, that brought eugenic programs for the retarded to an abrupt halt among "freedom loving peoples" (Williams, 1957, p. 84). Curiously, the constitutionality of involuntary sterilization was upheld by the courts in *Buck* v. *Bell*,[6] long before the outbreak of World War II, whereas a somewhat more circumspect judicial view of sterilization was apparent in *Skinner* v. *Oklahoma*,[7] a decision rendered in 1942. Justice Jackson's concurrence in *Skinner* referenced sterilization as motivated by the eugenic plan to eliminate certain characteristics from the race. It would be difficult to avoid making connections between judicial thinking and certain dramatic political events, especially when one considers that the most powerful arguments for sterilization of particular retarded clients are basically non-eugenic! As Williams has observed, sterilization of those clients for whom an unplanned pregnancy, if not terminated, would involve the birth of children incapable of receiving proper care is far from inadmissable. Objections to sterilization typically reference presumptive "rights" of retarded clients capable of procreation to have children. However, many abolitionist opponents of sterilization are silent about the drawbacks of social arrangements designed to achieve functional sterilization through segregation by sex. Such strategies, even if successful, drastically reduce the client's opportunity for sexual contact. The problem is especially poignant for the familial retardate, many of whose handicaps may be environmental, motivational, or iatrogenic (Stuart, 1968; Bogdan and Taylor, 1976). If so, the disadvantage of being sexually restricted due to the real or fancied inability to handle parenthood or birth control contributes further to a defectiveness status. While Kittrie's (1971) critique of the *parens patriae* tradition of the therapeutic state is also extended to sterilization programs, both he and others (Slovenko, 1965) acknowledge it as a non-eugenic therapeutic tool in appropriate cases (Kittrie, 1971, p. 334).

Just as lingering attitudes against sterilization cannot remain un-

---

[6] 274 U.S. 200 (1927).

[7] 316 U.S. 535, 541 (1942).

influenced by the racial purposes to which it was put by, for example, the Nazi regime, countervailing ideological climates may serve to move thinking in the opposite direction. For example, the women's movement has created a climate sympathetic to voluntary vasectomy. This may have future effects on the acceptability of sterilization as a therapeutic intervention, although it has its own meaning within the context of a rather different set of moral issues.

The women's movement also exerts a significant influence on attitudes toward abortion. At present this movement is the most powerful and sustained bulwark of the pro-abortionist position. Indeed, according to the view I am presently arguing, it is only a historical force like the women's movement to which legal thinking in *Roe* may be indirectly attributed. In this decision, the court affirmed the right of women to terminate pregnancies because the right is implied by the right to determine what shall be done with one's own body. However, the dilemmas posed by the abortion issue have too many philosophical intricacies (Wertheimer, 1971; Tooley, 1972; Warren, 1973; Brody, 1975; Hare, 1975; Jaggar, 1975; Thomson, 1975) to render the arguments of *Roe* alone as being decisive. There is, after all, the considerable moral issue of the rights of the unborn, against which the right of control over one's body may be interposed. Understandably, the former "rights" in turn hinge on the clarification of such thorny issues as the status of the fetus in relation to personhood,[8] or as a morally classifiable, hence disposable, part of the mother's body.

The abortion controversy, whatever its resolution, is the focal issue in a cluster of problems revolving around our ethical obligations to the unborn. It would be a mistake to confine the latter to the

---

[8] Werner (1976) has made a useful distinction between the status of a fetus as a "person" versus "human being." He identifies the former as that concept figuring in philosophical discussions concerning personal identity or other minds, and the latter as membership in the biological class *Homo sapiens*. He uses this distinction to challenge Hare's (1975) contention that, since the abortion issue hinges on the classification of the fetus as a "person," its resolution will necessarily involve additional normation, since the unborn lie on the fuzzy edges of the concept "person." Werner's anti-abortionist argument thus assumes an unarguable inclusion of the unborn in the class "human beings," and their unarguable exclusion from the class "persons," undercutting the necessity of further normation in Hare's sense. The pro-abortionist position has suffered a recent set-back through the impact of Pope Paul's *Humanae Vitae*, an encyclical proscribing birth control measures (Greeley et. al., 1976). Apparently, this encyclical left many American Catholics disaffected with the church, which had been moving in the direction of reform, sparked by the Second Vatican Council under Pope John. As a result, such indicators as church attendance, parochial school attendance and belief in apostolic succession from Christ have fallen off quite markedly.

ethical status of procedures undertaken on the fetus, since sizable dilemmas already exist in relation to the effect of our decisions on future generations. In essence, they involve ethical problems over genetic counseling of carriers of inherited disease. For example, Huntington's Chorea (HC) is inherited through a dominant auto-somal gene with complete penetrance. Accordingly, 50% of the children of a carrier will be expected to contract the disease. Since its symptoms usually develop during middle-age, a carrier will ordinarily have had children before discovering whether or not he has passed the disease on to them. Recent experiments with the drug L-dopa have led physicians to believe that a pre-morbid test for being a carrier is indicated by the dyskinesias produced in 36% of subjects with a positive family history of HC and none of the controls (Hemphill, 1973). Should this procedure get confirmed as a reliable way to determine the pre-choreic presence of HC, what ethical obligations do we have to discourage carriers from having children? That is, if it is obligatory to acknowledge our moral responsibilities to the fetus, can we in the last analysis fail to do so in relation to future generations? Can we accordingly ignore 50% of the future children of carriers who will pass on to them an incurable disease characterized by mental and physical deterioration in later life? We can, of course, object that discouraging carriers from procreating is the consequence of an unexamined moral assumption about the lesser value of lives plagued later by HC. However, such objections may be nourished equally by hardcore resistance to genetic coun-seling because it curtails procreating freely. If so, exercise of the latter right might be seen as one against which our moral obligation to future persons inheriting the disease should get balanced. Similar questions arise for transmitters of retinoblastoma, a malignant eye condition formerly resulting in death but now remediable by early radical surgery requiring removal of the eye and all cancerous tissue (Glass, 1972).

It was mentioned before that abortion will loom larger in clusters of significant ethical issues for the developmentally disabled. This is because there are at present about 33 diseases of genetic origin, some of which, like Down's Syndrome, PKU, Lesch-Nyan, Tay-Sachs, and sickle cell trait and anemia, can be determined prenatally by amniocentesis, or cytological examination of a speci-men of amniotic fluid withdrawn from the mother (Fuchs, 1966; Jacobsen and Barter, 1967; Nadler, 1969). The operation is not without its hazards (Ayd, 1970), and its contraindication may be defined by that proportion of risk outweighing the benefits of under-taking it (Littlefield, 1970). Nonetheless, determination of genetic or congenital defect by means of amniocentesis serves to dramatize the importance of the issue of abortion as it relates to developmental handicap. Obviously, if the pro-abortionist position comes to prevail while advances in prenatal detection continue, there may come a time when ethical issues over behavioral approaches to certain kinds of handicapped children may not even arise.

A controversial issue in pre-and post-natal genetic screening is its voluntary versus involuntary character. Clearly, the weight of scientific opinion is away from the belief that such programs, how-ever sophisticated in scope, can achieve complete eradication of genetic handicap (Lappé, 1972). In spite of the mandatory nature of PKU screening in over forty states, and mandatory premarital testing for sickle cell anemia in New York and Maryland, voluntarists (Murray, 1972; Lappé and Roblin, 1974) regard aspects of such programs as infringements on the right to privacy alluded to in *Gris-wold* v. *Connecticut*[9] and *Stanley* v. *Georgia.*[10] However, these legal rulings cover governmental intrusion into private matters, the con-duct of which does not inflict harm on others. It may be argued that the context is significantly different for transmitters of genetic defects, since "intentional" transmittal embraces the notion of harming another individual. Indeed, even if the law does not move in this direction for serious genetic disease like HC, the anti-abor-tionist, who also prizes the right to privacy against presumptive invasions of it by genetic screeners, is on the horns of a dilemma. To the extent that his arguments against abortion based on the humanhood of the fetus prevail, he will find himself even more compelled to balance the right of privacy against the obligation to undertake whatever measures ensure the health of the fetus. The same reasoning applies for postnatal screening programs.

The abortion issue might be viewed as one not easily classifiable as preventive or remedial. The pro-abortionist sees abortion as a way of offsetting the problems attendant on the birth of a seriously handicapped child. In this sense, it may be viewed as a preventive measure, since the individuality of the fetus is not acknowledged as a moral presupposition of the intervention. On the other hand, since the anti-abortionist classifies abortion as an instance of killing in

---

[9] 381 U.S. 479 (1965).
[10] 394 U.S. 557 (1969).

utero, he regards it as a morally unacceptable remedial measure in dealing with defective children.

Remedial Issues

Because there are a variety of conditions of a congenital or traumatic nature leading to retardation or developmental handicap in the earliest stages of life, it is obvious that genetic counseling or prenatal screening will not bear on the ethical problems they pose. The most poignant of these are that group of issues arising about the nature of our commitments to surviving defective children, especially those involving life and death decision-making (Fletcher, 1967; Veatch, 1972; Duff and Campbell, 1973; Reich and Smith, 1973; Shaw, 1973; Fletcher, 1974). Such issues have been the subject of extended ethical and legal discussion attributable to erosion of belief in the obligatory principle of preservation of life at all costs. In spite of the fact that objections to such interventions as euthanasia have been related back to the Sixth Commandment, an equally compelling religious tradition that recognizes exceptions can be documented. As firm a Catholic as Sir Thomas More made provisions for the rational administration of euthanasia in his *Utopia*, while the most entrenched opponents of the practice nevertheless acknowledge the dilemmas raised by, for example, the terminal cancer patient. The fascination of these dilemmas is indicated by the public interest in such cases as the Quinlan family. While the indefinite comatose condition is something of a rarity, it commands perhaps an undue share of public notice, considering the fact that decisions resulting in the death of defective children are rather commonplace. For example, Duff and Campbell (1973) indicate that fully 14% of infant deaths in a special-care nursery of the Yale-New Haven Hospital could be directly attributed to decisions to withhold treatment from neonates with congenital anomalies ranging from short-bowel syndrome to meningomyelocele. Physicians placed on the firing line with respect to decision-making and counseling in these matters (Lorber, 1971, 1973; Shaw, 1973) are in an unenviable position. They are exempted from avoidance maneuvers by virtue of their professional calling, yet subject to criticism by those who are strangers to the immediacy of such problems. By the same token, it would be premature to invest the practical judgment of the physician with ultimate moral significance, while jurisdiction under the auspices of one profession would be shortsighted. Williams (1957) thus refers to the "pretension" of the moral theologian who derives his "dictatorial" power of interpretation from pronouncements made "in the calm of his study" (Williams, 1957, p. 317). Surely, the agony over decisions about the killing of innocent individuals is itself a testament to the humanity of persons confronting them. The issue would appear to be one for which the forfeiture of input from theologians, lawyers, and philosophers would be tragic. It is precisely because the physcan or parents are closer to the furnace of practical decision-making that they must not be abandoned by others falsely reputed to have no important role. It is an unendurable burden to be compelled to make such decisions without the support of those whose very distance from the situation favorably equips them to shape ethical policy. The contribution is an enormously important one. Ultimately, it will aid those on the front line of making weighty decisions to approach them with a sense of security forged by the consistency of moral policy.

According to the Catholic doctrine of double effect, the functional equivalent of euthanasia is made ethically permissable only if the primary purpose of intention is to treat. Thus, a defective child who is in pain may be killed by the administration of a lethal amount of a certain drug if that amount is minimally necessary to relieve the pain. Williams (1957) feels that the admissibility of exceptions to euthanasia under the doctrine of double effect are "casuistical" (Williams, 1957, p. 321). That is, he feels it is altogether artificial to base moral guilt or innocence on distinctions between physicians who commit the same act, but who in one case have the intention to kill in the forefront of their minds and in the other case have the intention to treat. Williams asserts that there is no "legal difference between desiring or intending a consequence as following from your conduct, and persisting in your conduct with a knowledge that the consequence will inevitably follow from it, though not desiring that consequence" (Williams, 1957, p. 322). The argument is not persuasive, for two somewhat different reasons. First, that a "legal" distinction between guilt or innocence as provided by double effect cannot be maintained may be agreed to by Catholics, as this pertains to judgments in law. They would, however, maintain that a moral distinction can and must be made, since the making of it is what is partially meant by being a Catholic. Second, the conflict here is between two value systems, both of which recognize the urgency of accommodating our intuitions about particular situations to broader principles about the sanctity of life. We thus may feel a compelling moral urge to end an innocent life, while attempts to resolve the tension between these feelings and higher principles may take the form historically of doctrines like double effect. Indeed, what strikes Williams as "artificial" in Catholic doctrine nevertheless has its counterpart in American law. I refer to the distinction between omission and commission. While it is true that certain acts of omission may be subject to the same legal penalties as those incurred for acts of commission, the distinction between an intentional infliction of harm and the harm resulting in default of acting would have never been drawn had they always been viewed as morally equivalent. With respect to infanticide practiced on defective or seriously handicapped children, one might well draw parallels between Williams' assessment of the doctrine of double effect and the omission-commission dichotomy in law. Thus, is it not equally "artificial" to distinguish the moral gravity of withholding medication from a child with spina bifida from that of detaching tubes that deliver needed medication or sustenance? The foregoing remarks are not intended to obscure any distinction of legal importance between acts of omission and commission. They only aim to underscore the fact that the moral significance of the distinction may be illuminated by a better appreciation of human attempts to resolve the collision between intuitions in pragmatic situations and abstract ethical principles. For example, Fletcher (1967) attempts to assimilate a physician's discontinuing aid to a terminal patient to the legal notion of an omission. The validity of his argument is, for the moment, irrelevant. It is the function of the argument that is significant: permitting a greater degree of flexibility for physicians undertaking otherwise rational decisions to discontinue a patient's life. That is, it is precisely the prior acknowledgment of moral necessity for flexibility that motivates Fletcher to fashion legal arguments that will circumvent the classification of some medical interventions as "acts" of murder. In light of the recent ruling of the New Jersey Supreme Court in the Quinlan case, the flexibility Fletcher argues for is even further extended to acts of commission. Specifically, the New Jersey court ruled that turning off Karen Ann Quinlan's respirator is not subject to civil or criminal prosecution. The ruling involved an interesting combination of legal principles, including the right to privacy, legal guardianship, and standards under which terminally ill patients may now be allowed to die.

Most discussions of euthanasia revolve around cases of terminal patients whose voluntary killing is said to be justified in the light of the needless suffering they experience if they continue to live. This would not apply to the comatose patient, for whom euthanasia is undertaken on different grounds. Despite the fact that the term "euthanasia" still figures prominently in discussions of the ethical propriety of letting defective children die, this population poses a rather dissimilar set of problems. It is questionable whether allowing a defective child to die through an act of omission can be justified on the basis of its being "merciful" to the child in question. The failure to medicate a newborn with Down's Syndrome for a respiratory complication can hardly be regarded as relieving suffering. Mongoloids, like other types of handicapped children, "suffer" only in the eyes of others. While letting such children as those with meningomyelocele die may plausibly be undertaken with an eye toward the relief of future suffering, pediatric "euthanasia" is for the most part motivated by the social stigma and burden of care defective children place on parents and health agencies. It is consequently an undertaking which, even if it is classified as being in the "best interests" of the child, is so in a rather different sense of the term than is employed in connection with the problem of the terminal patient.

Shaw (1973) has drawn attention to some fairly acute ethical problems surfacing in the area of pediatric euthanasia. Among these are the following: If we are to permit variants of the practice in special circumstances, what rule should be applied about the magnitude of defect required in order to judge the act as ethically permissable? Should such criteria consist in the noncorrectableness of the anomaly, its severity, or a combination thereof? Should another criterion be the psychological burden placed on the mother caring for a defective child? If so, what is the moral danger inherent in acknowledging such a criterion if it can be used to terminate the life of a child whose anomaly constitutes an ethically tenuous deviation from normalcy?

Recent court rulings have marked a trend in legal thinking more and more concerned with the individual rights of retarded persons in connection with the possibility of various kinds of infringements. Retarded persons have been plaintiffs in rulings abolishing peonage and guaranteeing: 1) a minimum wage for institutional work;[11] 2) protection from deterioriation attendant on receiving mere custodial care in institutions legally mandated to provide more than this in the way of treatment;[12] and 3) free access to education or special classes

---

[11] *Souder* v. *Brennan* 367 F. Supp. 808 (D.C. 1973).

[12] *The New York State Association for Retarded Children* v. *Rockefeller* 357 F. Supp. 752 (E.D.N.Y. 1973).

structured to meet their particular needs.[13] These rulings aim not only at preventing exploitation or abuse, but also at an arbitrary conferral of defect status. Indeed, the damage that may be perpetrated by indiscriminate use of the label "retarded" is further dramatized by the fact that clients so labeled are persons of distinguishable capabilities. At least three-quarters of them have probably been handicapped to some extent by social assumptions about their alleged limitations.

Developmentally retarded institutional clients as a population pose special ethical problems. Unlike mental patients and prisoners, moderately and profoundly retarded clients as a rule are incapable of giving informed consent to therapeutic or experimental procedures legally requiring it. One is tempted to make comparisons between the legal status of the retarded and that of children in connection with informed consent, but there are differences. The common law tends to view children or legal minors as incapable of giving informed consent because of "immaturity." The latter concept is not strictly synonomous with "being underage," since the immaturity of children is *presumptive*. That is, a person who is younger than 21 (18 in jurisdictions like New York State) is presumed unable to give his informed consent to a therapeutic procedure unless there is evidence of an ability to comprehend certain information. In such cases, being a legal minor would not preclude being able to give informed consent. In rulings like *Bishop* v. *Shurley*[14] and *Bakker* v. *Welsh*,[15] for example, the courts ruled that legally underage boys were nonetheless capable of consenting to medical treatment of direct therapeutic benefit to them. In spite of the presumptive nature of "immaturity" in connection with normal minors, one wonders whether the label "retardate" is in effect judged as synonomous with "immature." If so, this and assumptions like it may contribute to an overgeneralized picture of the retarded client that gets transformed into a self-fulfilling prophecy.

The stringency of requirements for obtaining informed consent increase as interventions become "experimental" in nature. It is frequently difficult to determine the scope of a procedure as "experimental" or "therapeutic." In *Kaimowitz*, the court ruled that psycho-

---

[13] *Pennsylvania Association for Retarded Children* v. *Commonwealth of Pennsylvania* 334 F. Supp. 1257 (E.D. Pa. 1971); *Mills* v. *Board of Education of the District of Columbia* 348 F. Supp. 868 (D.C. 1972).

[14] 237 Mich. 76, 1926.

[15] 144 Mich. 632, 1906.

surgery was an "experimental technique," although it is hardly an innovative one, nor one that was known to most of the medical profession. Martin (1975) has addressed some of the legal complexities of distinguishing between therapeutic and experimental measures, while Kopelman (1975), in opposition to the views of Jonas (1969), argues that the two may only be distinguished as regards their goals in contrast to their methodological features.

Any strict interpretation of the Nuremberg Code's first princi- ple—that experimentation requires the voluntary and informed consent of participating subjects—would preclude those who do not have the capacity to consent. Whether the strict interpretation should further allow for the transfer of consent to legal guardians in contrast to a *de facto* prohibition is a cloudy issue. Prohibition of nontherapeutic experimentation on clients incapable of informed consent may be seen as having to be balanced against the benefit to others of properly conducted experimentation. Here the ethical issue is whether or not individual rights take precedence over the possi- bility of future benefits to numerous others. Kopelman (1975) raises the same question in connection with hypothetical cases in which experimentation is necessary to *protect* the immediate public interest, in contrast to *serving* its long-term future interests. Hence, she cites cases in which the infringement of personal rights is presumptively outweighed by an "overriding social need" (Kopelman, 1975, p. 6). Examples would be the "isolation of a carrier of a communicable disease" (Kopelman, 1975, p. 6). She concludes that such compulsory interventions remain unethical because, despite the social benefits they reap, they nonetheless treat persons as objects of study, as nonpersons. In doing so they patently represent more than merely a temporary inconvenience. Kopelman's argument may beg the ques- tion, since her conclusion is based on the premise that the use of unwilling subjects for urgent experimental missions is dehumanizing, when the issue seems to be whether what is or would be dehuman- izing in most contexts is nevertheless justified in the face of compel- ling societal needs. At any rate, a closer look at cases that are putative exceptions to the rule that compulsory experimentation is never justified will for the most part reveal them to be time-honored procedures for public protection, hence non-experimental in scope. For example, the justification for compulsory inoculation for the public's protection can hardly be judged as "experimental." One should, of course, be wary of the tautological nature of defining as "non-experimental" every intended intervention of "compulsory" character, a move we can hedge against by the development of independent criteria of "experimentation."

BEHAVIOR MODIFICATION

Definitions of the Field

A problem confronting anyone wishing to be informed about the ethical issues of behavior modification is an acceptable definition of the field. Treatment specialists who call themselves "behavior therapists," "behavior modifiers," or "applied behavior analysts" claim to identify with a tradition of treatment or experimental practice fundamentally *psychological* in nature. Accordingly, they react sharply to criticisms of "behavior modification" that are not divorced from reactions to the use of such modalities as ECT, chemotherapy, or psychosurgery. These biomedical techniques are considered the special province of the non-behaviorally oriented physician. They are consequently felt to fall outside "behavior modification," according to behaviorists (Brown, Wienckowski, and Stolz, 1975). Moreover, like others (Breggin, 1972; Salter, 1972; Wexler, 1972), behaviorists tend to frown on psychosurgery, feeling its use is promoted by physicians who may have defaulted on the ethical mandate to develop more effective, less drastic methods of treatment.[16]

In a way, behaviorists themselves must take partial responsibility for confusions over definitions of the field. In the face of attacks on "behavior modification" (Lucero, Vail, and Scherber, 1968; Carrera and Adams, 1970; Matson, 1971; Spece, 1972; Opton, 1974), they often fashion rebuttals, the deferred consequences of which are thereafter identified as someone else's confusion. For example, in

---

[16]Mark and Neville (1973), writing months after the *Kaimowitz* decision was handed down, asserted that psychosurgery "should never be performed on persons in any context in which they are under the jurisdiction of a court as the result of alleged criminal activity" (Mark and Neville, 1973, p. 772). They also favor extending this exclusionary principle to mental hospital inmates, as well as to those who refuse treatment. To the extent that these authors' criterion of suitability for psychosurgery is met (repeated acts of a violent nature), it would appear to characterize those who are already under some kind of jurisdiction. Yet Mark and Neville maintain that psychosurgery, if administered judiciously, would be a significant contribution to the solution of the problem of violence! Furthermore, and in line with a principal hypothesis of the present paper, the availability of a continued non-institutional pool of clients who would give their voluntary consent to the operation is probably less related to arguments in favor of its use, and more to whether or not the client had seen the movie "One Flew Over the Cuckoo's Nest."

response to the frequent criticism that behavior modification is unacceptable because it involves "control," behaviorists draw attention to the fact that most human endeavors, from child rearing and education to psychotherapy and politics, are forms of "behavior modification." Admittedly, such semantic gymnastics contain an important point and aim at lessening antagonism by revealing parallels between behavior modification and other recognized practices. However, if every instance of attempted influence on people suddenly becomes "behavior modification" in order to reform public prejudice about it, it seems unfair to attribute the alleged error of classifying ECT, chemotherapy, or psychosurgery as "behavior modification" to the uninformed. In hearings conducted preparatory to the court's decision in *Clonce* v. *Richardson*,[17] the Director of the Bureau of Prisons pointed out that, in what he called "the broadest sense," all the Bureau's programs were designed to "modify behavior."

In previous publication (Begelman, 1975a) I discussed four proposed definitions of behavior modification, to wit: 1) behavior modification is a set of specialized techniques historically classified as behavioristic, and administered by professionals who have identified themselves as behavior therapists; 2) behavior modification is the administration of therapeutic techniques producing major change, usually in relatively brief periods of time; 3) behavior modification is applied learning theory (or applied experimental psychology); and 4) behavior modification is the development of techniques of behavior change whose effectiveness can be explained in terms of learning theory or experimentally derived psychological principles. Despite the fact that I favored definition 4, I am now inclined to believe that it too is inadequate as it stands.

For example, does the psychologist who develops or applies the technique have to be the one who explains its efficacy behaviorally? Truax (1966) showed that Rogers, contrary to assumptions concerning "unconditional positive regard" made by client-centered psychotherapists, was in effect operating like a differential reinforcement machine with clients. Yet we would be unwilling to categorize Rogers as a behavior modifier, indicating a weakness in definition 4 if it did so classify him. On the other hand, we might be willing to classify as "behavior modification" as unlikely a candidate as a technique based upon reinforcements delivered before emission of the target behavior,

---

[17] 379 F. Supp. 338 (1974).

providing the practitioner conceptualized this a certain way. Thus, if the therapist in question were to say, "I believe I have hit upon a therapeutic illustration of the success of backward conditioning," we would tend to put him in the behavioralist camp.

There is something peculiar about the notion of a technique that cannot be said to derive from behavior theory, for the simple reason that the success or failure of any technique can be analyzed in behavioral terms. I conclude that any psychological technique is potentially a behavior modification technique. Indeed, if behavior theory or experimental psychology is that body of knowledge or principles accounting for acquired behavior change, what conceivable meaning can be attached to the notion of a technique that produces the change, yet can never be construed as an application of those principles? To constitute such an application, it is only necessary to use behavioral units of analysis in speaking about the change in question. The muddle here is the confusion between 1) the question of whether or not a technique represents an application of behavioral principles, and 2) the question of whether or not a therapist who cannot analyze the justification for, or operation of, a technique in behavioral terms deserves to be called a behavior modifier. In a very real sense, the difference between "behavior modification" and other effective behavior change techniques is not their distinctive features, but the language game (Wittgenstein, 1953) played by their respective practitioners.

The significance of the language game cannot be overestimated. Woolfolk and Wilson (1976) have shown that reactions to a videotape of a teacher were more favorable when she was described as practicing "humanistic education" than when she was described as administering "behavior modification techniques." The Woolfolk and Wilson experiment thus tends to confirm the notion that a significant variable in reactions to the ethics of behavior modification is the theoretical approach (most often identified by the language game) of the practitioner. Accordingly, a common reaction outside the profession is that it is, for example, ethically permissable for psychotherapists to encourage clients to explore feelings of resentment against one's parents in group psychotherapy, whereas it is felt there is something illicit in reinforcing group control over an individual's verbal behavior. However, the latter only amounts to playing a different language game in describing the same facts. If the likelihood of reactions to the ethical aspects of behavioral and nonbehavioral interventions is in part based upon the language games of their practitioners, other issues arise. First ethical criteria of treatment intervention should be divorced from the nature of a theoretical language game. That is, the ethical status of a treatment technique should be established independently of the way its practitioners conceptualize it. For example, a technique should not be assessed as "ethical" simply because it is referred to as an "exploration of inner motives" in contrast to "reinforcement of verbal behavior." Second, it is a moot question whether or not using a familiar behavioristic strategy in lessening public apprehension about behavior modification will prove successful. This is the ploy of attempting to shape a more sympathetic public response to behavior modification by drawing parellels between it and other permissable practices, such as psychoanalytically oriented therapy. The effect of the strategy may be to itensify fear of all kinds of psychological treatment, rather than to reduce apprehension of behavior modification.[18] Is the lonely target of liberation attack behavior modification per se or, rather, a much wider tradition of therapeutic approach, questionable aspects of which behavior modification is seen rightly or wrongly, as exemplifying?

Behavioral versus Ethical and Legal Concepts

Behavioral concepts are scientific units of analysis whose usefulness depends on their precision of meaning. Legal concepts, on the other hand, are useful only if they possess substantial open texture (Waismann, 1963), permitting an expansion of meaning in the light of new cases they are held to cover. Behaviorists sometimes display a degree of concern about this aspect of ethical and legal discourse. If the meaning of "good," "just," "rights," "informed consent," "voluntary," "ought," and so forth cannot be permanently fixed, how will the applied scientist be able to fulfill his obligation to provide the most effective service while being governed by proper ethical principles? Occasional attempts to bridge the gap between behavioral and ethical principles can be seen in, for instance, Skinner's (1971) contention that the adjectives "good" and "ethical" function as oblique refer-

---

[18] The prospect of an analogous backfiring in therapy was the subject of a limerick composed by the present author:

> A behaviorist named Peter
> Paired shock with the pangs of
>   an eater;
> The procedure was wasted
> On amounts the chap tasted:
> It merely made electricity sweeter.

ences to contingencies of reinforcement. The implication here is that the scientist is the ultimate authority on ethical matters because he is the most qualified to assess present and future contingencies. Limitations of space do not permit a detailed examination of the drawbacks of such a position. Suffice it to say that the Skinnerian analysis seems to systematically confuse what *is* valued with what *ought* to be valued. Skinner's ethical naturalism thus confuses "Killing Jews was a value for the Nazis" (because killing them was reinforced by the approval of fellow Nazis), with "The Nazis ought to have killed the Jews." Obviously, one may grant the former and still deny the latter.

A characteristic of ethical and legal, in contrast to behavioral, concepts is what Hart (1963) has called their *ascriptive* character. The failure to recognize the fact that even ordinary language has a variety of functions aside from the descriptive one has been characterized by philosophers as "the descriptive fallacy." In law, statements of the type "This is yours" are ascriptive, in the sense that they are blend of facts and law (Hart, 1963). It would be doing violence to their meaning to attempt to supply a set of necessary and sufficient conditions for their application, such that all doubt is removed, as it were, about the properties of goods tagged "yours."[19] The charge that ascriptive statements like those in law suffer from imprecision stems from the prejudice that they are made in default of the operational specificity demanded in the behavioral sciences. However, ethical and legal discourse are not "scientific" language games. Consequently, a behavioral scientist's impatience with concepts such as "voluntariness," "due process," "contract," "experiment," "right," "obligation," "duty," "informed consent," and so forth is often symptomatic of a much deeper problem, which is the failure to realize that the law is not struggling to be a "science," and is falling short of

---

[19] Hart says: "Now there are several characteristics of the legal element in these compounds or blends which conspire to make the way in which facts support or fail to support legal conclusions, or refute or fail to refute them, unlike certain standard models of how one kind of statement supports or refutes another, upon which philosophers are apt to concentrate attention. This is not apparent at once: for, when the judge decides that on the facts that he has found that there is a contract for sale between *A* and *B*, or that *B*, a publican, is guilty of the offence of supplying liquor to a constable on duty, or that *B* is liable for trespass because of what his horse had done on his neighbor's land, it looks, from the terminology, as if the law must consist of a set, if not a system, of legal concepts such as "contract," "the offence of supplying liquor to a constable on duty," and "trespass," invented or defined by the legislature or some other "source," and as if the function of the judge was simply to say "Yes" or "No" to the question: "Do the facts come within the scope of the formula defining the necessary and sufficient condition of "contract," "trespass," or "the offence of supplying liquor to a constable on duty"?" (Hart, 1963, p. 146).

this ideal. To expect it to define *operationally* "therapeutic obligation" would be analogous to a lawyer arguing that there must be
something unnecessarily petrified about the concepts "pulsar," "he-
terozygote," "response rate," or "normal distribution" because their
meaning is not continually expanded on the basis of fresh cases they
are ruled to cover. What is wrong with such diagnoses is, of course,
not the concepts in question, but an analysis of them calling for their
assimilation to discourse with rather different properties. Behaviorists
often approach notions like "informed consent" or "voluntariness" as
if the law could benefit from a bit more of that kind of operationalizing that is a workaday phenomenon in behavioral science. The assumption that the law is sophomoric science would appear to be suggested by such confusions as the argument that the M'Naughten
Rule[20] for insanity should be replaced by more "scientifically" based
criteria, such as those propounded in Durham,[21] or the frequently
heard argument that legal criteria of "voluntariness" are miscon-
ceived if determinism is true.

Conferences on the ethical issues of behavior modification
(Wood, 1975) include participants likely to refer to such odd-sound-
ing aspirations as the "shaping of ethical behaviors." The implication
seems to be that "ethical behavior" may be likened to a kind of com-
modity emerging from workshops, or a category of responses belong-
ing to the same logical type as, for instance, "reinforced behavior,"
etc. A corollary to the confusion that the adjective "ethical" is a
name for a set of descriptive behaviors that will be defined if and
when lawyers disambiguate their terms is that the real problem is a
behavioral, not conceptual one. That is, many behaviorists are con-
vinced that the problem of how to keep professional practices within
the boundaries of ethical imperatives is being delayed by scientifically naive or unsophisticated debate in legal quarters.

CONCLUSION
At present, and as the principal hypothesis of the present paper suggests, the delineation of ethical issues concerning the developmentally
disabled will be influenced by any number of significant external developments. The law is a sensitive measure of the way the ideological
wind blows, because it will register the impact of both remote and
immediate events of import. Especially significant will be develop-

---

[20] 10 Clark & Fin. 200, 9 Eng. Rep. 718 (1843).
[21] 214 F. 2d 862 (D.C. Cir. 1953).

ments in psychology itself. While psychologists often imagine their methods ensure a degree of insularity from ideology which they deemed the recurrent plight of other social forces, this is not the case. At present, for example, American psychology runs the gamut of intellectual fashion from those who insist that no one should be held responsible for anything to those who feel holding everyone (including and especially oneself) responsible is obligatory. In a reasonable legal system, persons generally assume responsibility for certain acts, and are relieved of it only when compelling grounds arise. A system that does not grant at least this much latitude is — as Charles Dickens' Mr. Bumble indicated — "a ass." Then again the law's being "a ass" is explicity what we must consider a principal motive behind all commendable efforts to change it.

REFERENCES

Arendt, H. 1963. Eichmann in Jerusalem: A Report on the Banality of Evil. Viking Press, New York.

Ayd, F. J. 1970. Fetology: Medical and ethical implications of intervention in the prenatal period. Ann. N.Y. Acad. Sci. 169:376-381.

Begelman, D. A. 1975a. Ethical and legal issues of behavior modification. In: M. Hersen, R. Eisler, and P. Miller (eds.), Progress in Behavior Modification, Vol. I. Academic Press, New York.

Begelman, D. 1975b. Homosexuality and the ethics of behavioral intervention. Paper presented at a symposium at the Ninth Annual Convention of the Association for the Advancement of Behavior Therapy, San Francisco, December.

Bogdan, R., and Taylor, S. 1976. The judged, not the judges: An insider's view of mental retardation. Amer. Psychol. 31:47-52.

Breggin, P. R. 1972. The return of lobotomy and psychosurgery. Congressional Record 118: E1603-E1612.

Brody, B. 1975. Fetal humanity and the theory of essentialism. In: R. Baker and F. Elliston (eds.), Philosophy and Sex. Prometheus Books, New York.

Brown, B. S., Wienckowski, L. A., and Stolz, S. 1975. Behavior modification: Perspective on a current issue. DHEW publication N. (ADM) 75-202.

Carrera, F., and Adams, P. L. 1970. An ethical perspective on operant conditioning. J. Amer. Acad. Child Psychiatr. 9: 607-634.

Davison, G. C. 1974. Homosexuality: The ethical challenge. Presidential Address, Ninth Annual Convention of the Association for the Advancement of Behavior Therapy, Chicago, November.

Duff, R. S., and Campbell, A. G. M. 1973. Moral and ethical dilemmas in the special care nursery. New Engl. J. Med. 289: 890-894.

Fletcher, J. 1972. Prolonging life. Washington Law Review 42: 999-1006.

Fletcher, J. 1972. Attitude towards defective newborns. Hastings Center Studies 2: 21-32.

Fuchs, F. 1966. Genetic information from amniotic fluid constituents. Clin. Obstet. Gynecol. 9: 565.

Glass, B. 1972. Human heredity and ethical problems. Perspect. Biol. Med. 15: 237–253.

Greeley, A. M., McCready, W. C., and McCourt, K. 1976. Catholic Schools in a Declining Church. Sheed and Ward, New York.

Hare, R. M. 1975. Abortion and the golden rule. In: R. Baker and F. Elliston (eds.), Philosophy and Sex. Prometheus Books, New York.

Hart, H. L. A. 1963. The ascription of responsibility and rights. In: A. G. N. Flew (ed.), Logic and Language, First Series. Basil Blackwell, Oxford.

Hemphill, M. 1973. Pretesting for Huntington's Disease: An Overview. Institute of Society, Ethics and the Life Sciences, Hastings-on-Hudson.

Jacobsen, C. B., and Barter, R. H. 1967. Inrauterine diagnosis and management of genetic defects. Amer. J. Obstet. Gynecol. 99: 796.

Jaggar, A. 1975. Abortion and a woman's right to decide. In: R. Baker and F. Elliston (eds.), Philosophy and Sex. Prometheus Books, New York.

Jonas, H. 1969. Philosophical reflections on experimentation with human subjects. Daedalus 98: 219-247.

Katz, J. 1969. The right to treatment—An enchanting legal fiction? University of Chicago Law Review 36: 755-783.

Kittrie, N. 1971. The Right to be Different: Deviance and Enforced Therapy. The John Hopkins University Press, Baltimore.

Kopelman, L. M. 1975. Human experimentation and subject consent. Unpublished manuscript, University of Rochester Medical School.

Lappé, M. 1972. Moral obligations and the fallacies of "genetic control." Theological Studies 33: 411-427.

Lappé, M., and Roblin, R. O. 1974. Newborn genetic screening as a concept in health care delivery: A critique. Ethical, Social and Legal Dimensions of Screening for Human Genetic Disease 10: 1-24.

Lasagna, L. 1969. Special subjects in human experimentation. Daedalus 98: 449-462.

Littlefield, J. W. 1970. The pregnancy at risk for a genetic disorder. New Engl. J. Med. 282:627-628.

London, P. 1975. Ethical issues in behavior modification. Paper presented at a symposium at the annual meeting of the American Psychological Association, Chicago.

Lorber, J. 1971. Results of treatment of myelomeningocele. Dev. Med. Child Neurol. 13:300.

Lorber, J. 1973. Early results of selective treatment of Spina Bifida Cystica, Brit. Med. J. (October): 204.

Lucero, R. J., Vail, D., and Scherber, J. 1968. Regulating operant conditioning programs. Hosp. Community Psychiatry 19:53-54.

Mark, J. H., and Neville, R. 1973. Brain surgery in aggressive epileptics. JAMA 226:765-772.

Martin, R. 1975. Legal Challenges to Behavior Modification. Research Press, Champaign, Ill.

Matson, F. W. 1971. Humanistic theory: The third revolution in psychology. Humanist 31:7-11.

Murray, R. F. 1972. Problems behind the promise: Ethical issues in mass genetic screening. Hastings Center Report 2:10-13.

Nadler, H. L. 1969. Prenatal detection of genetic defects. J. Pediatr. 74:132.

Novak, M. 1976. The family out of favor. Harper's Magazine (April): 37–46.

Opton, E. M. 1974. Psychiatric violence against prisoners: When therapy is punishment. Mississippi Law Journal 45:605–644.

Ramsey, P. 1970. The Patient as Person: Explorations of Medical Ethics. Yale University Press, New Haven.

Reich, W., and Smith, H. 1973. On the birth of a severely handicapped infant. Hastings Center Report 3:10–12.

Risley, T. 1975. Certify procedures not people. In: W. S. Wood (ed.), Issues in Evaluating Behavior Modification: Proceedings of the First Drake Conference on Professional Issues in Behavior Analysis. Research Press, Champaign, Ill.

Salter, A. 1972. Psychosurgery vs. political psychiatrists. Medical Opinion 1:47–51.

Shaw, A. 1973. Dilemmas of "informed consent" in children. New Engl. J. Med. 284:885–890.

Skinner, B. F. 1971. Beyond Freedom and Dignity. Alfred A. Knopf, New York.

Slovenko, R. 1965. A panoramic view. In: R. Slovenko (eds.), Sexual Behavior and the Law. Charles C. Thomas, Springfield, Ill.

Spece, R. G. 1972. (Note): Conditioning and other technologies used to "treat"? "rehabilitate"? "demolish"? prisoners and mental patients. Southern California Law Review 45:616–684.

Stuart, R. 1968. Iatrogenic illness: causes, illustrations and cure. Paper presented at the Conference on Behavioral Technology, sponsored by the Department of Psychology, University of Oregon, Eugene, Oregon.

Szasz, T. S. 1961. The Myth of Mental Illness. Hoeber-Harper, New York.

Thomson, J. J. 1975. A defense of abortion. In: R. Baker and F. Elliston (eds.), Philosophy and Sex. Prometheus Books, New York.

Tooley, M. 1972. Abortion and infanticide. Philosophy and Public Affairs 2:45–49.

Truax, C. B. 1966. Reinforcement and nonreinforcement in Rogerian psychotherapy. J. Abnorm. Psychol. 71:1–9.

Veatch, R. M. 1972. Choosing not to prolong dying. Med. Dimensions (December): 9–10.

Waismann, F. 1963. Verifiability. In: A.G.N. Flew (ed.), Logic and Language, First Series. Basil Blackwell, Oxford.

Warren, M. A. 1973. Moral and legal status of abortion. The Monist 57:55.

Werner, R. 1976. Hare on abortion. Unpublished manuscript, Kirkland College.

Wertheimer, R. 1971. Understanding the abortion argument. Philosophy and Public Affairs 1:79.

Wexler, D. B. 1972. Violence and the brain. Harvard Law Review 85:1489–1498.

Williams, G. L. 1957. The Sanctity of Life and the Criminal Law. Alfred A. Knopf, New York.

Wittgenstein, L. 1953. Philosophical Investigations. Macmillan, London.

Wood, W. S. 1975. Issues in Evaluating Behavior Modification: Proceedings of the First Drake Conference on Professional Issues in Behavior Analysis. Research Press, Champaign, Ill.

Woolfolk, A. E., and Wilson, T. G. 1976. Language, labeling and biases against behavior modification. Paper presented at the 47th Annual Meeting of the Eastern Psychological Association, New York City, April.

ETHICAL RESPONSIBILITIES IN REDUCTIVE PROGRAMS FOR THE RETARDED

Alan C. Repp & Diane E. D. Deitz

Behavioral psychology has had an enormous and growing influence in mental health services during the last decade—an influence that was certainly greeted by its proponents with enthusiasm and unguarded optimism. With its emphasis on accountability and data, the *theory*[1] of behaviorism seemed to have met one of the major needs of both the government and the public and seemed collaterally to have outgrown its literary association with *1984* and *Brave New World* and other works warning of the dangers of mass behavioral control.

The dissociation, however, was either short-lived or in reality a non-event. As a result of many poorly trained persons claiming to be competent in behavior modification, many procedures have erroneously been included under this rubric, and the unfortunate associations are being restated. Furthermore, because of the extremely poor judgment[2] of some well-trained behaviorists, some unethical procedures are also being included.

A different version of this paper was presented at the Atlanta Conference on Current and Future Behavioral Trends for the Developmentally Disabled, Atlanta, Georgia, 1976.

[1]'Theory' as discussed by B. F. Skinner in *Are Theories of Learning Necessary?* (Midwestern Psychological Association, 1949).

[2] As was evidenced by the occurrences that led to the development of the "Guidelines on Behavior Management" by the Florida Division of Retardation.

One of the facilities in which both appropriate and inappropriate behavioral procedures are being increasingly used is the institution. Institutions for the mentally ill and the mentally retarded have long been guilty of abridging human rights for many reasons, two of which are: 1) that there is virtually always external pressure to maintain the patient's confinement, a pressure that bears a collateral approbation of the facility's practices, and 2) that the resident is usually incapable of, or is barred from, protesting. However, one of those who is quite capable of protesting is Janet Gotkin, who has charged that:

(mental hospitals) are not open to scrutiny, and that they consistently resist efforts by oursiders to make them truly accountable for what goes on inside their walls. The hospitals use a self-policing system which makes them, in practice, accountable to virtually no one but themselves. The purpose of the institution is not to provide 'treatment' for the 'mentally ill', whoever they may be; rather, mental hospitals are bins for society's refuse—poor people, the minorities, old people, children, women, the peculiar, the radical, the sad, the nonconforming, the eccentric. These human garbage dumps, masquerading as hospitals, are instruments for social control. Mental patients are deprived of freedom until they act the way a small, powerful, socially sanctioned group claims it is proper to act. They are confined only because their differentness is a threat and an affront to society. Mental hospitalization itself is, and always has been, the ultimate in behavior modification.[3]

PROBLEMS GENERATED BY
"THE HOSPITAL AS A BEHAVIOR MODIFIER"

There are several concerns with Gotkin's remark that hospitals are the ultimate in behavior modification. The first, and a concern for everyone, is that it is true. No private sector, even advertising, and no governmental group, with the possible exception of the military, is so dedicated to the principle that a particular person's behavior must be modified for that person's own good. At times that dedication results in an inactivity generated by pleadings of helplessness from staff and legislators; other times it results in an overly zealous attempt to treat the patient's malady in any form necessary to produce change—a change at any cost and a change produced by non-regulated methods; and at other times, too few times, it results in active treatment that all, including the patient, agree is appropriately directed.

___

[3] From "New words for an old power trip: A critique of behavior modification in institutional settings." *Arizona Law Review,* 1975 17(1), 29-32.

However, the problem is not so much that behavior is to be modified—that is a given, and behavior change *per se* is perfectly acceptable. After all, we all hope that our behavior changes as we mature, as we learn more about our profession and environment in general; we do, in fact, pay persons to modify our behavior (e.g., teachers and therapists), and we become very upset when our behavior is not modified to the criterion level we have set. The problem lies in the decisions about 1) what behaviors are to be changed, 2) what procedures will be used to generate the change, and 3) who will be involved in making the decision to change.

Another concern, particularly for behaviorists, is that insofar as the public is concerned, too many procedures qualify as behavior modification and much too little is required of other procedures before they are labeled behavioral procedures. Many programs include some of the basic components of a behavioral program, but we are all extremely tired of hearing poorly trained teachers, university personnel, and program administrators proclaim that "this is a behavior modification program" while we watch someone dispense M& M's to students. While we look for within-task data, between-task data, task sequencing, integrated objectives in more than one area, the reason for the task, the generalization procedure, the entrance requirements of the next service placement for that student, the results of reinforcer sampling, and the specified program to bring behavior under the control of natural stimuli, we see only someone fairly indiscriminately giving M&M's. It is no wonder that behaviorists are charged with being too simplistic.

Other procedures disregard behavioral principles, yet they are still drawn together by the public and placed under the rubric of behavior modification. As Martin (1974) has indicated, this group includes:

1. Psychosurgery, a surgical intervention with radical results, used primarily on aggressive persons
2. Chemotherapy, drug intervention with supposedly reversible and non-interactive effects
3. Neuropharmacology, a non-reversible technique that permanently alters the chemistry of the brain
4. Electrical stimulation of the brain
5. Electroconvulsive therapy, a neolithic procedure seemingly intended to render the patient a moving but essentially comatose being
6. Psychoanalysis, a long-term procedure now thought by many

professionals to be more for the benefit of the therapist than the patient

7.   Behavioral instrumentation, such as electrode implementation
8.   Genetic screening and manipulation.

A behaviorist would certainly find it hard to believe that Skinner's emphasis on the importance of naturally occurring environmental events has been taken to include procedures like psychoanalysis and radical drug and chemical intervention, but it has, and we have only our own field to blame. The term "behavior modification" is inappropriate, as we all know from the phrase we frequently use ourselves: "but everyone is changing behavior." The problem has been partially solved by the flight to the term "applied behavior analysis," but we may merely be in the business of changing titles every decade, and the real problem has not been solved for those for whom it really counts—the patients who are forced into accepting these interventions. We have had a very bad press, having been associated far to much with the Orwell and Huxley warnings about our society. We have also suffered from Skinner's (1971) wittily titled and incisively written *Beyond Freedom and Dignity*, the title of which was read by many, and the text of which was read by few and understood by fewer.

However, Skinner long ago offered a solution to these problems, a solution that is a cornerstone to the success of the inductive theory, that is: 1) to make all procedures and results public, and 2) to be fully accountable through data collection. An acceptable approach for us would be to examine our problems within those guidelines, and, as a beginning in that direction, the following components of reductive programs in institutions for the retarded are discussed herein: 1) the reasons for intervention, 2) protecting the rights of residents subject to intervention, and 3) protecting the rights of other involved persons.

OBJECTIVES OF REDUCTIVE PROGRAMS

Reducing Extra-Institutional Responding

The most dramatic and most significant reductive program is that which prevents any responding outside an institution; and that program of course begins with the admission procedure. The important point for our consideration is an obvious one, yet one that we often ignore: Admission to a mental retardation facility is usually requested by someone other than the future resident. Admission is much to the benefit of someone other than the applicant—sometimes the family, sometimes a judge, sometimes a politician; only occasionally is admission for the applicant's benefit. For that reason, we must be careful about the admission procedure, because, as those of us at institutions know, admission is much easier to arrange than release.

To guard both the right to admission and the right to be protected from admission, we must attempt to define objective criteria for admission, no matter how difficult this quicksilver objective is. In the majority of institutions, criteria for admission and release are too general and too subject to the *mood* of the admission committee's members—or to political pressures from those who may control next year's budget. Can we really continue to allow questions of admission to be decided by the vagaries of committee members? Can we continue to allow a resident to be forced to remain in an institution because the parents argue against release, and one is a Councilman while the other works for the Lieutenant Governor? (This actually happened at an institution in Georgia.)

Most admission committees are staffed by very good people who do want the individual to be in the best place for over-all progress. However, we all need objective, data-based criteria for decision, and these committees are certainly no different than teachers, who need to know what a student has already learned before he can be placed on an appropriate task sequence in class. Most committees have attempted to establish some criteria for admission, but what type of criteria are they? They are usually: "give 7 points if the family situation is very poor, 5 points if moderately poor, 3 points if not so bad," etc. But what is "very poor"? Are we judging a figure skating contest, i.e., generating scores sometimes severely affected by regionalism and politics, or are we deciding whether or not to restrict a *person's* right to expression in a life outside the restrictive confines of an institution?

In our pursuit of objectivity, we should not be fooled by data, which are numerical or categorical, and which therefore gain an aura of respectibility, objectivity, validity, and importance. Can we allow judgments about admission to be affected by the level of retardation when the category is predominently determined by the score on the IQ test? Hardly! We need to know what behaviors the person is and is not capable of, the behavioral deficits and anomalies of the person with the skills exhibited by the staff in treating these problems. Why is an admission committee not provided with this information? Usually because there is no administrative backing, there are no tests already developed (the Adaptive Behavior Scale is an embarrassment, and the Behavioral Characteristics Progression is unwieldy), and because many diagnosis and evaluation staff argue that a detailed analysis of the student's behavior would take too long to obtain—*too long to obtain*, when the life of that individual is to be decided by persons very external to him!

We must have criteria for admission *and release* that, in turn, have three criteria for their own formation: 1) they should be defined either in observable terms or, if not in observable terms, then at least in terms that allow assessment; 2) they should be weighted in a data-based manner that describes the successes and failures, both within and outside institutions, of individuals in similar situations; and 3) they must specify objectives for the resident that will allow the institutional staff to provide programs directed to release.

Reducing Socially Maladaptive Responding

The presenting problem for most admission requests is not really a problem of the individual, but rather a problem of those around him who are unable to cope with him and who desire him to be removed from their environment. This problem is the basic reason for seeking admission, whether the procedure is being pursued by the family, a judge, a politician, or a training center director. Unfortunately, the cause of the problem often exists within the individual's living environment (e.g., parental abandonment) rather than with the individual (e.g., severe physical involvement requiring continous medical attention).

Nevertheless, the institution is charged with ridding the admitting party of its problem and is usually charged conjointly with decreasing maladaptive responding. This objective presents extreme problems for institutions, several of which are legal and moral and require our protection of the individual's rights. Others, however, involve tactical problems that give question to whether placement for this reason is justified when an institution is: 1) populated by many persons with extremely bizarre behaviors who serve as models, 2) fraught with extremely high auditory and visual noise that leaves even staff exhausted at the end of eight hours (with what we are learning from environmentalists what several hours of noise per day will do to our nervous system, it is easy to comprehend how much it can affect residents continually exposed to it), 3) structured, with few and usually no available retreats to privacy, 4) unable or unwilling to offer opportunities for heterosexual relations and their accompanying release from tension, 5) managed with staffing patterns that will never provide enough staff for the private and gentle relations possible in a family, and 6) generally faced with high staff turnover that breaks social ties and teaches the resident to resist making them again. Instead of being the appropriate place for eliminating maladaptive responding, the institution may be the very worst, and, for this reason, placement is usually an extreme tactical error. Indeed, considering the many reasons promoting program failure, institutional staff should be lauded when they do succeed.

However, given that we do succeed sometimes and that we do try to succeed many other times, there are several considerations for those implementing programs to reduce socially maladaptive responding. The first concerns the classification itself. Who decides that a behavior is socially maladaptive, and on what basis? In order to determine what is maladaptive, there must be an examination of the present environment and the one(s) in which the resident will be placed upon release. Clearly, what might not be inappropriate in a family of three or four may be disastrous on a ward of 15, 30, or 60. If we can make a determination of the appropriateness of a classification, we have a better basis for programs that are meaningful to the individual instead of programs that are only meaningful to staff who are idiosyncratically annoyed with an otherwise innocuous behavior.

A second consideration is whether or not the maladaptive behavior interferes with the acquisition of appropriate responding. The behavior may occur at such a high rate that other behaviors tend not to occur or are incompatible, in that it is physically impossible to engage in both the maladaptive behavior and the task behavior. Examples are: high-rate stereotypic responding, such as finger-flicking and head weaving; counter-academic responding, such as being out of one's seat; and the many types of counter-social, oppositional behaviors.

Another consideration is selection of the procedure to be used. Practitioners *and administrators* must be familiar with the full range of available strategies and their advantages and disadvantages. Of those strategies available, the one with the least restrictive conditions is preferable *if it is the considered judgment of trained individuals that the procedure promises to be effective in the particular situation within a reasonable amount of time.* We simply must stop ignoring the fact that there are some types of behavior, such as self-abusive behavior, for which aversive techniques may be the most effective and ethical option for eliminating the behavior. A prime consideration in deciding whether or not to employ aversive techniques is the number of times it would be necessary to repeat the procedure to produce a positive behavior change; however, this answer is obviously difficult to determine. The ethical dilemma of the least restrictive method versus the shortest program duration is one that will continue to plague those in decision-making positions. Is an aversive treatment over a short time period really more punitive and unethical than milder treatment over a long time period?

Schwitzgebel (1975) said that "where duration is limitless, treatment is 'de facto' ineffective and cannot be allowed simply to continue." However, unless there is another procedure that proves to be totally effective, what is the alternative to limitless duration? While "garbage eating," "food stealing," and "aggressive acting-out" had not been eliminated from the active repertoire of one institutionalized student, through the use of "quiet training" the behaviors had been significantly reduced to the point where they occurred an average of three times a week. However, an administrator of the institution revoked approval of the procedure, labeling it ineffective, because it had not eliminated the behaviors. No alternative procedure was provided, and the frequency of the behaviors increased to forty-three in one week. While there should be concern for an unlimited continuance of reductive programs, one must obviously consider the alternative possibilities.

Reducing Counter-Institutional Responding

Counter-institutional responding is responding that interferes with the operation of the institution. When an inappropriate response is in the form of aggressive responding, such as one resident throwing another's food on the floor, it is called socially maladaptive, because it would be inappropriate both inside and outside the facility. However, when a resident's behavior is considered inappropriate only because it is occurring in the institution, it is called counter-institutional.

In institutions some truly sad restrictions of individual freedoms may be necessary—these restrictions are compulsory because institutional staff must work toward providing group services, no matter how individualized the treatment programs are intended to be. For example, residents within a living unit generally have to eat at the same time, and they generally are served the same food. A family usually eats at the same time, so that concept is not inappropriate; but a family can regulate the time of a meal in a particular day. In a family, if some members are hungry at 6:00, or are tired and prefer to take a nap, dinner can be postponed. However, such freedom is not possible in institutions, where food carts must, for example, arrive at 5:45 and leave at 6:45 because the residents are scheduled for another activity at 6:45. Refusing to eat at this time is a counter-institutional behavior, as is refusing particular food items, and these behaviors cannot be tolerated. How many of us have absolutely no choice in the foods served at a meal? The only choice the institutionalized retardate has is whether or not to eat what is served. Most kitchens provide one menu, three times (or four with evening snacks) per day, seven days per week. Any verbal or nonverbal behavior meaning "I'd rather have a cheeseburger than this mystery meat" is simply not acceptable because it is counter to the institution's sameness of operation.

Reducing Responding For Research Purposes

There are two issues of primary concern in research programs for reducing responding. The first is whether or not the needs of the resident are compatible with the needs of the research program. Is the decision to treat based on a need for treatment, or has a treatment program been designed and the subjects subsequently selected to fit the needs of the proposal? This consideration is discussed in the following section on the protection of resident's rights.

A second issue of concern is the methodology of the research proposal. Although the distinction is sometimes vague, we can usually identify two types of responses (insignificant versus socially significant) and two types of contingencies (innocuous versus significant). By the former distinction, we mean such things as the reduction of button pressing versus the reduction of talking; by the latter, we mean such things as paying subjects with trinkets for reduced responding versus applying shock when the behavior occurs. These distinctions provide a 2 x 2 matrix from which research committees, or the parents, or resident advocates have few easy choices in deciding whether or not to approve a proposal. The lack of quantifiable data promotes both ambiguity and a lack of referent for decision making.

A further problem of methodology involves the experimental design. Again, the distinction becomes vague at times, but, in general, experimental design involves two choices: either between-subject or within-subject. In the former, one group of subjects receives treatment while another group receives either nothing or a placebo; the results are then compared statistically to determine the effects of the treatment. There are concerns in this area for each of these groups.

For the treatment group, the concern is whether or not the intervention they receive is justified in the sense of: 1) whether or not there are other, reasonable, non-experimental methods available; 2) whether or not the intervention is commensurate with the severity of the response and its disruption of the resident's progress; 3) whether or not the intervention is implemented in sufficient length (or brevity) to ensure rapid reduction and generalization when the behavior is not innocuous and does interfere with the resident's progress; and 4) whether or not the resident is compensated for his essentially meaningless participation if the behavior is innocuous, and, if he is, whether or not he is compensated suitably (e.g., paid at the minimum wage rate).

In the control group, the overriding concern is whether or not the resident is deprived of intervention just to meet the needs of the experimenter for appropriate statistical analysis. If this is the case, then the experimenter should choose another design; if he cannot, then the decision between research benefit and human rights must be addressed. Additional considerations include just compensation for participation and the immediate availability of intervention for these residents if the treatment proves successful for those in the treatment group.

While the within-subject design does not have all the same concerns that the between-subject does, it shares some and has others indigenous to itself. Shared are concerns about matching treatment with response severity, about just compensation, and about length of treatment programs (a special concern for reversal designs). While there are many possible within-subject designs, three predominate, and they are discussed here.

The AB design is the simplest and is closely related to the between-subject design. It is merely a case in which an individual serves in both the control and the treatment conditions, usually in that order. The analysis then becomes a comparison of the control and treatment conditions as both affect the same individual's behavior, instead of a comparison of the conditions as each affects different persons' behaviors. The concerns here are similar to those in the previous designs; e.g., matching treatment with the problem, just compensation, a provision for generalization of the treatment effects if they are successful, and the length of the control (baseline) condition.

The ABAB, or reversal, design is merely an AB design repeated once on the same individual. All the problems of the AB design are also problems for the ABAB design. The major additional one for the latter is the same as its experimental strength—the concept of reversal. If, in the second phase, there is some treatment success, the design calls for the cessation of treatment for some period in the third phase. The change provides the experimenter with a comparison of the treatment effects with both the preceding and subsequent phases. However, it provides the resident with a period in which he is not receiving treatment that the experimenter believes is effective. The problem becomes a trade-off between lack of treatment for the resident and increased surety of treatment effectiveness for the experimenter. Again, we have no quantifiable basis for the decision of whether the ends justify the means—we have only a qualitative guess.

Inherent in the choice to reverse conditions in the ABAB design is the question of how long to continue the second baseline. For experimental purposes, the second baseline should be continued for a relatively long period of time, during which a careful assessment of effects can be made, while, for the purposes of the individual, the second baseline should continue for a very short time—a time used to assess whether or not the effect will generalize to those periods in which treatment is not available. Although the questions of both the researcher and the service provider are extremely similar, one requires a much longer time to answer than the other.

The third type of design frequently used is a multiple baseline, which can be an AB, ABA, or ABAB design in which the times at which condition changes are made are staggered across subjects, across situations, or across different responses. When only the AB design is used, and the initiation of treatment is staggered, the problems associated with reversal designs do not occur; the problems with the AB design, however, remain. In addition, because treatment begins on different days for the experimental subjects (e.g., day 10 for subject 1, day 15 for subject 2, and day 20 for subject 3), some residents are denied treatment for longer periods just to meet design requirements. The justifications for the length of this delay are often very difficult to make because, again, they must be made in the absence of data. Beyond simply justifying a delay, one must support a delay of a particular number of sessions for particular residents. When in a research proposal the experimental jargon of S_1, S_2, etc., is changed to "When she is not restrained Gloria picks her face until it bleeds," or to "Ronnie hits other residents about 20 times per day," the justifications become more difficult than when one is merely making phase change decisions and not having to interact with the residents.

PROTECTING THE RIGHTS OF
RESIDENTS WHO ARE SUBJECT TO INTERVENTION

Human Rights Committees

Once the decision has been made to attempt an intervention strategy in order to decrease a behavior emitted by a resident, there are in most institutions human rights committees operating to "protect" the rights of those residents. Unfortunately, those committees are too frequently comprised of persons with degrees in medicine, nursing, social work, and other discipline areas in which even those holding doctoral degrees usually do not receive any training in behavioral strategies for reducing behavior. This committee then has the power to determine whether or not proposed programs adequately protect the rights of residents, while very often those programs are written by persons specifically trained in the use of behavioral procedures. While ignorance may occasionally be bliss, it usually isn't for the recipients of services approved or disapproved.

In selecting a reduction procedure, we clearly have a responsibility to employ the method that, in the judgment of the best-trained individuals available, will be the best balance between effectiveness and restrictiveness. However, in this age of human rights committees generated by *Wyatt* v. *Stickney* and other court cases, we find it explicit in some, but implicit in all, committee policies that one must at least try non-negative approaches (e.g., reinforcing incompatible responding (DRI), differentially reinforcing low rates of responding (DRL), differentially reinforcing other behaviors (DRO), or extinction), before trying punitive approaches (e.g., positive punishment, time-out, response cost, and the various forms of overcorrection such as quiet training and oral hygiene). While the concept of initially trying the least restrictive methods is, at first glance, laudable, in reality it is 1) a camouflage to protect the committee as well as the administrators of the institution, 2) a procedure that is either seldom followed or presents such a time-consuming obstacle that practitioners give up on the proposed program, and 3) a procedure that is usually counter-productive to the resident's right to immediate treatment.

Let us consider a hypothetical case. Unless the behavior is extraordinarily disruptive, it will have been occurring for at least a week, and perhaps years, before anyone attends to it enough to define it as a problem requiring a program. The first step, of course, is to record baseline data for at least a week. Then the program team meets— another day—and decides to implement a DRI procedure—a decision requiring another day to inform all staff. This procedure is tried for a few days and is not effective; but, as any behaviorist knows, the first days are often the worst, so it is continued for a total of two weeks until consensus is that the data show it to be ineffective. Another two days pass with meetings and training and dissemination of program information, and a DRO program is then instituted, but with the same results; then DRL is tried, and then extinction—all without success.

The program team can now propose to the Human Rights Committee implementation of an aversive method (let's choose time-out) and is given time at the next meeting, which will be held in a week. Suppose the Committee approves the new procedure at this initial meeting—can we proceed? Of course not! The parents or legal guardian must sign informed consent papers approving the procedure—a step requiring at least another week. Now can we proceed? Still no! The facility's director must sign the form, but he is out of town and will not be back until next week. Now can we proceed? Yes, finally!

Our treatment program has taken 90 days to arrive at the introduction of a non-positive approach. Suppose all time requirements can be halved. Is even this really meeting the needs of the resident? Is it really protecting the rights of the resident?

Several years ago, we had an out-patient in our Early Childhood Program who engaged in head banging. A program consisting of extinction, DRO, DRI, tokens, and social reinforcement was developed and implemented for three class hours each day for four months. The behavior was reduced to 17% of the baseline level, but the child still banged his head on the concrete floor, and the furniture still vibrated when he banged his head on the floor. The treatment alternatives available had been exhausted and had failed.

However, another institution a few miles away could use faradic aversive stimulation and would be able to continue to do so for two more weeks before the Commissioner was going to prohibit its use throughout the state. Our head-banging student was quickly admitted there for two days. The program director videotaped each session for his and the student's protection and implemented a program in which he applied a brief electric shock each time the subject banged his head. He applied the shock three times the first day and not at all the second day. The student returned to our program for six weeks, during which time he did not bang his head again. He was then transferred to a public preschool program and maintained this level of non-behavior during the brief period we maintained contact before his family moved.

It is hoped that he did not begin to bang his head again, but the question of behavior recovery is irrelevant in this context. The point is that for months this child and his family had to undergo the trauma of his bruised and split forehead because we were not allowed to use what all of us felt would be the most effective means of reducing this behavior. A legal commitment may have been met, but a moral commitment certainly was not.

This general procedure of attempting positive approaches first, and having alternate methods approved by committees, by the director of the facility, and by the parents has been supported by legal authorities, by federal authorities (HEW), and by advocate groups (NARC) as delimiting the omnipotent doctrine of *in loco parentis* practiced by institutions. It is only an assumption, however, that changing the authority to authorize programs to committees, directors, and parents totally benefits the resident. These committees tend to be plodding and very removed from the daily problems of contending with, and providing services for, the resident. While committees may, on occasion, promote valuable objectivity, they also promote a lack of concern and lack of feel for daily occurrences. There simply are no contingencies on the committee's action or lack thereof, and we all know that such a situation eventually, if not immediately, leads to major problems.

One must also ask: What are the contingencies on the director's approval or disapproval of a program? Because the administrator is not generally answerable to those beneath him in the administrative structure, there are only rare contingencies operative in this area. The administrator need only be concerned with not approving methods that might lead to inquiry by his superiors, or by the press, or by federal or state surveyors. In general, this is probably the only contingency affecting his behavior, regardless of whether or not it is in the best interest of the resident.

Perhaps a viable attempt to implement contingencies would be to force administrators and committees to provide alternative approaches when they reject a treatment plan. This practice would force them to attend to behavioral practices, either through personal competencies in the area or through having associates who do have such competencies. In an effort to address this problem, our institution has recently formed a Behavior Modification Committee, comprised of persons with degrees in psychology and training in applied behavioral analysis. This committee forwards approved behavioral proposals to the Human Rights Committee and suggests improvements or alternative procedures for those proposals it does not approve. However, all recommended programs must still be approved by the Human Rights Committee, the director, and the parents or guardian.

And what of the parents? Parents pose a most curious problem, because most of us have found parents to be in one of two groups: 1) those who will consent to anything the institution asks, perhaps hoping for their child's progress; and 2) those who oppose anything that will help their child progress to the point at which he could be released. (The latter are an obdurate group who will engage in all types of political pressures and threats to maintain institutionalization; unfortunately, we all are familiar with these cases.) While we know that these groupings are a generalization, we find it remarkably easy to accurately classify our parents in them. The result is very interesting, whether it applies to all or to just some cases, because it promotes a "rubber-stamp" procedure, the major purpose of which appears to be protection of the institution rather than protection of the resident. When the parents are asked to approve programs, the institutional staff are not asking the parents to consider the problem; they are interested in having the program approved and, therefore, are asking the parents for rapid approval. With this as an objective, the plan is simple: parents in the first category are told that the program will help their child in the institution and will help them manage him when he returns home; parents in the second category are only told that life in the institution will be easier and more humane for their child—great care is taken to avoid discussion of the resident's potential for release. The whole procedure of parental approval has become a "political" one in which institutional staff quickly learn to guide questions to provide a "yes" answer.

Research Committees

The fundamental question for protecting a resident's rights in research programs to reduce behavior is whether the needs of the research program are compatible with the needs of the resident. If a research committee decides that they are, then there appears to be little conflict. If they are not, there are two alternatives. The first is simply to disallow any programs in which the needs of the individual and the researcher are not isomorphic. This attitude, however, would be disastrous for the progress of science and for the many who could benefit from the results of experiments involving relatively few.

The second alternative is to allow some research, even if the needs of the research program do not meet the needs of the individual. However, establishing a basis for deciding which research to allow is extremely difficult because there is no way to quantify on a cardinal scale either the benefits a research project can provide or how much benefit the subjects will not receive in other areas because of the time involved in participating in the research. The decision becomes one that must be based on qualitative information rather than on quantitative information and is therefore more difficult.

Because one of the proposed solutions is to demand that voluntary consent be obtained from the resident (if appropriate) or the resident's parent or guardian, let us consider the issue of consent as it relates to the use of reductive procedures still considered in the research stage. The Research Department at our institution employs three different consent classifications, the first of which is a form of blanket consent, which parents are asked to sign when their child is admitted. This consent approves, for research purposes, the use of data that is routinely collected as part of programming. This blanket consent also includes use of family background information, although of course, names cannot be used. Even once the form is signed, consent can still be revoked at any time.

A second form of consent is obtained when subjects are asked to participate in experiments that are outside of normal programming activities but that are risk-free, such as a lab study involving bar pressing. Parents are notified by mail that their child has been selected as a subject for such a research study and that they have five days in which to refuse permission. If no response is received from the parents, the student is included in the study.

For any procedure that could possibly involve risk to the subject, informed consent must be obtained. Express or informed consent is defined in the Florida Guidelines (1975) as:

consent voluntarily given in writing with sufficient knowledge and comprehension of the subject matter involved so to enable the person giving consent to make an understanding and enlightened decision, without any element of force, fraud, deceit, duress, or other form of constraint or coercion.

Informed consent involves a full explanation of the proposed procedure, an outline of both the risks inherent in the procedure and

the reasons these risks are outweighed by potential benefits or knowledge, an explanation of alternative procedures, and a statement
about the expected duration of the program. In addition, the con-
senter should be apprised that: 1) there will be no retribution of any
kind if consent is denied, 2) once consent is given, it can be revoked
at any time, and 3) feedback will be provided on a regular schedule.

Before a research project involving a procedure containing some
risk can be instituted at our institution, it must also be sent to the
Research Committee of the Department of Human Resources for
approval, and informed consent must be obtained. Certainly some
measures for protecting the rights of residents in research programs
are necessary, but does this protection of rights require such a time-
consuming procedure as the one we have outlined? Once again we
are faced with the resident's right to immediate treatment, in this
case through a behavioral reduction program. However, even if all
non-research alternatives have been exhausted, the procedure for
instituting a "risk" program can be much too time-consuming.

Actually, it is amazing that any research proposals are submitted
in institutions when there are so many obstacles facing a researcher
before a study can even be implemented — and the problems are not
over even then. One still has to contend with the problems intrinsic
in running a study in an institution, such as the scheduling of
subjects. Unfortunately, red tape generated to protect the rights of
residents in research may create a more dangerous situation, because
in order to circumvent research regulations and delays, researchers
may simply stop calling what they are doing "research" and do it
anyway. For example, in our institution, with a population of 480
residents, only twelve research proposals were submitted to the Committee from March of 1975 to March of 1976. Of those twelve
proposals, only two dealt with the reduction of behavior. These
statistics are even more interesting when one considers that there are
13 universities and colleges within a short driving distance of the
institution. There are constant inquiries about the possibility of conducting research at the institution, but, after listening to the requirements, most researchers either go elsewhere, conduct the project
without approval, or never conduct the experiments.

PROTECTING THE RIGHTS OF OTHERS

In the effort to protect the right of clients whose behaviors are targets
for behavior reduction procedures, the rights of other involved per-

sons are often ignored and are rarely protected. The other persons concerned include: 1) the other residents with whom the subjects come into contact, 2) the staff members who work with the subjects, and 3) those who financially support the operation of an institution, the taxpayers.

Rights of Other Residents

In considering the rights of other residents, let us contemplate the hypothetical case previously discussed in this paper, in which 90 days elapsed from the time a reduction program was initiated until it was implemented. Those 90 days were supposedly devoted to the protection of the target subject's rights, but in what ways were the rights of the other residents protected? Suppose that the undesirable behavior was hitting. For 90 days, the other residents' rights were infringed upon as they were subjected to occurrences of physical abuse from the target subject. Then suppose that the program was *not* approved for some reason. Perhaps a Human Rights Committee member delivered a polemic on the "atrocities of behavior modification and its effect on that which is internal to the individual"; or the parents of the subject decided that they did not want their child subjected to a time-out procedure; or, in the case of a subject who is judged capable of giving informed consent, he refused to do so. Do we not have the right to impose a program on the subject in order to protect the rights of the other residents?

The threats that aggressive behaviors pose to other residents are obvious, but nonaggressive inappropriate behaviors can also be damaging. If a resident is constantly in the company of fourteen other residents, each one engaging in his own particular behaviors, and the bureaucratic policies of the institution make submission of proposals for reductive procedures aversive to the staff, chances are that each resident will continue to be consistently exposed to many and various inappropriate behaviors. When residents are first immured in an institution, few are impervious to the behaviors that they see around them. However, because these behaviors impinge upon them time and time again, many residents, especially those who are passive, become habituated to the behaviors and accept them as a normal part of their environment. Are they given a chance to refuse to accept these bizarre behaviors as part of their environment? Because those *outside* the institution refused to accept those behaviors as part of their environment, they had the choice of institutionalizing those perpetrating the behaviors, but those *inside* the institution have no choice about whether or not those behaviors become part of their environment.

Eventually, some residents may even begin to imitate the inappropriate behaviors of other residents. In *New York State Association for Retarded Children* v. *Rockefeller* (1975), several residents, when evaluated some time after participating in an institution's program, were shown to be performing on a lower level than when they entered the program. The court ruled that residents have a right to protection from deterioration. However, not only is this right generally ignored, but also many human rights policies counteract this right.

The rights of other residents are infringed upon in other ways in addition to constant exposure to those clients who emit undesirable behaviors. For example, if three staff members are assigned to work with fifteen residents and two of those residents emit high rates of uncooperative and aggressive behavior, one can reasonably presume that the majority of staff time will be devoted to those two residents, while the other thirteen share the attention of one staff member. Consequently, most appropriate behaviors of the thirteen cooperative residents are ignored. In what ways do institutions protect the rights of those thirteen students to equal staff attention and time? They don't. Those residents are not only denied equal attention, they are also prohibited from achieving their programming goals, and they are the residents who could probably benefit *most* from staff time because their cooperative behaviors increase the probability of their return to the community. Yet, in most institutions the rights of those residents are ignored, while staff predominantly contend with problem students.

Those same thirteen residents would also be denied participation in "normal" outside activities, such as grocery shopping, going to the movies, and using the bus. Staff would either have to risk taking the two problem students or not go at all, because most institutions demand, and rightly so, at least one staff member for every four residents on any outing. The rights of residents to participate in these activities are again subjugated to the rights of the problem residents.

This discussion is not an attempt to promote the dismissal of those policies protecting the rights of clients who engage in undesirable behavior, but rather an attempt to point out the necessity for improving those policies to include protection of the rights of other residents. Granted that the implementation of many behavioral procedures to reduce behavior requires an initial investment of considerable staff time, eventual control of the behavior should, in the long run, afford more staff time for the other residents. The rights of the other residents should be considered in the selection of a strategy. Is it fair to them to select a procedure that could require four months of staff time if a procedure that could control the behavior in several weeks is available?

Rights of Staff

A second group of persons whose rights are often denied are the staff who work directly with residents of institutions. These persons are often told by administrators that they *cannot* do certain things when attempting to cope with undesirable behavior, but, when asked to give alternatives, the administrators evade the issue.

In a letter to a publication of the Georgia Regional Hospital in Atlanta, a staff member wrote the following:

In the past month on (one ward) alone, one staff member's leg has been broken while (he was) scuffling with a patient; another staff member was held in the bathroom by two female patients for over 15 minutes with two knives at her throat; another staff member was jumped from behind by another patient; a staff member was jumped by four female patients while trying to stop these patients from bashing another staff member with two chairs. Also, a patient took a metal strip off a chart rack to place it around the throat of a staff member. After each one of these incidents, the patients involved laughed and bragged about what they had done to the staff and what other things they were going to do in the future. We hear so much about the rights of patients, but how many people who come here have the right outside of the hospital to bash people's heads open with chairs, hold people at knifepoint, or threaten people within an inch of their life?

To the request for help, the administrator replied "I am acutely aware of all these problems and recognize that we cannot solve all of them at this hospital. However, we intend to do every constructive thing we can to find adequate solutions."

Certainly, staff members have the right to defend themselves when attacked by residents, but they are often so uncertain about what specific responses are permissable and what responses would be considered student abuse that they are rendered virtually defenseless. Administrators should be responsible for outlining very specifically what actions can and what actions cannot be taken by staff members in particular situations. Once guidelines are established, it is impera- tive that the information be effectively communicated to all staff and that their related questions be answered, and not circumvented. It is not enough to inform staff that they cannot employ five different procedures in a given situation and then not offer them any alternatives. Administrators must be held responsible for providing staff with some approved method of coping with aggressive behaviors. In *Carter* v. *Carlson* (1971), the court found that some administrators had violated their duty to supervise their subordinates by failing to institute a system of training, instruction, monitoring, and discipline that would prevent or discover and remedy wrongful action.

Surely staff have the right to training in self-defense. Everyone's rights, including the rights of those doing the acting out, would be better protected if staff were trained by experts in the application of procedures that 1) control aggressive behavior without harming the perpetrator, 2) protect other residents from physical abuse, and 3) protect staff from injury. A monitoring system that included frequent observations of staff could then be established to ensure that procedures are employed only when necessary and that they are applied correctly.

Staff also have the right to training in behavioral procedures to reduce responding; again it is the responsibility of administrators to provide that training. Staff who appropriately use positive reductive procedures, that is, those procedures employing positive reinforcement, can effectively reduce much of the inappropriate responding occurring in institutions. However, extremely aggressive behavior often requires to use of other procedures. If staff were trained to implement aversive procedures, they would then be ready whenever one of those procedures was approved by the necessary committees or persons. This would enable practitioners to begin programs immediately upon approval of a procedure without spending at least an initial time period training staff.

In addition to being provided with specific guidelines for handling particular behaviors, training in self-defense techniques, and training in behavioral procedures for decreasing responding, staff who work directly with residents *must* have an open line of communication with those persons making policy decisions. Too often, staff are frustrated because they are not given directions for dealing with problem students, yet each staff member must deal with them eight hours a day, five days a week. Because administrators so seldom come in contact with the pernicious behaviors of the residents, it is difficult for staff to believe that they understand the problems or even that they care very much. In a working situation like that in institutions, where there is so little communication between low level staff and high level administrators, a high rate of staff turnover becomes inevitable. Administrators must spend time in direct contact with residents so that they have first hand knowledge of behavior problems, and they must be held accountable for providing staff with effective methods for dealing with problem behavior. Administrators are not meeting their commitment as administrators if, when staff ask about *their* rights, the response is, "If you do not like the system, you have the right to resign."[4]

Rights of Taxpayers

The third group of persons whose rights should be considered is one whose money supports the operation of institutions— the taxpayers. Millions of tax dollars are allotted to institutions yearly, yet administrators are seldom if ever asked to account for resident progress as a product of that money. It is time for the public to demand their rights and to hold administrators accountable for actual changes in the residents' behaviors.

When seeking to decrease or eliminate undesirable behaviors, one should: 1) specify those behaviors when the resident is admitted to the institution, and 2) assign on paper the responsibility for each problem behavior to a specific person. That person should then be held publicly responsible for a reduction program being written and implemented and should have to show through data that there was a positive behavior change. If no change occurs, he should have to attempt alternative procedures, again showing their effectiveness or lack of effectiveness with data, until he successfully decreases the behavior.

All institution staff, from the lowest to the highest level, with the exception of support staff such as clerical workers and maintenance men, are publicly taking state and federal money to change the behavior of the residents. Yet few administrators are ever asked to show that any behavior is actually changed, and an even smaller number have instituted a method whereby changes in the residents' behaviors can be assessed through a viable data system. Too often, ineffective or non-existent programming is camouflaged by impressive-looking buildings with nice wallpaper and by playground areas with brightly colored sculpture. As long as the residents are dressed decently and do not engage in any obscene behavior, visitors go away impressed with the wonderfulness of the institution. They seldom if ever ask to see any data on the students' behavior.

Why are taxpayers willing to continue to allocate state and

---

[4] The actual response of an administrator at our institution during a meeting with residential care staff concerning human rights, on February 25, 1976.

federal money to pay salaries for people who are charged with changing behavior when in fact those people may not change behavior at all? Why pay these salaries if people are not doing their jobs? Indeed, unless they can show with data that they are changing behavior, they are not doing their jobs. If those who direct institutions cannot staff their facilities with persons who possess the expertise that is necessary to establish a data-based system for changing behavior, then they should be replaced with those who can. However, until the public cares enough to demand an accountability system based on data, those who take tax money for producing little if any change in residents' behaviors will continue to do so.

SUMMARY

In discussing ethical issues in programs to reduce responding of institutionalized persons, this chapter concentrates on the following four aspects:

1. The institution as the ultimate in behavior modification
2. Objectives of reduction programs, which are a) reducing extra-institutional responding, b) reducing socially maladaptive responding, c) reducing counter-institutional responding, and d) reducing responding for research purposes
3. Protecting the rights of residents subject to intervention programs, a) through Human Rights Committee and b) through Research Committees
4. Protection the rights of other involved persons, that is, a) other residents, b) staff who work directly with residents, and c) taxpayers

The moral or ethical problems raised in this chapter will not be solved quickly or easily, and, in this day of the courtroom, these problems either have, or will, become legal issues. While most legal cases have until now focused on the right to treatment or to be left alone, future cases will hopefully be concerned with the *quality* of treatment. This places a responsibility on administrators and those persons working to change behavior, that is, a responsibility to keep abreast of the changing guidelines and legal aspects of intervention. In *Wood* v. *Strickland* (1975), the Supreme Court ruled that those in charge of a program cannot claim ignorance. Part of their jobs is to know the rights of those in their charge, and, while that is a time-consuming endeavor, it is certainly one of the most important aspects of their positions.

The frustration that accompanies not knowing all our moral, ethical, and legal commitments is sometimes overwhelming as we receive vague directions from our supervisors and read legal decisions that seem to conflict with each other and the policies of our facilities. However, this period of change is also a fascinating time to be part of this field.

REFERENCES

Carter v. *Carlson,* 447 F. 2'nd 358 (D.C. 1971).

Guidelines for the Use of Behavioral Procedures in State Programs for Retarded Persons. 1975. The National Association for Retarded Citizens.

Martin, R. 1974. Behavior Modification: Human Rights and Legal Responsibilities. Research Press, Champaign, Ill.

New York State Association for Retarded Children v. *Rockefeller,* 357 F. Supp. 752 (E.D.M.Y. 1975)

Schwitzgebel, R. K. 1975. Implementing a right to effective treatment. Law and Psychology Review (Spring): 117–130.

Skinner, B. F. 1971. Beyond Freedom and Dignity. Alfred A. Knopf, New York.

Wood v. *Strickland,* 95 S. Ct. 992 (1975).

Wyatt v. *Stickney,* 344 F. Supp. 373, 374 F. Supp. 387 (M.D.Ala. 1972) aff'd sub nom. *Wyatt* v. *Aderholt,* 503 F. 2'nd 1305 (5'th Cr. 1974).

Section II

Toward Effective Programming and Service Delivery

EDITORIAL
INTRODUCTION

Although the pessimism typically associated with the treatment of the developmentally disabled is being replaced by frequent and impressive demonstrations of success, it is clear that we still have a long way to go. If the goal of normalization is to be realized, alternative strategies will continually need to be identified and implemented. In the search for effective educational programs and service delivery, a number of factors will need to be addressed, including: 1) a model for organizing service delivery, 2) staff and paraprofessional training, 3) program implementation and monitoring, 4) research and development objectives, and 5) selection of priority target behaviors. The chapters in this section are, therefore, an attempt to assist the reader in acquiring perspective on such conceptual and practical concerns.

In the first paper, Lent considers some of the crucial tasks involved in formulating service delivery systems for the severely disabled. He appropriately points out that the traditional emphasis on diagnostic aspects has resulted in an impressive knowledge of who the retarded are, but has provided us with very little in the way of effective programming. Stressing the need for replicable and cost-efficient procedures that can be used by direct care personnel, a *pro*active, rather than a *re*active, approach to the task is advocated.

Given the multiple behavior deficits of the severely handicapped and the necessity for providing individualized instruction, the creative use of paraprofessionals or "teaching associates" can significantly reduce student-teacher ratios to more promising and workable levels. While providing an overall model for competency-based teacher training programs, the paper by Hollis, Tucker, and Horner presents a model for training paraprofessionals that is based on a strong practicum component, certification requirements related to specific informational and performance competencies, and opportunities for career advancement.

Although they are well-intended, many human service programs for the developmentally disabled have often failed to achieve their goals, and in some cases they have even exacerbated the problems they were designed to solve. For these and other reasons, increased attention is being paid to quality control procedures and to measures of service delivery accountability. After a discussion of the existing constraints and the prior attempts to ensure adequate service delivery, the chapter prepared by Boles and Bible describes the development and implementation of management procedures designed to maintain the performance of previously trained staff at acceptable levels. In addition to focusing on the expected outcomes of programming, this paper emphasizes the importance of ongoing process measures of service delivery.

One of the most important ways of addressing the gaps in our knowledge and ensuring improved educational programs is through innovative research efforts. Bricker's excellent paper discusses current dimensions of research and emphasizes an applied research orientation with a specific focus on seeking procedures to improve the instructional process. A "test-teach" research orientation, illustrating a strong inference model, is proposed as a research design alternative that deals with many of the problems associated with groups and individual subject designs.

Finally, the selection of meaningful target behaviors, particularly those that enhance the learning of other crucial behaviors and that introduce students to "natural communities of reinforcement," cannot be overemphasized. Thus, the development of functional language skills for the developmentally disabled is an essential requirement. This is especially important if public school systems are to begin providing services to all members of the population. The last chapter, by Kent, describes practical strategies for implementing language programs for accomplishing these objectives.

ORGANIZING SERVICE DELIVERY FOR THE SEVERELY RETARDED
A Futurist's View

James R. Lent

We know who the severely and profoundly retarded are, but we do *not* know *what* they can do or how to help them do it. We have spent many years and dollars on diagnostic instruments and behavior scales, and consequently we have many ways of labeling them and categorizing their handicapping conditions.

We now must become *pro*active, rahter than *re*active, in devoting our time and money to programming for the retarded. We must use all our technology and all our art in designing and developing programs that will enable us—and the retarded—to discover their adaptive limits.

The task is stupefying in its enormity, but we must get at it. The first requisite must necessarily be a change in our attitudes toward the job itself. The undertaking is not one of diagnostics, however complete and esoteric we might conceive such a goal to be; rather, it is one of individual, deficit-specific programming. This objective is further compounded by the fact that such programming *must* be designed to be cost-efficient and replicable. We must subscribe to the idea that what we do to help the severely retarded help themselves *must* be done well enough so that others—even untrained others—may be enabled to immediately and successfully multiply our effects. Only then will we be able to bring about a real "delivery system."

THE HISTORY OF THE PROBLEM

In the past, despite noteworthy attempts to better the lives of the retarded, the prevailing attitude precluded instruction beyond that which amounted to custodial care. Training that could contribute to the personal growth and satisfaction of the retarded in the community was not a primary goal for most programs. Until recently, too little attention was paid to daily-living behaviors that win acceptance in a normal community.

Before the 1950s, some of the higher-functioning retarded were allowed in the public school systems of some states. It was in that decade, however, that several forces produced a concerted effort to make this practice more universal. Among the forces changing the public attitude toward the handicapped were: the disabled veterans of World War II, research findings concerning the dynamic nature of intelligence quotients, and the increasing use of an adaptive-behavior philosophy—all of which combined to help modify some earlier attitudes about the educability of the retarded. Perhaps even more important were the efforts of the parent groups who banded together to seek support and recognition for mentally retarded offspring. Beginning with experimental programs and schools that were privately financed, this movement affected, and continues to affect, local school systems, state legislatures, and federal government agencies.

Local organizations were ingenious in their efforts to secure space wherever possible—in churches, in community buildings, and in abandoned school buildings. Even more impressive was their ability to get financial assistance from local service groups to help finance day-care centers. These early efforts were not philosophically coherent, but they were important for solving immediate problems. As they grew in number and variety, there was increasing communication between the various parent groups, and this resulted in increased effectiveness.

The growth in numbers of special education classes within the public school systems of this country has been steady, but special education has been beset with serious problems, including a lack of technologically trained teachers, a shortage of university-level personnel qualified to train them, the financial burden of such programming, an inadequate number of appropriate facilities, a scarcity of specific curriculum guides, and, most important of all, a dearth of validated, replicable program materials. Too often, special education classes offer a watered-down academic curriculum or are a "dumping ground" for heterogeneous problem children who are taught by an unqualified teacher in unsuitable, leftover, or improvised space.

SOME STEPS TOWARD SOLUTIONS

The community can serve as a "classroom" for those retarded who are not institutionalized by providing a learning environment filled with examples of acceptable behavior. Such models can help each person achieve a degree of normality. As the individual learns to adjust to the normal community, adopting the behavior patterns he learns there, he becomes more acceptable to that community.

The need for a more individualized instruction has been acknowledged, but it has not been provided. Most state departments of education and local school districts recommend a teacher-pupil ratio for the trainable retarded of 1 to 10 or 1 to 12. That ratio may be as advantageous as can be expected, but it is not realistic. A provision for a teacher aide in the special class is the most hopeful development of recent times. It makes the professional teacher twice as effective by allowing him or her to provide instruction to small groups and individuals while the aide is occupied with the remainder of the group. It should be made clear, however, that a proper number of adults in the classroom is not the only condition for better learning. Many day-care centers and institutions can provide a favorable teacher-pupil ratio without being able to provide functional, measurable changes in pupil behavior. This fact is attributable to poor organization, a lack of systematic program materials, a poor choice of instructional objectives, or all of the above.

In a properly engineered classroom, or, as Skinner would put it, if the total learning environment is properly arranged, the problem of individualizing training is markedly lessened. It is possible for the teacher to devote attention to a single student or to small groups while other students are productively employed elsewhere in any "classroom."

It would be impossible to stress too greatly the role systematic teaching, appropriately programmed materials, and suitable resource materials—not to mention resource personnel and training aides—can play in facilitating the learning process, *whatever the teacher-student ratio*. In fact, if the prognosis for the number of teachers immediately available from training institutions is considered, along with the prognosis for the number of students to be immediately serviced by public institutions, it is clear that our concentration *must* be on systematic training procedures and appropriate materials developent. Drucker (1969) has said that any technology consists of only two factors: appropriate tools and the organization of work.

One of the most conspicuous reasons for lack of success in preparing the mentally retarded for life in the community is that most training environments are not natural. They are limited in both scope and realism of experiences offered. Although recent research findings suggest that the mentally retarded are indeed capable of generalizing some kinds of learning from one situation to another, in a real-world, non-laboratory setting, they generalize less than persons with a higher mental ability do. Although persons who work with the retarded are aware of this, they seldom make provisions for it. Even the highest quality education provided in an institution does not provide sufficient skill for adjustment to life in any other special environment.

Not all training can take place in a natural setting, because we cannot arrange conditions in the real world to provide repeated lessons at convenient times. On the other hand, certain adjustments can be made. First, nearly all training environments can be designed to more nearly simulate required community experiences. Second, *more* training *can* take place in the real environment. Our present problem is attributable to the fact that too few programs are committed to community transition and most facilities were constructed without considering a community-transition philosophy. Education still relies on the patterns the don system established in the years shortly following the Gutenberg press: the person who owned the book was paid to read from it to the assembled students. (In fact, the word "lecture" originally meant a reading!) How far has education come? Has it been forced to adapt? How does it accomodate change? How does it account for itself when human priorities and their concomitant cost factors are the basics in our new age?

A FUTURISTIC PHILOSOPHY

Education must become consumer-oriented. The successful "enterprises" of today—whether or not we insist on the labels "public" or "private" is of no consequence in an interdependent Post-Industrial Age—already predict the tasks of the future: according to Drucker, they all consider marketing their "crucial task." Education is our only "enterprise" that is rooted in two age-old prejudices: the Puritan ethic, which insists that the learner can be "wrong," and what

Drucker calls the traditional European social prejudice against market, customer, and selling, which says that, in effect, the teacher and the school are "noble," and that the client, who must be able to respond to them according to rule, should be grateful for the chance to do so. These two belief systems combine to make what seems to be an insurmountable resistance to the need for new attitudes and alternatives and, indeed, to the notion that accountability to the consumer must determine these alternatives.

We must attend to two facts: 1) we cannot afford the societal solution that we invented in the past two centuries and which we have not examined with respect to cost-benefit since—i.e., institutionalization; 2) we cannot afford the standard model for education that we invented in the early Rennaissance and which we have not examined for cost-benefit since—the scholar-as-teacher. Both these inventions are obsolete, inefficient, and ineffective. In the future, our pursuits in educational technology must be directed toward imaginative, alternative, and humane solutions to our present problems.

As we have already noted, the community can serve as a "classroom" for those retarded who are not institutionalized by providing a learning environment filled with examples of acceptable behavior. Along with astute programming, such models can help each person achieve a degree of normality. As the individual learns to adjust to the normal community, adopting the behavior patterns he learns there, he becomes more acceptable to that community.

THE IMPLEMENTATION OF THIS PHILOSOPHY

Whether or not he is institutionalized, the severely retarded individual can best learn to adapt to community life through daily-living experiences in that community. Such experiences help him appear more normal and prepare him for at least somewhat semi-independent living in the comminity.

Truly successful adjustment from the institution to the community has not occurred on a large scale for three reasons:

1. The target behaviors necessary for success have not been delineated or specified in a manner to make them teachable
2. There has been no realistic plan of implementation with specific program materials
3. Few institutional administrative structures ideologically or functionally support such behavior specification and training materials

It should nevertheless be remembered that there are concerted efforts by many groups to return to a "restoring" philosophy for retarded persons either in or out of institutions. Special classes are being mandated, and community facilities are being provided. The mere commitment to a philosophy of normalization will guarantee a measure of success to any program. In addition, there is quite a bit of new technology available to assist in selecting target behaviors and implementing them.

The process of writing instructional objectives has received considerable attention in recent years. Such objectives lay the foundation for putting together instructional materials so that others may use them and expect the same results as the program writer. There are three terms used to describe educational outcomes: educational goals, educational objectives, and instructional objectives. In this classification scheme, an educational goal reflects the ideal purposes of education. It is an abstract statement of future educational outcomes, e.g., "to produce citizens who have an appreciation of their American Heritage." The next category, in terms of degree of specificity, is an educational objective. "Upon completion of the reading program, students will enjoy recreational reading," is an example of an educational objective. Such a concept is not directly observable; as a result, its use is potentially hazardous. It could be assumed that exposure to the reading program will produce the desired outcome. Although the outcome could be more accurately inferred from other observations, it would still be only an inference. Despite the built-in dangers, educational objectives can be helpful. A careful analysis of educational objectives will allow the educator to determine which objectives *are* observable and therefore teachable.

This process necessitates an attempt by the educator to make components of instruction more specific in terms of one or several *instructional* objectives—the final and most functional category. There are three main features of an instructional objective:

1. It contains a description of the behavior in observable terms
2. It contains a description of the conditions under which the behavior may be observed
3. It contains a description of the criterion by which the behavior may be judged

The other problem in selecting instructional goals arises from our concept of what constitutes an "important" behavior. It is easy to say, "Whatever contributes to community adjustment," but it is diffi-

cult for the public to believe that for certain individuals toothbrushing or spoon-holding should take priority over knowledge of income
tax laws. Daily-living skills that contribute to normality may be the
most important skills needed by the retarded because they make
them less distinguishable from other citizens of the community.

Assuming that target behaviors have been chosen wisely, the
next most important consideration is to remember that the goal of
teaching is successful, *independent* performance by the student. It is
very easy to be deceived into thinking that our students are capable
of performing totally without help. Teachers in public schools, for
instance, are often deceived by the appearance of their children. It
is not unusual for the children to be delivered to school neat, clean,
and well-groomed. If the teacher were to put these same children
to the test, she would discover that few of them could dress or groom
themselves or care for their personal hygiene without help. If they
cannot do these things alone, they have not learned—they have not
been taught. Parents are anxious to help, and they try to avoid negative reactions. Teachers feel they cannot take the time to teach to a
criterion of independent performance. Nobody is to be blamed, but
the child needs more help than he is getting.

The skills required for acceptance, or toleration, are mostly social—especially in the case of the retarded. They must not offend,
and, if possible, they must please. Normal children are often tolerated in spite of deviant, offensive behavior. This is because the non-
retarded person is far more likely to have compensatory skills. This is
not the case with retarded persons, today, and especially not in the
future—*any* future.

The skills required for the future resemble those required for
adjustment to the community today. The most notable categories,
although they are not recognized by many educators as legitimate
major parts of a curriculum, are personal appearance, personal hygiene, and contributive use of leisure time. Use of leisure time will
assume increasing importance in any world of the future, and not
just for the retarded, yet educators have not made this area one of
their research priorities.

A phenomenon to be considered by the decision-makers of today, and therefore of tommorrow, is the placement of mentally retarded children in the public schools. There are two main practices
today, and there is argument about which is more appropriate. First,
there is the special class, the self-contained classroom. There are special classes for every category of handicapping condition, and for

the retarded there are classes for the educable, classes for the train-able, and classes for the more severely retarded. The other policy is usually referred to as mainstreaming. Mainstreaming has a nice ring to it, and, besides that, it is new—or is it? Conley (1973), sheds an interesting light on the subject.

> In 1968 and 1970 there were approximately 1,936,000 and 1,975,000 children who were 5 to 19 years of age with IQs below 70. We have esti-mated that about 631,000 and 690,000 were in special education pro-grams. On the basis of previously computed information, it is estimated that the number in institutional care was 108,000 in 1968 and 110,000 in 1970. This leaves about 1,197,000 who must have been in regular aca-demic classes or not in school in 1968, and 1,175,000 in 1970, a slight de-crease.
>
> Most retarded children who are not in special classes or in residential care attend regular academic classes. Of over 11,000 schoolage children identified as mentally retarded in New Jersey in 1953, 41% were in special education classes, 49% were in regular classes, and only 10% were not attending school. In the 1970 survey of special education pro-grams conducted by the National Center for Educational Statistics, an estimated 28% were attending regular classes on a full-time basis. Un-doubtedly in both cases many more retarded children attended regular classes but were not identified as retarded.

In other words, mainstreaming has been going on for years. This is not to say that mainstreaming is not a good idea, especially since later efforts have included a resource room to supplement the offerings of the regular class. At this point, however, it can only be regarded as another *re*active measure—a reaction to the failure of special classes and the pressures from the right to education move-ment. Every year, in fact, new thousands of young, normal persons are pushed from the traditional processing of the public schools into a world that is too difficult and complex for their management. In regular education as well as in special education, new teaching skills have not been brought to bear on old problems.

Because the public schools are failing with an incredibly large number of non-retarded pupils, the simple expedient of regular-class placement is not going to help the retarded to the degree that is required. The concept of the resource room is a step in the right direction because it gives promise of prescriptive help, but the pres-ent state of the art in education is not sufficient, and many children will not be given specific community-required skills.

There are two main reasons for this: first, the community-re-quired skills are rarely taught in regular schools to a useful extent— even in resource rooms. Second, whatever is being taught is depend-ent upon the artfulness and dedication of available teachers. This means that a few lucky children will be helped, while the rest will remain in trouble. Clearly what is required is a whole new *system* of education for the retarded. A system that teaches the *most needed* behaviors and that guarantees that each child demonstrates proficiency in the skills selected as priorities for that particular child. We need a system that will not accept the child's failure to learn as simply the child's fault. The system and the people in it will have to accept the blame for child failure.

The writing of functional, usable, and validated program materials has become more feasible with recent advances in educational technology. Ultimately, the solution to the materials shortage will be met by professional program developers, such as those associated with Project MORE. Such program development is being encouraged by the United States Offices of Education, Bureau of Education for the Handicapped. In the meantime, the crises brought on by mandatory education rulings will have to be met by developing teacher-made materials.

Because we are all aware that we cannot possibly train enough teachers to handle even our present education load in the traditional training mode, in which the teacher is considered to be the "expert" who can process all possible inputs into learning bits, the primary task for educational technology is to train others to teach. *We must train-to-train.* It is possible for one professional-level person, teacher, if you like, to manage the activities of several non-professional trainers. These trainers, teacher aides, if that is a more comfortable term, can perform nearly all the skill-training required by the retarded if they are given adequate direction and functional teaching materials. Significantly less time is required for training these trainers.

This kind of training/learning arrangement calls for new skills for old administrators. The techniques of systems analysis are invaluable in planning, organizing, and evaluating such an undertaking. This means that systems managers may be more appropriate than teachers, and that skill trainers may be more appropriate than teacher aides. The consoling thought is, however, that such a system can be wholly accountable, including a requirement for data-based evidence, for the only mission that education has ever had—socially appropriate behavior change.

THE FUTURE OF TEACHER TRAINING

The considerations discussed above have vast implications for teacher training. New skills for a new age will have to be learned and mastered by all of us in higher education if we do not wish to become outmoded and valueless in a world that no longer recognizes *intrinsic* value in college degrees and teaching certificates. In spite of powerful traditions and enormous bureaucracies, we must master Post–Industrial Age technology and put it to use to build new, relevant, efficient, and humane educational models. In the not distant future, the term "teacher" will have to have a very different connotation— one that carries the meaning and respect that it did in ages past.

Providing more trainers does not comprise a total solution. We need to rearrange the training/learning environment so that intensive, individualized instruction and appropriate group activities can occur both simultaneously and sequentially. This calls for a recognition that no one teacher can do all things for all children—as in the self-contained, self-defeating classroom model. There are many arrangements that would be an improvement over present practices, but the one that holds the most promise is an adaption of the circuit-training model. In this arrangement, a variety of learning centers appropriate to different teaching targets are established. The centers are arranged in logical relation to each other according to program content and developmental level of the learning task. For instance, in one room there may be a variety of learning stations at which several pairs of trainers and learners are concentrating on personal appearance and personal hygiene skills. Although many of the children may be relatively young, there is no stigma attached to older children receiving instruction in the same environment.

Next to the intensive individual training room there may be a group activity room for children who have earned credits or other reinforcers in skill training. In this space they may spend small periods of free time playing with games, with each other, or with the trained adult in charge of this activity. Another nearby room may be arranged for individual presentations of preacademic and academic learning tasks, such as discrimination of colors, sizes, and shapes. Obviously, the combinations and permutations of the circuit-training model are endless—and exciting.

The challenge of technology is to make the *ordinary* person capable of *extraordinary* performance. This challenge has been understood and met in business and industry, but not in education. Although there is an awareness in the educational arena of the many successful and exciting developments in behavior modification, the full exploitation of these developments in educational models has not been forthcoming. Such developments, in order to be used efficiently and effectively, require the adoption of a systems approach and, indeed, the concomitant evolution of a comprehensive technology. What has been learned about human behavior and the techniques of managing and changing behavior cannot be translated into practice by ordinary persons in ordinary circumstances *unless such information is delivered to them in practical formats.*

CONCLUSION

If one were to view today's practices as predictive of tomorrow's shape and style, the vision would be very depressing. The field of special education is not reacting to the problems of yesterday and today. It is merely coping. Some of the practices are concrete, some semi-solid, and others fluid, but if they are continued indefinitely, they guarantee that in twenty-five years the field will be a hopeless anachronism rather than "just behind." It helps to remember that the shape of the future is in our hands and that we are not bystanders, but participants. It helps to remember that there are *alternative* futures.

The most important development since the end of World War II is unquestionably the right to education movement. It must be seen as a *re*active event. It is not *pro*active. It will not in and of itself bring about a more enlightened future for the disadvantaged. The movement is a reaction against cultural lag, mishandling, and inattention. As cultural analogs we have the specific thrusts of the civil rights movement—and these seem to be succeeding, although slowly. It is dangerous, however, to use other areas of the civl rights movement as predictive analogs. The gains that have been achieved in human rights are not attributable to belated although enlightened *legislation* alone. They are attributable to the creativity and stubbornness of disadvantaged Blacks and other minority groups, who have themselves followed up in establishing relevant civil-action precedents. They have persevered, and in so doing they have actively shaped the implementation of civil rights practices.

What if the future of the civil rights movement had been left in the hands of others, i.e., bureaucrats, school administrators, college professors, and school teachers? Can the right to education movement really change things? Certainly it cannot provide its own leadership. The persons most affected by this movement, the retarded, must rely on advocates. The fate of the movement is in the hands of these advocates. The tools that legislation and civil action have provided us can be used to serve the representatives of the movement in the name of the "cause." We should not use these tools willfully, of course, but, because there is not a direct built-in corrective mechanism, i.e., the voice of the retarded, we must not hesitate to use all available tools in their behalf.

We must devise and operate a technology that will give the retarded the skills that will allow them citizenship in the Post–Industrial Age. We do know that the retarded can only "get along" by successfully *reacting* to the world of the normal, and we know that the world of the normal will continue its rapid-pace change.

However, we must also keep in mind that some requirements for life in the future are going to be the same as in the present. For instance, the severely retarded still will be dependent upon normal persons, in spite of any legislation or any technology. This means that they will be accepted or tolerated in this world *because of skills they possess*—not *in spite of their deficits.*

REFERENCES

Barnes, R. 1974. Toward Alternative Futures. The Menninger Foundation, Topeka, Kansas.

Commission on Instructional Technology. 1970. To Improve Learning. United States Government Printing Office, Washington, D.C.

Comptroller General of the United States. 1973. Report to Congress: Educational Laboratory and Research and Development Center Programs Need to be Strengthened. General Accounting Office, Washington, D.C.

Conley, R. W. 1973. The Economics of Mental Retardation. The John Hopkins University Press, Baltimore.

Drucker, P. F. 1969. The Age of Discontinuity: Guidelines to Our Changing Society. Harper & Row, New York.

Lent, J. R. 1975. Developing daily-living skills for the mentally retarded. In: J. M. Kauffman and J. S. Payne (eds.), Mental Retardation: An Introduction and Personal Perspectives. Charles E. Merrill, Columbus, Ohio.

Lent, J. R. 1968. Mimosa cottage: experiment in hope. Psychol. Today 2 (June): 51–58.

Lent, J. R., and McLean, B. M. 1976. The trainable retarded: the technology of teaching. In: N. G. Haring and R. L. Schiefelbusch (eds.), Teaching Special Children. McGraw-Hill, New York.

Lippman, L. and Goldberg, I. 1973. Right to Education: Anatomy of the Pennsylvania Case and Its Implications for Exceptional Children. Teachers College Press, Columbia University, New York.

TRAINING STAFF AND PARAPROFESSIONALS TO WORK WITH THE DEVELOPMENTALLY DISABLED

John H. Hollis, Dennis J. Tucker, & R. Don Horner

Sontag, Burke, and York (1973) have stated, "In our view, there is a direct relationship between the level of the students' disability and the competencies of the teachers, i.e., the more pronounced the level of disability, the more specific and precise are the competencies required of the teachers" (p. 23). Thus, providing education and training services for the severely handicapped should necessarily require the bringing together of all factual information currently available in the area of programmed human learning—including knowledge of basic learning principles, techniques for precise measurement, and the application of a problem-oriented, objective task-analysis approach. Programming for the severely handicapped should include a developmentally programmed sequence of instruction, a rapid time schedule under optimally motivating conditions in application of the programs, and a continued data feedback system for accurately charting progress across time. The severity of the behavioral deficits manifested by these children, in addition to a number of physical and

Preparation of this chapter was supported in part by the Division of Personnel Preparation, the Bureau of Education for the Handicapped, USOE, Grant OEG-0-74-2766, and the Bureau of Child Research, University of Kansas.

sensory disabilities that complicate the learning process, demand that their education and training experiences not be left for unattended "natural" development, but, indeed, should be precisely programmed through the systematic manipulation of organism-environment relationships. Thus, a technological approach in the education and training of the severely handicapped must encompass empirical findings from previous and ongoing research efforts in the field, and include the collection and the application of sound training programs that have evolved from these efforts. Fortunately, there exists a vast amount of new information pertaining to the training of the severely handicapped. The task remains, however, to bring this information together in training packages that can be used by direct service personnel for the severely handicapped.

The application of a technological approach in servicing the needs of the severely handicapped requires the joint participation of many individuals, including the classroom teacher, the teacher aide, the child's parents, and others who provide direct services for the child. To be effective, each contributing member must be trained, although to differing degrees, to implement and maintain the often rigorous teaching programs for individual children. The trained teacher must know *both* how to apply existing programs appropriate to the area of training and how to develop his own programs or program variations based upon the idiosyncratic needs of various children. Additionally, the trained teacher must know how to train others, in turn, to follow the instructions and procedures inherent in the application of these programs.

The teacher aide, or teaching associate, must know basic learning principles to the degree that they can be applied effectively in accordance with the procedures of a training program. Similarly, the child's parents (or parent surrogates) must be trained to maintain and monitor the various training programs that extend into the home (or agency) environment. In essence, any major endeavor to provide direct education and training services for the severely handicapped must materially extend to all significant adults who come into contact with the child on a daily basis. To do less would only serve to prolong and possibly to sidetrack the progress made by the child.

The major emphasis in this chapter is on the training of paraprofessionals (teaching associates) to work in educating severely handicapped children. However, it will become apparent that the chapter provides an overall model for a competency-based special education teacher training program.

BACKGROUND TO PARAPROFESSIONAL TRAINING

Paraprofessional: Definition

The term "educational paraprofessional" is used to refer to any salaried or non-salaried person, other than a teacher, who is providing educational opportunities for children (e.g., parents of handicapped children who are involved in educational programs for their children, direct care staff within state institutions for the mentally retarded, physical therapy aides, vocational specialists in sheltered workshops, houseparents in sheltered group homes, etc.) (Tucker et al., 1976).

The program described here is designed to train a particular kind of educational paraprofessional, a "teaching associate" (formerly referred to as a "teacher aid") who works directly with a teacher in providing educational opportunities for severely handicapped individuals.

Legal Authority for Paraprofessionals in Special Education

Ultimately, the authority for certification and employment of paraprofessionals in special education must come from the various state legislatures. For example, in 1974, the Kansas legislature enacted the Special Education for Exceptional Children Act (K.S.A. 72-962), which defined and specified the role of the paraprofessional in special education. The act refers to paraprofessionals functioning as assistants to special education teachers in public schools, state institutions, and other facilities that provide accredited special education programs. It also specifies that the standards for program approval are the same, irrespective of the classroom site.

Overview of Paraprofessional Training Literature

The utilization, roles, and duties of paraprofessionals in special education have been controversial issues for many years (Cruickshank and Haring, 1957; Esbensen, 1966; Blessing, 1967; Reid and Reid, 1974). Reid and Reid (1974) have summarized the literature and classified paraprofessional duties into four major categories: clerical, housekeeping, non-instructional, and instruction-related duties.

Specifically with regard to instruction-related duties (Reid and Reid, 1974), the tasks include: observe children and write reports, assist in preparing instructional materials, reinforce learning with small groups, and read and tell stories. Implicit in the tasks is that teachers will do the "teaching" and paraprofessionals will prepare materials and "manage" the children while the teacher teaches. Perhaps with normal children and mildly and moderately handicapped children, where teaching can take place in relatively large groups, these duties are practical and feasible for paraprofessionals. However, such is not the case for classrooms for the severely, profoundly, and multiply handicapped. Fredericks et al. (1975) appropriately stated that:

"Because of the wide range of individual differences in the severely handicapped population and oftentimes their unmanageability because of previous ineffective home training, effective instruction can oftentimes only be achieved in a one-to-one relationship. Therefore, the utilization of paraprofessionals to provide individualized instruction in the classroom is considered mandatory" (p. 2).

In acceptance of the role of the paraprofessional as a "teaching" role, it is a purpose of this personnel training project to prepare paraprofessionals, or teaching associates, using behavioral procedures (Panyan, Boozer, and Morris, 1970; Gardner, 1972; Hursh et al., 1973; Panyan and Patterson, 1974; Fredericks et al., 1975; Clark and Macrae, 1976), for the education of the severely and profoundly handicapped.

Staff Training Objectives

1. To develop, establish, and operationalize a technologically oriented training model with practicum in a residential resource center, for teachers, teacher retrainees, and teaching associates who will be engaged in serving the educational needs of severly handicapped children in the community and in various service centers, and to provide technical support to special education departments across the country who need assistance in developing programs for the severely handicapped.

    New Teachers The objective is to develop, in conjunction with area colleges and universities, a practicum experience and supporting college-based curriculum aimed at equipping and providing an immediate source of personnel who will enter classrooms and agencies dealing with severely and profoundly handicapped children, and who will thereby be in a position to actualize measurable behavioral objectives toward better levels of self-care and self-fulfillment of such children in society.

    Teacher Retrainees The objective is to provide additional instruction and supervised practicum training for teachers who are currently working with the severely handicapped, and yet who have not been trained in this area, having been awarded degrees in fields other than special education, or having been prepared for other areas of exceptionality within the field of special education.

Teaching Associates The objective is to provide explicit practicum-oriented instruction in the application of training programs for the severely handicapped, thus enabling teacher aides to carry out meaningful programs under the direct supervision of the trained teacher.

University Faculty Resources The objective is to provide technical support to the faculty members from special education departments in universities and colleges across the country, as a mechanism for disseminating the training model to other states and regions. Short-term institutes will provide the vehicle for making the program visible at the national level.

2. To assemble, analyze, package, and enable delivery of relevant aspects of an existing technology for training and education of the severely handicapped, and to pinpoint areas where additional programs are needed—hence, the development of curricula to enlarge upon and expand the scope of educational programs presently constituted in the State of Kansas as outlined in the Kansas Plan (Thorsell, 1971).

3. To firmly anchor the teacher-training component of the project on behavioral demonstrations of teacher competencies appropriate to the areas outlined as essential to training of the severely handicapped.

CURRENT ISSUES IN PARAPROFESSIONAL TRAINING

In the development of state-wide programs for the training of paraprofessional personnel, several issues arise. When dealing with severely handicapped children, should the personnel training program be oriented toward nursing care or toward education? Should we certify paraprofessional personnel? Another issue involves the provision for career advancement in the field. Finally, what type of relationship should be established between teachers and paraprofessional personnel?

Nursing versus Educational Training

Other than in cases of total custodial care, and even then it shall be questioned, is the nursing approach relevant to the training and education of handicapped children? The nursing type of program, in addition to health care, provides only a cursory overview of child development, and that with a considerable amount of psychoanalytic jargon. This point was very evident from our review of the literature. On the other hand, if educators are to succeed in their endeavor to use paraprofessionals, they must of necessity develop comprehensive training programs and relevant and functional uses for parapro- fessional personnel. If teachers persist in using paraprofessionals as people who take children to the bathroom and collect meal tickets, it's a lost cause!

Certification

Certification provides a vehicle for establishing regulations to carry out the intent of the law developed by various states (see Public Law 94-142). It provides a basis for the establishment of minimum train- ing and experience levels for teachers and teaching associates. To some degree, certification provides teachers and administrators with a degree of confidence that the personnel they employ are competent and able to carry out their responsibilities (also see Risley, 1975). In most cases, certification is a necessary prerequisite in order to es- tablish eligibility to be paid from public funds. Table 1 provides a summary of recommendations for certification of special education paraprofessionals.

Career Advancement

The total program presented here provides comprehensive, perfor- mance-based training across a common set of competencies for both teachers and teaching associates, and an educational career ladder whereby teaching associates may advance across ranks to become teachers.

A program designed to train teaching associates for the severely handicapped will probably fail to attract many applicants unless some visable and objective method for advancement is built into the program.

Current salaries for teaching associates are inadequate in rela- tion to the educational opportunities they will be able to provide severely handicapped students upon completing a functional per- formance-based training program. Thus, potential career advance- ment is currently the only viable source of motivation for acquiring the competencies taught through a rigorous training program.

Table 1.   Certification recommendations

Recommendation	Rationale
1. It is recommended that a training program be established at the community college level as well as at the university level to prepare instructional paraprofessionals for classrooms for the mentally and physically handicapped.	Since the primary responsibility of the instructional paraprofessional is to provide functional teaching assistance to the classroom teacher, that individual will need to be trained in the requisite skills necessary to accomplish such tasks.
2. It is recommended that the State Board of Education refer to the formerly defined "instructional paraprofessional" for special education as "teaching associate" for special education.	Included in the national mandate for the education of all handicapped children has come to the "professionalization" of many personnel trained to work with the handicapped. The term "teaching associate" has become the accepted term for those individuals who engage in functional teaching duties with a special education teacher.
3. It is recommended that full certification requirements be adopted for teaching associates (instructional paraprofessionals) in the area of special education.	Through certification, teaching associates (instructional paraprofessionals) will be eligible for legal support from the LEA and for other fringe benefits, such as medical coverage.
4. It is recommended that the State Board of Education survey the certification requirements, or the equivalent, for special education teaching associates (instructional paraprofessionals) in the remaining 49 states.	It is anticipated that a number of states will have certification or licensing requirements that meet or exceed those of Kansas. With an established list, Kansas certification personnel and a prospective special education teaching associate from approved states considering a teaching associate position in Kansas can immediately determine eligibility for certification in Kansas.
5. It is recommended that basic requirements be common to all special education teaching associates unless otherwise noted: "Specific competencies directly related to successful performance as a special education teaching associate (instructional paraprofessional) in the classroom to be acquired through at least 20 semester hours of course work and practicum experiences prescribed by the accredited teaching associate education institution." This training program will include:	Specific competencies directly related to successful performance as a special education teaching associate in the classroom is considered to be most relevant. Additionally, as opposed to the teacher requirements of 8 to 12 semester hours, it appears that an individual with less academic experience will generally require the additional 8 to 12 semester hours to acquire the requisite performance and informational competencies for educating handicapped individuals.
A. At least six semester hours of credit leading to competencies in behavior management, including the following: Measurement of behavior, evaluation of behavior, strengthening behavior, weakening behavior.	Specific competencies in behavior management are prerequisite skills for instructing handicapped individuals.

Table 1.—*continued*

Recommendation	Rationale
B. At least two semester hours of credit leading to competencies in assisting teachers in organization of learning environments, e.g., classrooms, home, and work environments.	Competencies in knowledge of learning environments is essential for providing functional assistance to the classroom teacher.
C. At least three semester hours of credit leading to competencies in assisting teachers in curriculum development, including methods and materials.	Competencies in curriculum development are essential for providing functional assistance to the classroom teacher.
D. At least three semester hours of credit leading to competencies in each of the following areas: Motor development, self-help skill development, language development, social development, and academic or pre-academic skill development.	Competencies in knowledge of skill development are essential for providing instruction to handicapped individuals.
E. At least 240 clock hours of supervised practicum experiences with handicapped individuals (includes approximately six semester hours of credit in practicum courses).	Actual training experience with handicapped individuals is essential for acquiring performance skills for classroom instruction.
6. It is recommended that specialized training for teaching associates in areas of special education, such as learning disabilities, emotionally disturbed, educable mentally retarded, trainable mentally retarded, and multiply or severely handicapped, be acquired by either of the following options: A. At least three semester hours of credit leading to competencies in the specific area of specialization; or, B. At least 16 weeks of supervised inservice training in the specific area of specilization.	The aforementioned basic requirements for special education teaching associates are essential for all areas of exceptionality; however, specific training in a given area can be acquired with minimal additional training. Also, specifying general or basic requirements for teaching associates increases the number of possible directions for career advancement across several disciplines of exceptionality.

Although there may be a multiple number of solutions to the advancement problem, we will only consider two at this point. First, advancement within the teaching associate ranks, and second, advancement to the teacher ranks. Briefly, the advancement within ranks could be based on experience (years on the job and number of children's behavior changed) and additional training (workshops and advanced courses with objective testing at critical points). Such continuation of training could lead to an Associate Degree (Community Junior College). A natural step from teaching associate to teacher could then be taken by attending a four-year college for completion of a degree and certification as a special education teacher. It should be noted that the authors are aware of the fact that most programs for certified special education teachers are at the graduate level. This is due to the fact that in most cases certification and experience in elementary or secondary education is a prerequisite to certification in special education. The authors believe the rationale for this to be more myth than fact. That is, there appears to be little if any valid data to support this type of program for training teachers of the handicapped. We have fast been approaching the absurdity of requiring special education teachers to have a Ph.D. and to plan their certification program from birth—nonsense!

Teacher and Teaching Associate Relationship

The educational teaching associate, in order to effectively supplement the educational opportunities for severely handicapped students provided by a teacher, must have acquired the informational and performance competencies directly related to changing the behavior of such students. The teaching associates will be directly supervised by the teacher and carry out educational programs developed and implemented by the teacher. Thus, the teacher becomes a classroom "manager" or "coordinator" instead of just a "teacher" (Fredericks et al., 1975). In order to enhance implementation of educational programs, both the teacher and teaching associate should receive similar training in those competencies directly related to the education of severely handicapped students. This approach suggests that, during training, the teacher, should be provided practicum training in supervising paraprofessional personnel in working with children.

PARAPROFESSIONAL TRAINEE
SELECTION AND PLACEMENT FACTORS

In the selection, training, and placement of persons to be trained as paraprofessionals, consideration should be given to the selection population pool, job placement situation, and geographical areas. Figure 1 illustrates the components that make up each factor and their respective relationships.

Demographic Considerations

In the selection of persons to be trained as paraprofessionals, we should give consideration to three factors: educational background,

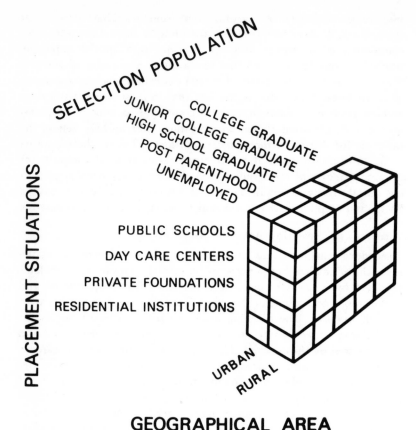

GEOGRAPHICAL AREA

Figure 1.   Paraprofessional trainee selection model.

age group, and geographical locale. First, in view of the difficulty of the task, it is doubtful that anyone could be successful in a competency-based paraprofessional training program who did not have a high school diploma or the equivalent (e.g., G.E.D.). However, at the other extreme we may find that there are college graduates that for one reason or another wish to be employed as paraprofessionals. Age becomes a critical factor when considering the size of the population pool from which we can draw prospective students. At first glance, two groups emerge — young or recent high school graduates and the post-parenthood adult. These two groups typically have large numbers of unemployed and can afford to work for salaries well below those required to support a family. For the young person with an effective career ladder, paraprofessional training and experience could serve as an entry into the professional level. For the post-parenthood adult, paraprofessional training could provide a worthy contribution to society as well as an added income. The final factor to be considered in personnel selection is the geographical residence of the prospective trainee. Depending on the state, we are confronted with the problem of urban or rural residence. This may not be a serious consideration for the young trainee; however, for the adult, area of residence could provide a significant barrier to training and work placements because of permanent family ties in a small rural community. In addition, handicapped children needing special education services span the breadth and width of a state. In view of these facts, it would appear logical to locate paraprofessional train-ing programs in, or as close as possible to, the community where the prospective trainee resides and subsequently would be employed (see Figure 1).

The Training Institution

If one considers the demographic factors involved in the selection and placement of paraprofessional personnel, it would appear that the community junior college provides a natural training site. These junior colleges are frequently strategically located throughout the various states and in many cases have had experience in conducting programs for paraprofessional personnel. For example, many junior colleges have already developed programs for nursing, mental health workers, and medical technicians. Because many of these programs are aimed at providing community services, it would appear likely that they would or could be interested in developing programs for educational personnel.

The use of community junior colleges or training sites has been discussed with several college administrators. They all indicated interest; however, they would not consider pursuing the issue until the Kansas State Board of Education had set the certification stand-ards for paraprofessional personnel. Another concern they voiced is: Would there be sufficient students to warrant a program?

Job Placement

Where is the job market for educational paraprofessionals? At first glance it would appear that the largest utilization of educational paraprofessionals would be in public school special education classes.

Since there are other facilities that serve the needs of handicapped children, we have included the following list:

1. Special education classes — unified school districts
2. Residential institutions — e.g., state hospitals for the mentally retarded
3. Private foundations — those serving handicapped children
4. Day-care centers — those serving handicapped children

Irrespective of the job setting (Figure 1), it would be anticipated that the educational paraprofessional would be supervised by a certified special education teacher.

CAREER TRAINING MODELS

The competency-based training program for teaching associate personnel for the severely handicapped may be implemented in any of four possible career training models: 1) inservice training (on-the-job training); 2) preservice training at the junior college level; 3) two-year preservice training at the university level; and 4) four-year preservice training at the university level (see Table 2). The four levels of training programs are listed in a potential hierarchy of "career ladder" benefits, beginning with inservice training, with potentially the least amount of career benefits, and culminating with the four-year university preservice training, resulting in the greatest amount of potential career benefits.

Inservice Training

The teaching associate training program may be implemented as an inservice training program at the local educational agency, e.g., local public school district. The primary terminal objectives for the trainees in the program would be the obtainment of: 1) the specified applied skills for educating handicapped children by demonstration of criterion performance in the practicum training; and 2) the informational competencies to criterion in the academic training.

The specified prerequisite for entry into the training program is a high school diploma or the equivalent, e.g., G.E.D. However, if an individual can demonstrate the required competencies without the formal prerequisites, a high school diploma is an irrelevant issue. Nevertheless, the fact remains that most school districts have established a high school diploma as a minimum qualification for employment.

Table 2. Career training models for teaching associates

Training program	Terminal objectives	Prerequisites	Certification
I. Inservice	A. Applied skills: Practicum modules B. Infomation: Academic modules	A. High school diploma or equivalent	A. Complete modules B. 1 year on-the-job training
II. Preservice: Junior College	A. Applied skills: Praticum modules B. Information: Academic modules C. Associate degree	A. High school diploma or equivalent	A. Complete modules B. Associate degree
III. Preservice: Pre-university	A. Applied skills: Practicum modules B. Information: Academic modules C. Associate degree or equivalent	A. High school diploma or equivalent	A. Complete modules B. Associate degree or equivalent
IV. Preservice: University	A. Applied skills: Practicum modules B. Information: Academic modules C. Bachelor degree	A. High school diploma or equivalent	A. Complete modules B. Bachelor degree

If certification of teaching associate personnel is a relevant issue, it is proposed that minimum requirements for certification be the successful completion of both the academic and practicum training in addition to one full year of supervised on-the-job training.

Preservice Training: Junior College

The training program may also be implemented at the preservice level at a local junior or community college. The terminal objectives for the teaching associate trainee would be the successful completion of: 1) the performance competencies specified in the practicum training; 2) the informational competencies specified in the academic training; and 3) the general curriculum requirements for an Associate Arts degree (e.g., 60 credit hours).

The prerequisites for entry into the program would be qualification for admission to the community college, which is typically a high school diploma or the equivalent.

Certification as a teaching associate would be contingent upon successful completion of the practicum and academic training, in addition to fulfilling the general requirements for the Associate Arts degree.

The career advantages for completing a preservice training program in a junior college are basically: 1) increased probability of higher beginning salary in local educational agency; and 2) completion of general requirements for entry into the specialized component of a four-year degree program at the university level.

Preservice Training: Pre-university

A pre-university preservice training program would be essentially the same as that for a junior college except that the program would be coordinated and administered through a four-year university for a two-year duration. The only advantages of this model over the previous model would be: 1) the facilitory transition between Associate degree level and continued study toward a Bachelor's degree; and 2) an additional geographical source for obtaining college-level education.

Preservice: University

Once again, the basic objectives, prerequisites, and certification requirements would remain the same as in the previous models, with the added requirement of successful completion of a Bachelor's degree. The additional advantage of this model would be the completion of requirements for admission to a graduate training program facilitating *across-ranks* career advancement.

COMPETENCY-BASED CURRICULUM MODEL

The Kansas program (Sailor et al., 1975) is designed to provide comprehensive performance-based curricula for the preparation of both teachers and teaching associates who will provide educational programs for severely handicapped individuals, in accord with the national mandate for equality of access to education for all handicapped children and youth.

The competencies identified through this program provide both teachers and teaching associates with the performance skills required to provide functional educational programs for individuals who are severely and profoundly handicapped, including those with severe or profound orthopedic impairments, behavior disorders, perceptual, psychomotor, and/or medical disorders.

The competency-based curriculum model (Figure 2) was developed around two training components: informational competencies and performance competencies. The identified competencies have been organized into training modules. Each training module has a format that includes the specification of the criterion required to successfully demonstrate the acquisition of the informational and performance competencies.

Courses

The training modules are subsumed under a sequence of courses leading to college credit hours (see Table 3). The general curriculum requirements, or the "core" curriculum for the Paraprofessional Multiply/Severely Handicapped Program, consists of 11 courses, including practicum courses, sequenced across a five-semester period of training (approximately two years). This "core" program comprises about 24 of the approximate total 60 credit hours of an Associate Arts degree.

The primary purpose for the academic courses is to provide the teaching associate trainee with the informational competencies necessary to increase the generality of the requisite skills for education of the severely and profoundly handicapped. A secondary purpose is to lay the groundwork for a common, and hopefully a more "professional," language system to be used with the teacher, psychologist, counselor, etc.

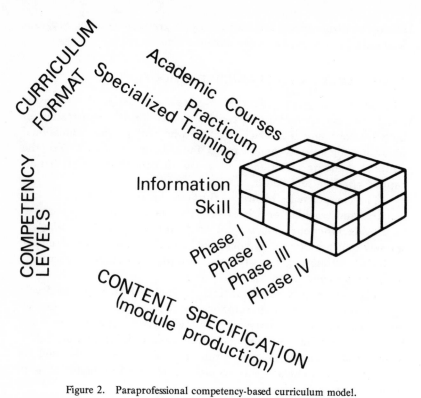

Figure 2.   Paraprofessional competency-based curriculum model.

Practicum

The practicum courses serve the purpose of providing the teaching associate trainee with a structured program in which to obtain the performance competencies, or skills, necessary for directly teaching the severely and profoundly handicapped.

The practicum courses are sequenced throughout the training program to provide the trainee with a gradual increase in the amount of time spent in the classroom, working directly with the children, as he acquires more and more informational competencies. In the first practicum the trainee spends approximately one hour per day per week, or the equivalent, in the classroom, whereas in the last practicum the trainee spends approximately three hours per day each week, or the equivalent, working with children in the classroom. The number of credit hours assigned to each practicum course may be determined by the local educational agency according to its individual guidelines. Nevertheless, the practicum courses remain the most important and functional aspect of the training program regardless of the credit hours awarded for successful completion of the course.

Specialized Training

The purpose of specialized training is to provide training in specific competencies for a specific task. The main advantages of specialized training lie in the expedience and inexpensiveness of providing training for a specific set of competencies for a specific environment as compared to training and general competencies. The response cost involved in training a teaching associate in, for example, the procedures of a specific language training program with a given group of children is considerably less than the cost of training that same teaching associate in the basic components and concepts in all language training, per se. The time involved in training, the financial cost of implementation, and the latency between training and proficient performance of the trainee are all factors that are more advantageous for specialized training.

However, there are important factors to be considered that are disadvantages of specialized training. From the standpoint of preservice instruction, specialized training is relatively impractical to implement. It is nearly impossible to know exactly what type of job placement each individual trainee is going to have. Is the trainee going to be teaching language development, motor development, etc.? Is the trainee going to be working in a classroom for severely handicapped, moderately handicapped, learning disabled, deaf and blind, or all combinations of handicaps? Training each individual in specialized skills for each position is obviously impractical and economically unfeasible. A disadvantageous by-product of obtaining only specialized skills is that it limits opportunities for employment.

The 23 modules of this training program are intended to provide "general" competencies for teaching associates. Although the program is geared for providing skills for educating the severely handicapped, it is our opinion that the program provides generic competencies for teaching individuals with any or all handicaps in general.

The advantages of training in generic competencies are apparent. First, it is feasible to implement through preservice programs, since all trainees are provided the same information and skills. Academic information can be provided on a group basis or through self-paced instruction. Each method is practical for a limited number

Table 3. General curriculum requirements: Paraprofessional Multiply/Severely Handicapped Program[a]

Fall Semester

Course 1 (2 hr)	Introduction to Mental Retardation and Behavior Management	Module A: Right to Education	A
		Module B: Introduction to Operant Behavior	A
Course 2 (1 hr)	Classroom Participation with Exceptional Children	Module D: Basic Classroom Participation – Practicum I	P

Spring Semester

Course 3 (2 hr)	Methods in Classroom Measurement and Evaluation	Module E: Measuring Operant Behavior	A
		Module F: Evaluation of Operant Procedures	A
Course 4 (3 hr)	Methods in Classroom Management and Programming	Module G: Strengthening Operant Behavior	A
		Module H: Weakening Operant Behavior	A
		Module I: Schedules of Reinforcement	A
		Module J: Generalization and Discrimination	A
Course 5 (2 hr)	Classroom Participation with Exceptional Children	Module O: Intermediate Classroom Participation – Practicum II	P

Summer Semester

Course 6 (2 hr)	Techniques in Programming Learning Environments	Module L: Programming Prosthetic Environments	A
		Module M: Programming Engaging Environments	A

Fall Semester

Course 7 (3 hr)	Curriculum Development for Exceptional Children	Module P: Assessment Scales	A
		Module Q: Writing Instructional Objectives	A

Course 8 (2 hr)	Laboratory in Developing Instructional Programs	Module R:	Curriculum Planning	A
		Module S:	Task Analysis	A
		Module Y₁:	Advanced Classroom Participation 1 — Practicum III	P
Course 9 (2 hr)	Seminar in Basic Skills Programs for Exceptional Children	Module T:	Motor Programs	A
		Module U:	Self-Help Programs	A

Spring Semester

Course 10 (2 hr)	Seminar in Advanced Skills Programs for Exceptional Children	Module V:	Language Programs	A
		Module W:	Socialization Programs	A
		Module X:	Pre-academic Programs	A
Course 11 (3 hr)	Advanced Practicum with Exceptional Children	Module Y₂:	Advanced Classroom Participation 2 — Practicum IV	P

[a] A = Academic Skills; P = Practicum or Applied Skills. Modules C, K, N, Teacher Training Program, are not applicable to Para-professional Training Program. Course titles are examples and are not intended to be exclusive. Approximately 24 total credit hours.

of instructors. Performance competencies can be provided through practicum exercises on individual practicum sites, which not only trains the students in specific competencies, but also exposes them to specialized environments. It is assumed that, with specific competencies in the basic learning principles and teaching procedures, a teaching associate should have increased probabilities for employment beyond those of an individual with a specialized skill. Although it is an empirical question, another working hypothesis is that an individual with generic training should be able to generalize to new and novel teaching environments more effectively than an individual with specialized training.

As a result, this project recognizes the importance and advantages of specialized training, but does not, however, promote the exclusive development of a systematic program of specialized training for national dissemination. Nevertheless, specialized training still remains an important component of training and should best be provided at the local level through inservice training programs for specific educational environmental needs.

COMPETENCY LEVELS

Analyzing the Student's Learning Task

The salient product of an educational program is the student's knowledge of the subject matter and on-the-job performance. There are many kinds of knowledge (symbolic learning) and performance skills required of teachers and teaching associates in order to survive in the classroom. As has already been discussed in this chapter, it appears advantageous to have teachers and their teaching associates trained in the same content core areas. However, it has been suggested that the depth of knowledge need not be as extensive for the teaching associate as for the teacher. Therefore, by specifying the kind of skills and knowledge required of teachers and teaching associates with some degree of precision, it would be possible to obtain real advantages in their education and training. The basic training model provides for a dichotomy of learning into two functional parts: 1) symbolic learning and 2) skill learning. This training model was developed by Woolman (1954) for the systematic analysis of Air Force pilot training programs. At this point it is appropriate to outline and apply Woolman's analysis to the training of teachers and teaching associates in special education.

In general, the preceding section has presented a competency-based curriculum model in which the curriculum format specifies: 1) academic courses, 2) practicum, and 3) specialized training. In the development of specific competencies, *the first criterion for identifying the student learning task is to relate the area of instruction to on-the-job performance required by the teacher.* Thus, the analysis of the student's learning task is concerned with two broad areas, as follows:

1. *Information learning*—which involves learning of names and symbols, locations, relationships, etc.
2. *Skill learning*—which involves learning how to physically manipulate a child's limb (e.g., with the physically handicapped), select and set up various educational materials, properly deliver reinforcers, etc., while using established procedures.

It should be understood that symbolic learning (language) may take place without skill learning, but skill learning always has some symbolic component. That is, there are always names, locations, sequences, etc., in a skill learning task.

Information Competency Levels

In order to develop functional information competency levels, it is necessary to objectively analyze the curriculum content area. It is then necessary to state the information or knowledge objectives explicitly. The kinds of information and knowledge required of a teacher or teaching associate may be classified into six levels, as outlined in Table 4.

Table 4.   Information levels

Level	Kind of knowledge	Definition
1	Names	What it is called
2	Location	Where it is
3	Function	How something works
4	Relations	How several things work together
5	Abstractions and principles	Understanding equations and general scientific laws
6	Theory	The formulation of hypotheses

Skill Competency Levels

In the training of personnel to work with handicapped children, it is necessary to provide them with more than information. That is, in addition to having information they must be competent in skills that directly modify the child's behavior in the appropriate directions. Therefore, they must be able to develop the ability to assist children directly in making simple movements and developing imitative behavior, and to deliver social or tangible reinforcers and to engage in many more complex demonstrations. Skill competencies have been broken down into five levels and are outlined in Table 5.

CURRICULUM CONTENT SPECIFICATION

Course Modules

Competency Blocks   Three basic blocks of "teaching" competencies have been identified (see Figure 3): 1) those competencies that are directly related to changing student behavior (e.g., measuring behav-

Table 5.   Skill Levels

Level	Kind of skill	Definition
1	No skill required	Exists where only information is necessary for the student to know (operational indoctrination)
2	Single skill	A single movement on the basis of simple information (grasping a child's hand)
3	Compound skill	This, for example, is a number of simple skills bundled into a common task (a response chain, e.g., reach-grasp-pull-drop)
4	Complex skill	The combination of a number of simple skills where feedback information requires interpretation and judgment (in vocational training, teaching a student to operate a drill press, table saw, etc.)
5	Multiplex skill	This requires the combination of a number of complex skills where large quantities of information must be judged and actions performed (for example, driving an automobile, operation of camera equipment for a TV show, and so forth)

ior, strengthening behavior, weakening behavior, etc.); 2) those competencies that are indirectly related to changing student behavior (e.g., writing instructional objectives, curriculum planning, task analysis, etc.); and 3) those competencies that have an unknown relationship to changing student behavior (e.g., issues in "right to education," "normalization," counseling with parents, etc.) (Tucker and Horner, 1976).

Training Modules   Twenty-five modules, covering the three basic blocks of instructional competencies for teacher training, were targeted for initial development (cf. Horner, 1976). The project has developed a Module Production Lattice (see Figure 4) that illustrates the sequenced procedure for developing each individual module. The procedure consists of four basic phases of development: 1) the development of the instructional competencies; 2) the development of the prototype module; 3) the revision and production of the final module; and 4) the publication and dissemination of the final module. The major subcomponents of the procedure are emphasized in Figure 4.

The topic covered by each training module was subjected to a content analysis, and the informational and performance competencies identified (Horner, Holvoet, and Rinne, 1976). The informational and performance competencies for teaching associates were

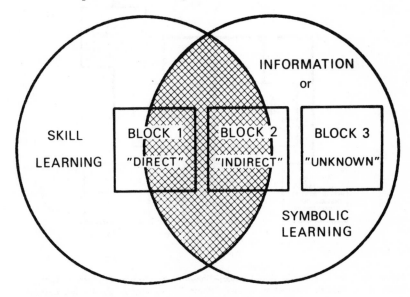

Figure 3.   Teaching competency blocks.

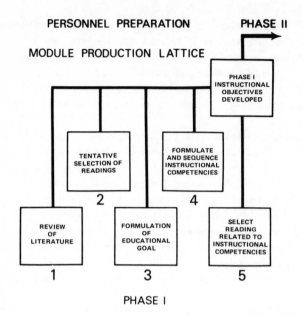

PHASE I

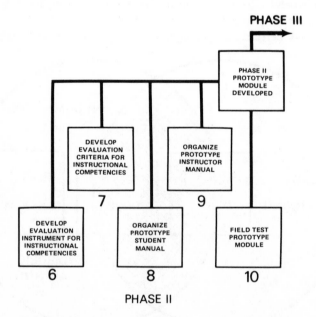

PHASE II

Figure 4a: Module Production Lattice—Phase I. b: Module Production Lattice—Phase II. c: Module Production Lattice—Phase III. d: Module Production Lattice—Phase IV.

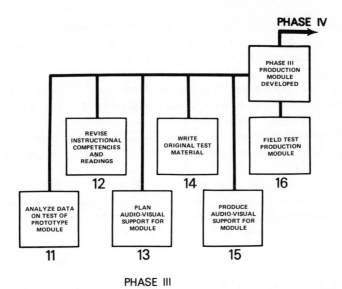

PHASE IV

PHASE III
PRODUCTION
MODULE
DEVELOPED

REVISE
INSTRUCTIONAL
COMPETENCIES
AND
READINGS

WRITE
ORIGINAL TEST
MATERIAL

FIELD TEST
PRODUCTION
MODULE

12   14   16

ANALYZE DATA
ON TEST OF
PROTOTYPE
MODULE

PLAN
AUDIO-VISUAL
SUPPORT FOR
MODULE

PRODUCE
AUDIO-VISUAL
SUPPORT FOR
MODULE

11   13   15

PHASE III

PRODUCTION
MODULE
COMPLETED

PHASE IV
PRODUCTION
MODULE
PUBLISHED

REVISE
ORIGINAL
MATERIAL FOR
MODULE

ARRANGE FOR
PUBLICATION OF
PRODUCTION
MODULE

18   20

ANALYZE DATA
ON TEST OF
PRODUCTION
MODULE

REVISE
AUDIO-VISUAL
SUPPORT FOR
MODULE

17   19

PHASE IV

specified by determining on an *a priori* basis which competencies would provide functional classroom teaching assistance to teachers. Table 6 illustrates the relationship of the teacher and teaching associate training modules.

It was determined that the teaching associate should receive: 1) rigorous training in those competency areas that are *directly* related to changing student behaviors (i.e., concentration on competencies related to actual teaching skills); 2) training in some component parts of the areas *indirectly* related to changing student behav-

Table 6.   General competency area curriculum requirements: Teacher and Teaching Associate Multiply/Severely Handicapped Program

Module	Title	Teacher	Teaching Associate
Module A:	Right to Education	X	X
Module B:	Introduction to Operant Behavior	X	X
Module C:	Behavioral Approach to Special Education	X	
*Module D:	Basic Classroom Participation: Practicum I	X	X
Module E:	Measuring Operant Behavior	X	X
Module F:	Evaluation of Operant Procedures	X	X
Module G:	Strengthening Operant Behavior	X	X
Module H:	Weakening Operant Behavior	X	X
Module I:	Schedules of Reinforcement	X	X
Module J:	Generalization and Discrimination	X	X
Module K:	Programming for Normalization	X	
Module L:	Programming Prosthetic Environments	X	X
Module M:	Programming Engaging Environments	X	X
Module N:	Training Teacher Aides and Parents	X	
*Module O:	Intermediate Classroom Participation Practicum II	X	X
Module P:	Assessment Scales	X	X
Module Q:	Writing Instructional Objectives	X	X
Module R:	Curriculum Planning	X	X
Module S:	Task Analysis	X	X
Module T:	Motor Programs	X	X
Module U:	Self-Help Programs	X	X
Module V:	Language Programs	X	X
Module W:	Socialization Programs	X	X
Module X:	Pre-academic Programs	X	X
*Module Y:	Advanced Classroom Participation: Practicum III	X	X

*Practicum modules consist of exercises designed to teach performance competencies.

iors; and 3) minimal exposure to those areas that have an unknown relationship to changing student behaviors (see Table 7).

Informational and Performance Competencies An example of the relationship between teachers and teaching associates with respect to informational competencies for a module is presented in Table 8.

Module A (right to education) represents a competency area that falls into Block 3, having an unknown relationship to teaching students. Out of 20 informational competencies for teachers, only six apply to teaching associates. In addition (not illustrated), Module A contains four performance competencies for teachers, as opposed to none for teaching associates. On the other hand, Module B (intro-

Table 7. Relationship of modules to competency blocks

Module	Title	Direct	Indirect	Unknown
Module A:	Right to Education			X
Module B:	Introduction to Operant Behavior	X		
Module D:	Basic Classroom Participation— Practicum I	X		
Module E:	Measuring Operant Behavior	X		
Module F:	Evaluation of Operant Procedures		X	
Module G:	Strengthening Operant Behavior	X		
Module H:	Weakening Operant Behavior	X		
Module I:	Schedules of Reinforcement	X		
Module J:	Generalization and Discrimination	X		
Module O:	Intermediate Classroom Participation—Practicum II	X		
Module L:	Programming Prosthetic Environments	X		
Module M:	Programming Engaging Environments		X	
Module P:	Assessment Scales		X	
Module Q:	Curriculum Planning		X	
Module R:	Writing Instructional Objectives		X	
Module S:	Task Analysis		X	
Module Y_1:	Advanced Classroom Participation 1—Practicum III (Laboratory)		X	
Module T:	Motor Programs	X		
Module U:	Self-Help Programs	X		
Module V:	Language Programs	X		
Module W:	Socialization Programs	X		
Module X:	Pre-academic Programs	X		
Module Y_2:	Advanced Classroom Participation 2—Practicum IV	X		

duction to operant behavior) exemplifies a competency area categorized as a Block 1 area. Module B contains 20 informational competencies for teachers that are all applicable for teaching associates. The informational competencies are accompanied by ten performance com-

Table 8.   Teacher and teaching associate informational competencies: Module A—right to education

Informational competencies (abbreviated)	Teachers	Teaching associates
Prepare a written definition, description statement of:		
1. Concept of "zero rejection"	X	X
2. Origins of "rights to treatment and education"	X	X
3. Constitutional provisions establishing "rights to treatment and education"	X	
4. Legal exclusion of handicapped from public education	X	
5. Difference between "class action" and "private action" suit	X	
6. Rationale for legal issue of equality of *access to* education	X	
7. Stages in *Wyatt* v. *Stickney* litigation	X	
8. The salient provisions of the Pennsylvania consent agreement	X	
9. Application of "least restrictive means" principle	X	X
10. "Cascade system" of educational placement	X	
11. Status of institutional residents in relation to "right to education"	X	X
12. Legally prescribed minimum standards for educational programs	X	
13. Economic aspects of court ordered minimum educational standards	X	
14. Court decision challenging use of testing instruments for special class placement	X	X
15. Negative aspects of purchasing special education services	X	
16. Concept of "institutional peonage"	X	X
17. Distinction between therapeutic and nontherapeutic work assignments	X	
18. Legal approaches to remediating "institutional peonage"	X	
19. Statutory definition of exceptional children	X	
20. Legal exceptions to providing special education services	X	

pentencies for teachers, eight of which apply to teaching associates (see Table 9).

With respect to Block 2, areas *indirectly* related to teaching students, an example is Module P (assessment scales). A teacher is expected not only to administer assessment scales, but also to interpret the results for formulating instructional objectives and planning the curriculum. The teaching associate, on the other hand, is trained only in the mechanics of administering the assessment scale.

In addition to the informational and performance competencies, each module contains a reading list (academic modules only) that corresponds to the informational competencies and a system for evaluation. Both of the personnel training programs use written examinations for evaluating informational competencies.

Practicum Modules

As illustrated in Table 7, the program contains four practicum mod-

Table 9.   Teacher and teaching associate performance competencies: Module B — introduction to operant behavior

Performance competencies (abbreviated)	Teachers	Teaching Associates
Apply academic information by:		
1. Translating target behaviors from assessment scales into behavioral definitions	X	
2. Engaging in a procedure for identifying potential reinforcers	X	X
3. Using a measurement instrument to record performance of target behavior	X	X
4. Determining inter-observer reliability of measurements	X	
5. Computing and plotting data points on a graph	X	X
6. Presenting programmed discriminative stimuli	X	X
7. Immediately presenting contingent reinforcers during training	X	X
8. Withholding the presentation of reinforcers during training contingent upon nontargeted responses	X	X
9. Interrupting responses that are incompatible with targeted responses	X	X
10. Following a specific programmed teaching sequence	X	X

ules. Three of the modules pertain directly to the training of the children, whereas the fourth module (Module Y_1) consists of actual instructional program development.

The purpose of the practicum modules is to provide specific applied exercises, allowing the trainee to demonstrate the performance competencies identified in the preceding academic modules. For example, the second performance competency in Module B (introduction to operant behavior) is:

A teaching associate of the severely and profoundly handicapped should apply the information acquired through the readings of the Introduction to Operant Behavior Module by ... 2) engaging in a procedure leading to the identification of conditioned and/or unconditioned stimuli which may serve as reinforcers when made contingent upon and presented immediately after a target behavior.

The teaching associate trainee is then provided the opportunity and trained, if necessary, to follow, with a child in the classroom, the procedure of identifying potential reinforcers specified by Striefel (1974). Because effective reinforcers for severely handicapped children are often transient, the procedure is generally a relevant and functional task for the praticum site classroom as well as for the trainee.

The practicum exercises guide the trainee across the five-semester training program through a series of activities based somewhat on a continuum of task complexity. The first practicum module concentrates primarily on instructing the trainee to teach *one* specific child *one* specific skill. The second practicum module expands the trainee's responsibilities and skills across different skill domains (e.g., motor development, self-help development, language development, etc.). The third practicum module instructs the trainee to teach several children one particular skill as a function of testing the instructional program assigned for development. The fourth and last practicum module essentially provides the trainee with realistic on-the-job responsibilities and duties. These duties test the trainee's competence in instructing severely handicapped children across several skill programs. In addition to specific structured programmed sessions with the children, the trainee is provided experience with unstructured free operant activities with the children, such as snack time, holding activities, "recess," etc. Thus, the practicum exercises are designed to provide the teaching associate trainee with an array of singular to more complex skills and experiences in a functional classroom setting.

TRAINING METHODS

Because there are two basic categories of competencies identified for training teaching associate personnel, there is a need for two separate training methods: 1) a set of procedures for training informational competencies, and 2) a set of procedures for training performance competencies.

Information

Each informational module contains a list of primary readings and supplemental readings. The reading list is accompanied by a chart identifying the sequence in which the readings should be covered and which competencies are included in each reading. Thus, the method for completing a given module is self-explanatory within the module. As a result, the teaching associate could, in fact, proceed through each module on his own at his own rate, i.e., he could use self-paced personalized instruction. However, the possibility remains that the readings may not be adequate for an individual trainee to acquire the competencies without additional or remedial assistance.

This project has found that, for teaching associates, that is the case for many of the modules, since there is a deficit of published material directly related to a behavioral approach to teaching severely and profoundly handicapped individuals. The method being used is a combination of personalized competency-based instruction and a traditional approach to college education. The courses consist of the self-contained modules plus regularly scheduled class meetings in a seminar format. The seminar sessions serve the purpose of providing verbal feedback to the trainees in addition to frequent written examinations.

The following is the procedure for teaching the seminar sessions for each module (see Figure 5 for a flowchart illustrating the procedure).

1. Before directing the seminar sessions for a module, the instructor should thoroughly read the readings, both primary and supplemental. The supplemental readings contain additional and more comprehensive information to be added to the instructor's resources for discussion and remedial sessions.

2. Assign teaching associate trainees (students) to the seminar class. It is suggested that no more than ten students be assigned

to a class in order to promote an informal class environment
and to facilitate discussions.

3. At the outset of the first class session, distribute the Student
    Manuals and explain the course procedures.

4. For the remainder of the first class session, explain the purpose

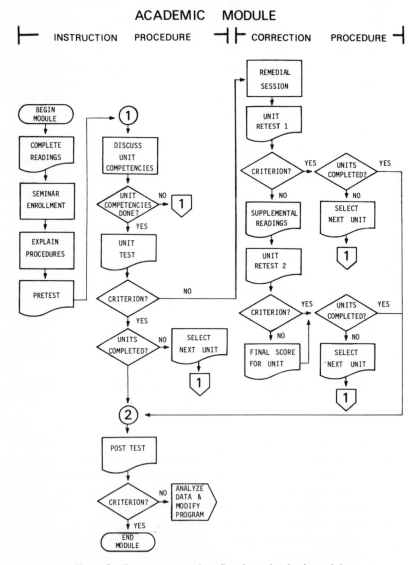

Figure 5.   Instructor procedure flowchart: Academic module.

of the pretest (to compare pretest and posttest differences for determining effectiveness of training material). Then assign readings for the first unit (if more than one unit) and administer the pretest. (After a comprehensive pretest is further developed and tested in the future, the pretest will also provide the opportunity for the student to "test out of" the module.)

5. In the second class session, begin discussion of the competencies in the first unit, using the test questions and answers as a discussion guide. The guide is recommended because the test questions and answers may provide more information and definitions than are included in the primary readings.

6. Once all of the competencies within the unit have been covered in the seminar, administer the unit test.

7. If a student reaches criterion on the unit test, cycle the student back to the discussion of the next unit; if all units have been covered, then administer the posttest.

8. If a student fails to reach criterion on the unit test, then cycle to the "correction procedure."

9. Correction procedure:

    a. Re-discuss those competencies for the questions the student responded to incorrectly,

    b. Administer the same unit test again (Retest 1).

    c. If the student reaches criterion on the unit retest, cycle to the next units. If all units have been covered, then administer the posttest.

    d. If the student again fails to perform to criterion, assign the supplemental readings over the pertinent competencies and administer Retest 2 for that unit,

    e. If the student reaches criterion on Retest 2, cycle to the next units. if all units have been covered, then administer the posttest,

    f. If the student again fails to perform to criterion, record the highest score for the unit and proceed to the next unit or posttest.

10. Once all units have been tested, administer the posttest to each student.

11. If criterion is reached on the posttest, the student has successfully completed the module.

12. If criterion is not reached on the posttest, analyze the data and modify the program accordingly in order to meet the needs of training environment and/or the individual students.

In addition to the discussion, the instructor can utilize various audiovisual aids as well as behavior rehearsal. Fawcett et al. (1975) have recently demonstrated the effectiveness of behavior rehearsal, consisting of an opportunity to practice followed by feedback on practice performance, as an important link between information acquisition and performance acquisition of specific competencies by "low-income paraprofessionals." In this present primitive state of instructional technology for training paraprofessionals, the skill-fulness and resourcefulness of the instructor will play an important supplemental role to published instructional material for trainers of the severely and profoundly handicapped.

Skill

The training methods for the practicum skills are being adapted from procedures developed by Carpenter (1976), which are similar to those suggested by O'Brien and Azrin (1972) and Horner and Keilitz (1975) for training handicapped persons. The procedure consists of five basic components: 1) providing explicit instructions to the trainee; 2) providing the opportunity to perform correctly with no assistance from the instructor; 3) providing immediate corrective verbal feedback; 4) modeling or demonstrating the skill to be learned; and 5) providing verbal guidance to the trainee in successive approximations to criterion performance.

Instructions At the outset of a skill task, the practicum instructor provides explicit instructions on the procedures and components of the task, or instructional program for the child. For example, if the skill task consists of an imitation program (cf. Striefel, 1974), the instructor gives a copy of the program to the trainee for study and systematically goes through the program, step by step, until the trainee is familiar with what cues to give, what child responses to expect, how to reinforce correct responses, correction procedures for incorrect responses, criteria for correct responses, data collection procedures, etc.

No Assistance The instructor then provides the trainee the opportunity to conduct the task correctly without assistance. If the trainee does in fact perform correctly, the instructor provides positive feedback, or praise for correct responses. If the trainee makes an error, the instructor proceeds to the next component of the training procedure, i.e., immediate corrective verbal feedback.

Immediate Corrective Feedback Immediately following an error by the trainee, the instructor provides corrective verbal feedback. Corrective feedback is defined as: "Stating the trainee's error in response to the child behavior, and/or giving corrective feedback why the child response required a certain response from the trainee" (Carpenter, 1976). Stating the trainee's errors include listing, describing, or providing additional information about what trainee behaviors are needed to make a correct response. This statement is put in positive form, never negative, and instead of pointing out what the trainee did wrong, the instructor explains the child's error and what is the correct trainee response. The trainee is then provided the opportunity to correct his error by "practicing" the appropriate response.

Model   Usually, immediate corrective feedback with positive practice and praise is sufficient to obtain and maintain desirable performance by the trainee. However, if the trainee continues to make errors, the instructor models or demonstrates the appropriate response. After the model, the trainee is, once again, allowed to practice the task correctly.

Verbal Guidance   If the trainee responds incorrectly, the instructor task analyzes the skill and verbally guides the trainee through successive approximations of the task until criterion performance is achieved. It should be emphasized that the verbal guidance method is an alternative procedure that is rarely, if ever, needed in eliciting correct performance by teaching associate trainees. Should this procedure be needed frequently, the skill task should be broken down into component parts as a means of simplifying the required activity.

In addition to this systematic training procedure, the trainees are in the presence of other appropriate models in the classrooms throughout the duration of practicum training. It is assumed that these models in addition to required exercises, have an important effect on the "teaching" behavior of the trainees.

EVALUATION OF TRAINEE PERFORMANCE

The ultimate goal of the trainer of the severely handicapped is, of course, to increase the number of functional skills of the child being trained. However, a teacher or teaching associate can perform perfectly according to academically structured objectives, and yet the child may still fail to learn. Any number of programmatic variables may be responsible for this failure. Therefore, not only is it necessary to evaluate competencies during and at the completion of training, but also it is necessary to establish their validity at the job placement site. This can be accomplished by monitoring on-the-job performance by "site visits" following placement.

Course Modules—Information Proficiency

Written tests, including objective questions as well as questions requiring written statements, have been developed for each training module within specified courses. A proficiency criterion, such as 90% correct responses for test completion, is necessary for demonstration of informational competencies of each module. The difference in proficiency criteria between teachers and teaching associates is a quantitative difference as opposed to a qualitative difference. For example, in a given competency area, such as "right to education," a teacher is required to obtain 20 informational competencies, whereas the teaching associate is required to obtain only six of those 20 competencies. Nevertheless, 90% correct performance is required of both teachers and teaching associates.

Practicum Performance—Skill Proficiency

In determining skill proficiency, the difference in criteria for demonstration of performance competencies remains the same, i.e., quantitative instead of qualitative.

Skill proficiency is evaluated with the same tool for all teaching personnel. Our project utilizes the Trainer Proficiency Checklists (for example see Table 10), developed by R. Don Horner (Department of Special Education, University of Kansas, and the Personnel Training Program, Kansas Neurological Institute) for evaluation of practicum performance. The checklists provide an objective evaluation of the trainer's ability to: 1) establish the child's baseline performance; 2) engage in appropriate teaching procedures for acquisition of a new behavior by the child; and 3) engage in appropriate procedures for maintaining learned behavior by the child. Reliability for skill proficiency is established in two ways: 1) by independent evaluations by separate instructors for the same competency using the checklists, and 2) by evaluation of the trainer's performance on teaching a second new behavior to the child.

Table 10 illustrates the evaluation procedure of the trainer teaching the acquisition of a new skill. The instructions for the use of the Acquisition Trainer Proficiency Checklist are described below.

The first seven items are information items. They are as follows:

1. The name of the student teacher conducting the acquisition session is entered in the space after "Teacher."

2. The name of the practicum site supervisor is entered after "Observer." If a second observer is also present for reliability checks, one observer places "primary" after his name. The observations made by the primary observer are used for determining the teacher proficiency score.

3. The month, day and year are entered after "Date."

4. The name of the handicapped student receiving acquisition training is entered after "Student."

5. The name of the program being used for acquisition training (e.g., use of spoon, self-dressing, grasping, etc.) is entered after "Program."

6. The number of the acquisition session is entered after "Session No." For example, a student who has had nine prior acquisition sessions (exclusive of baseline sessions) would be on session ten. If the student teacher has no record of prior acquisition sessions, a question mark (?) is placed in the space (unless it is the first acquisition session). The student teacher is asked for the training record to determine the session number. The student teacher is not asked the session number as this might encourage a false report to cover the absence of a training record.

7. If the observer witnessed the procedure (conducted before the first acquisition session) to identify reinforcer(s) for the student to be trained, the reinforcer(s) determined to be most effective is entered after "Reinforcer(s)." If the observer did not witness the procedure or none was conducted, a question mark (?) is placed in the space.

The next three items are behaviors that are to be performed by the student teacher before he conducts the acquisition session. They are scored as follows:

8. If the student teacher *has* the program or program steps in the immediate training area before starting the acquisition session, the observer circles YES after "has list of program steps." If the student teacher does not have the program or program steps in the immediate training area, the observer circles NO and instructs the student teacher to obtain the program or program steps. If it is unavailable or none exists, the observation is terminated and the session is scored "unacceptable."

9. If the student teacher *has* the required materials (e.g., data

Table 10.   Teacher proficiency checklist — Acquisition

1. Teacher _____   2. Observer _____
3. Date_____   4. Student _____
5. Program _____   6. Session No. _____
7. Reinforcer(s)_____

BEFORE CONDUCTING EACH ACQUISITION SESSION THE TEACHER:

8. has list of program steps	YES	NO	9. has prepared training area	YES	NO
10. has reinforcers	YES	NO	11. records time acquisition session is started	YES	NO

DURING EACH ACQUISITION SESSION THE TEACHER:

12. begins acquisition session as specified in program   YES   NO

13. presents programmed discrimina-
    tive stimulus for each response as   YES
    specified in program   NO

1	2	3	4	5	6	7	8	9	10	11	12	13	14	15

14. presents reinforcer for each
    response that conforms to   YES
    behavioral definition   NO

1	2	3	4	5	6	7	8	9	10	11	12	13	14	15

15. withholds presentation of rein-
    forcer for each response not   YES
    conforming to behavioral definition   NO

1	2	3	4	5	6	7	8	9	10	11	12	13	14	15

16. interrupts each response
    incompatible with conformance   YES
    to behavioral definition   NO

1	2	3	4	5	6	7	8	9	10	11	12	13	14	15

17. records results of each trial

    YES
    NO

1	2	3	4	5	6	7	8	9	10	11	12	13	14	15

18. proceeds to next step
    as specified in program   YES
    NO

1	2	3	4	5	6	7	8	9	10	11	12	13	14	15

19. records time acquisition
    session is ended   YES   NO

AFTER EACH ACQUISITION SESSION THE TEACHER:

20. computes data point   YES   NO

21. plots data point on chart   YES   NO

Total YES _____
—————————— × 100 = _____%
Total YES & NO

90-100% = Excellent
80-89% = Good
70-79% = Fair
60-69% = Poor
59-below = Unacceptable

sheet, counters, etc.) and equipment (e.g., toothbrush, spoon, etc.) before starting the acquisition session, the observer circles YES after "Has prepared training area." If the student teacher does not have the required materials and equipment, the observer circles NO and instructs the student teacher to obtain the required materials and equipment. If they are not available, the observation is terminated and the session is scored "unacceptable."

10. If the student teacher *has* "tangible" reinforcer(s) (e.g., candy, cookies, juice, etc.) physically present in the immediate training area, the observer circles YES after "has reinforcers." If the student teacher does *not* have any tangible reinforcers physically present in the immediate training area, the observer asks, "What reinforcers do you plan to use?" If the answer is a "tangible" reinforcer, the observer circles NO and instructs the student teacher to obtain the tangible reinforcers. If they are not available, the observation is terminated and the session is scored "unacceptable." If the answer is an "intangible" reinforcer (e.g., hugs, praise, etc.), the observer circles YES and instructs the student teacher to proceed with the session.

The next eight items are measures of behaviors that are to be performed by the student teacher during the acquisition session. They are scored as follows:

11. The acquisition session is officially started when the student teacher enters the time of day on the data sheet. If the student teacher enters the time before beginning the acquisition session, as specified in the program, the observer circles YES after "records time session is started." If the student teacher starts the acquisition session without entering the time on the data sheet, the observer circles NO. If the student teacher has no data sheet, the observer circles NO and instructs the student teacher to obtain the data sheet. If no data sheet exists, or it is not available, the observation is terminated and the session is scored "unacceptable."

12. The observer must determine from the acquisition record the point in the program at which the student teacher should start the acquisition session (e.g., beginning, step one, step two, etc.). If the student teacher starts at that point, the observer circles YES after"begins session as specified in program." If the student teacher starts at a different point, the observer circles NO. The observer must carefully note the criterion for moving

the student ahead in the program. An example of a criterion is three sessions with 90% correct responses or better on a specific program step; if this has been met on the acquisition record, the correct beginning step for the session would be the next step in the program.

13. The programmed discriminative stimuli are the instructions (as specified in the program) presented by the student teacher to set the occasion for a response by the student. This could be a verbal discriminative stimulus, such as "John, say 'cup'"; a visual discriminative stimulus, such as the student teacher pointing to an object; a tactile discriminative stimulus, such as guiding a student's hand; or any combination or variation of instructional stimuli. Before using the checklists, the observer must determine the instructional discriminative stimuli to be presented by the student teacher during acquisition for each step in the program. The first 15 minutes of instruction are divided into one-minute intervals. The observer places a tally mark after YES in the appropriate interval (e.g., interval five during the fifth minute of instruction) each time the discriminative stimulus *is* presented by the student teacher exactly as specified in the program. The observer places a tally mark after NO in the appropriate interval each time the discriminative stimulus *is not* presented by the student teacher exactly as specified in the program.

14. The reinforcer(s), as determined and entered in item seven and/or determined to be present through item ten, must be given by the student teacher within three seconds of the termination of a response by the handicapped student that conforms to the behavioral definition of the response specified in the program. Before using the checklist, the observer must have determined the behavorial definitions specified for each step in the program. The observer places a tally mark after YES in the appropriate interval each time a response conforming to the behavioral definition occurs and *is* followed within three seconds by the predetermined reinforcer. The observer places a tally mark after NO each time such a response occurs and *is not* followed within three seconds by the predetermined reinforcer.

15. If the observer determines that a response by the handicapped student does not conform to the behavioral definition, item 15 is scored instead of item 14. The observer places a tally mark after YES in the appropriate interval if the response does not

conform to the behavioral definition and the student teacher *withholds* the reinforcer, or a tally mark after NO if the student teacher *presents* the reinforcer.

16. If the observer determines that a response by the handicapped student not only does not conform to the behavioral definition but also is incompatible with the response required by the behavioral definition, then item 16 is also scored. The observer places a tally mark after YES in the appropriate interval each time the student gives a response that is incompatible with the response required by the behavioral definition and *is* interrupted or stopped by the student teacher before it can be completed. The observer places a tally mark after NO in the appropriate interval if such a response occurs and is *not* interrupted by the student teacher before it can be completed. Examples of incompatible responses might be attempts to leave the training area, to throw equipment or materials, to crawl under a table, to resist physical assistance, etc.

17. Before using the checklist, the observer must determine from the program what constitutes a trial (e.g., each presentation of a discriminative stimulus, or each time a response occurs, or each time an opportunity is provided by events occurring in the individual's environment, or each time a specified time interval expires, etc.). The observer places a tally mark after YES in the appropriate interval each time the trial occurs and the student teacher marks the results of that trial on the data sheet. The observer places a tally mark after NO each time a trial occurs and the student teacher does not mark the results of that trial on the data sheet.

18. Before using the checklist, the observer must determine what steps are in the program. The steps might be each behavior in a sequence of behaviors to be completed by the handicapped student. If the program specifies that the student is to be trained on all the steps in the program at each acquisition session, the observer places a tally mark after YES in the appropriate interval each time the student teacher advances the handicapped student to the next step in the program sequence. The observer places a tally mark after NO in the appropriate interval each time the student teacher advances the student to a step that is *not* the next step in the program sequence. If the program specifies the handicapped student is to be trained on one step at a time, this item would be scored only if the student

reached criterion on a step during the observed session and should be advanced to the next step. The observer places a tally mark after YES in the appropriate interval if the handicapped student reaches criterion on a step within the observed session and *is* advanced to the next step by the student teacher. The observer places a tally mark after NO in the appropriate interval if the handicapped student reaches criterion on a step within the observed session and is *not* advanced to the next step in the program by the student teacher. When only one step is taught at a time, the decision to move to the next step in most programs is based on criterion performance over one or more entire sessions. In this event, the decision to move to a new step would only occur before the start of a session and would be scored in item 12, "begins session as specified in program."

The last three items are behaviors that are to be performed by the student teacher to end the acquisition session. They are scored as follows:

19. Training during each acquisition session is officially ended when the student teacher enters on the data sheet the time of day the training ends. If the student teacher enters the time on the data sheet, the observer circles YES after "records time session is ended." If the student teacher does not enter the time on the data sheet, the observer circles NO.

20. The student teacher should summarize the data into either total frequency, average frequency, rate, total duration, average duration, percent correct, percent of total possible, or other score(s) for the session as specified in the program. If the student teacher computes the data point(s), the observer circles YES after "computes data point." If the student teacher does *not* compute the data point(s), the observer circles NO.

21. The student teacher should plot the summary score(s) on the chart at the point where vertical line up from the number of the session just conducted intersects with a horizontal line across from the number(s) that represents the score(s) for the session. If the student teacher plots the data point(s), the observer circles YES after "plots data point on chart." If the student teacher does not plot the data point(s), the observer circles NO.

In scoring, one point for each YES circled and one point for each mark tallied after a YES is summed and entered as total A. One point for each NO circled and one point for each mark tallied after a NO is summed and entered as total B. The total of A (YES scores) and B (NO scores) is summed and entered as total C. The total of A (YES scores) is divided by the total of C (YES and NO scores) to obtain the percentage of YES scores. The category (excellent, good, etc.) that contains the percentage of YES obtained by the student teacher is circled by the observer. Ideally, total C should be around 100 (Guilford, 1965) in order for the computation of percentage of YES to be a sensitive measure of student teacher performance. A percentage should not be computed if the divisor (total C) is less than 20. In this event, the data from such a session should be combined with the data from subsequent sessions until total C is greater than 20.

$$\frac{B_y + B_{sn}}{A + D_1 + D_2} \times 100$$

Reliability between observers should be determined by dividing the sum of the number of times both observers circled YES, or both observers circled NO, and the number of times both observers entered the same number of YES or NO in an interval (agreements), by the number of agreements plus the sum of the number of times one observer circled a YES and the other circled a NO and the number of intervals in which one observer entered a different number of YES or NO than the other observer (disagreements), and multiplying by 100. Any interval in which neither observer enters a YES or NO tally should not be counted as either an agreement or disagreement, in order to avoid inflating the reliability quotient (Kazdin, 1975).

SUMMARY

The training of "teaching associates" or other paraprofessional personnel must be specific and precise if the goal of such training is to reduce the level of disability of those identified as developmentally disabled. The role a teaching associate should play in the classroom has been the subject of considerable debate. There are many who believe that teaching should be the sole responsibility of the professional teacher. The absolute necessity of individualized instruction for the more severely developmentally disabled render such beliefs impractical. The successes of well-trained teaching associates in teaching the developmentally disabled show such beliefs are unfounded.

The training model for teaching associates should be based on strong practicum experience, should be supported by certification requirements emphasizing the attainment of specific comptencies, and should provide the opportunity for career advancement. The mode should stress the cooperative interaction of teacher and teaching associate and should be based as close as possible to the community in which the prospective teaching associate resides.

The possible models include an inservice training program through the local educational agency, preservice training at the junior college level or a two-year program at a four-year college or university, and a four-year degree program facilitating across-ranks career advancement, through graduate training, up to the level of full teacher.

The model should be competency-based, with specific informational and performance competencies organized into a sequence of training modules with a system for delivering instruction, evaluating performance, and reporting the level of competency acquired by each teaching associate. The practicum experiences should be sequenced so that each teaching associate acquires, and is asked to perform with an increasing degree of sophistication, those competencies required for effective performance as a teaching associate. The program should culminate by teaching associates demonstrating criterion performance in a situation as similar as possible to the one they will assume upon completion of the program.

ACKNOWLEDGMENT

The authors express their appreciation to Ruth Staten for typing the manuscript.

REFERENCES

Blessing, K. R. 1967. Use of teacher aides in special education: A review and possible implications. Except. Child. 34:107–113.

Carpenter, J. C. 1976. An experimental analysis of descriptive feedback and corrective practice as a paraprofessional training technique. Unpublished doctoral dissertation, University of Kansas.

Clark, H. B., and Macrae, J. W. 1976. The use of imposed and self-selected training packages to establish classroom teaching skills. J. Appl. Behav. Anal. 9:105.

Cruickshank, W. M., and Haring, N. C. 1957. A Demonstration: Assistants for Teachers of Exceptional Children. Syracuse University Press, Syracuse, N.Y.

Esbensen, T. 1966. Should teacher aides be more than clerks? Phi Delta Kappan 47:237.

Fawcett, S. B., Mathews, R. M., Fletcher, R. K., Morrow, R., and Stokes, T. F. 1975. A community-based personalized instructional system: Teaching helping skills to low-income paraprofessionals. Unpublished manuscript. University of Kansas.

Fredericks, H. D., Baldwin, V. L., Grove, D. N., Riggs, C., Furey, F., Moore, W., Jordan, E., Gage, M., Levak, L., Alrik, G., and Wadlow, M. 1975. A Data Based Classroom for the Moderately and Severely Handicapped. Instructional Development Corporation, Monmouth, Oregon.

Gardner, J. M. 1972. Teaching behavior modification to non-professionals. J. Appl. Behav. Anal. 5:517–521.

Guilford, J. P. 1965. Fundamental Statistics in Psychology and Education. McGraw-Hill, New York.

Horner, R. D. 1975. Teacher proficiency checklist. Personnel Preparation Program, Department of Special Education, University of Kansas. (Unpublished.)

Horner, R. D. 1976. Competency based approach to preparing teachers of severely and profoundly handicapped: perspective II. In: E. Sontag, J. Smith, and N. Certo (eds.), Educational Programming for Severely/ Profoundly Handicapped, pp. 195-209. Division on Mental Retardation, The Council for Exceptional Children, Reston, Virginia.

Horner, R. D., Holvoet, J., and Rinne, T. 1976. Competency specifications for teachers of the severely and profoundly handicapped. Personnel Preparation Program, Department of Special Education, University of Kansas. (Unpublished.)

Horner, R. D., and Keilitz, I. 1975. Training mentally retarded adolescents to brush their teeth. J. Appl. Behav. Anal. 8:301–309.

Hursh, D. E., Schumaker, J. B., Fawcett, S. B., and Sherman, J. A. 1973. Training behavior modifiers: A comparison of written and direction instructional methods. Department of Human Development, University of Kansas, (Unpublished.)

Kazdin, A. E. 1975. Behavior Modification in Applied Settings. The Dorsey Press, Homewood, Illinois.

K.S.A. 72-962, Special Education for Exceptional Children Act. Topeka, Kansas, 1974.

O'Brien, F., and Azrin, N. H. 1972. Developing proper mealtime behaviors of the institutionalized retarded. J. Appl. Behav. Anal. 5:389-399.

Panyan, M., Boozer, H., and Morris, N. 1970. Feedback to attendants as a reinforcer for applying operant techniques. J. Appl. Behav. Anal. 3:1-4.

Panyan, M., and Patterson, E. F. 1974. Teaching attendants the applied aspects of behavior modification. Ment. Retard. 12: 30-32.

Reid, B. A., and Reid, W. R. 1974. Role expectations of paraprofessional staff in special education. Focus Except. Child. 6:1-14.

Risley, T. R. 1975. Certify procedures not people. In: W. S. Wood (ed.), Issues in Evaluating Behavior Modification. Research Press, Champaign, Illinois.

Sailor, W., Guess, D., and Lavis, L. W. 1975. Preparing teachers for education of the severely handicapped. Educ. Ment. Retard. 10:201-203.

Sontag, E., Burke, P., and York, R. 1973. Considerations for serving the severely handicapped in the public schools. Educ. Train. Ment. Retard. 8:20-26.

Striefel, S. 1974. Managing Behavior—7: Teaching a Child to Imitate. H & H Enterprises, Inc., Lawrence, Kansas.

Thorsell, M. 1971. Kansas State Plan. Kansas State Department of Education, Special Education Section, Topeka, Kansas.

Tucker, D. J., and Horner, R. D. 1976. Competency based training of paraprofessional "teaching associates" for education of the severely and profoundly handicapped. In: E. Sontag, J. Smith, and N. Certo (eds.), Educational Programming for Severely/Profoundly Handicapped, pp. 71-83. Division on Mental Retardation, The Council for Exceptional Children, Reston, Virginia.

Tucker, D., Hollis, J., Sailor, W., Horner, D., Kelly, P., and Guess, D. 1976. Preparing "paraprofessional" personnel for education of the severely handicapped: The teaching associate. Educ. Train. Ment. Retard. (October):274-280.

Woolman, M. A. 1954. A Method of Training Aide Selection. Training Analysis and Development Division, 3520th Combat Crew Training Group (MBOM) McConnell Air Force Base, Wichita, Kansas.

THE STUDENT SERVICE INDEX
A Method for Managing Service Delivery in Residential Settings

Shawn M. Boles & Gary H. Bible

One measure of the health of a culture is the type of living environment provided for its most deviant members. The definition of who
is deviant is culture-specific, but it is usually specifiable in terms of
the frequency and intensity of certain operant classes exhibited by
an individual as compared to the values of these same classes for the
culture of which the individual is a member (Boles, 1969). The solution of what to do about deviant members that has been implemented
by Western culture within the last 100 years has been an increasing
use of institutions to provide restricted living environments for them.
Depending upon the operant categories used for defining deviancy,
those institutionalized may be labeled retarded, psychotic, aged and
infirm, delinquent, or disturbed, etc. For retarded citizens alone, the
number of public residential institutions in the United States has almost doubled—from 96 in 1950 to 190 in 1971, while the cost of
maintaining these institutions has become more than ten times greater
—increasing from 92 million dollars in 1950 to over one billion dollars in 1971 (Statistical Abstract of the United States, 1976).

Institutions for these groups were developed with the overt rationale that they would comprise an environment that would pro-

vide training and life-support services for the populations they were to serve. Although this is a laudable goal, the fact is that institutions have for the most part provided training only in the acquisition and maintenance of deviant response classes, and life support that is of subhuman quality and which fosters the resident's dependence upon the institution. The person who spends even a limited amount of time in residential institutions occupied by abandoned children, the old, the psychotic, prisoners, or retarded citizens cannot fail to be impressed by the consistently inhumane treatment these groups receive under the guise of service. This inhumanity of treatment has resulted, in recent years, in an increasing emphasis being placed upon the development of alternative living and treatment arrangements for institutionalized citizens. This emphasis is resulting, and hopefully will continue to result, in the gradual replacement of institutional environments with environments that are closer approximations to the less restrictive ones enjoyed by a majority of the society. However rapid such a replacement process might be, it is highly unlikely that it will occur at a rate that would eliminate traditional institutional facilities anytime soon (e.g., within the next ten years). *What then are we to do about the institutional living and treatment environments that we have already created?* This chapter addresses this question from the perspective of a front line manager[1] working within the conditions encountered in an institutional environment.

The chapter is divided into three sections, the first of which attempts to identify some of the conflicting forces that are present and must be resolved in an institutional setting. These forces are identified as a series of constraints to which the manager must respond in attempting to repair a particular residential setting. The second section briefly reviews some of the approaches used (primarily by those of a behavior-analytic persuasion) in providing institutional service programs. The third section provides a detailed analysis of a method (The Student Service Index) used, within the constraints described in the first section, to provide consistent, defined, quality service to a residential treatment unit serving 60 profoundly retarded citizens. This section covers an initial diagnosis of the unit, a general description of the Service Index method, and the results of using the method in the unit for a period of 78 weeks.

---

[1] A front line manager may be defined as an institutional staff member charged with supervisory responsibilities involving three shifts of personnel and associated staff who are serving a specified subgroup of the institutions' residents in a residential treatment facility for the developmentally disabled.

CONSTRAINTS OPERATING IN A RESIDENTIAL INSTITUTION

Environmental Repair

The first constraint on the manager of a residential institution is that he is *not* faced with a problem in environmental design. By definition, the environment is already present, and, at best, assuming that the manager can identify *all* of the contingencies operating within an open environmental system *and* that he can control them, he is dealing with a problem of environmental re-design. Because this assumption cannot now be made, perhaps a more modest conception of the manager's role should be considered—specifically, that the manager is engaged with others in the *repair* of the environment to meet the needs of those who must use it (Alexander, two unpublished papers—see references). Such a conceptualization has at least two advantages over the concept of environmental design: 1) it implies a gradual process of environmental change similar to that manifested by other organisms on this planet; and 2) it allows for a focusing of work activities on achieving many concurrent changes in the total environment rather than a few large changes in limited portions of the environment. The thrust of this argument is that institutional environmental change constrains the manager to use an evolutionary, rather than a revolutionary, process.

Subsystem Complexity

A second constraint to be taken into consideration is the complexity of the social subsystems of which the environment is composed. Most persons would agree with Atthowe (1974, p. 181) that "... human behavior does not occur in a vacuum; it occurs within the context of many on-going, intrapersonal, interpersonal, social and cultural systems of behavior." Recognition of this fact carries with it the necessity of recognizing that the manager is not able to specify all these subsystems. At best he (like everyone else) can obtain limited experiential and empirical information about some of the products and processes associated with the subsystems. When such information is required about the rate of attainment of a specified target goal by an individual client, the measurement process is relatively trivial; when information is required about the attainment, by many clients *and* by staff, of many goals, each of which affects the attainment of other goals, things become much more complex and less amenable to consistent measurement. This is particularly true when the managers must rely on pencil and paper information processing methods.

Subsystem Balance

The third constraint that must be considered has to do with the extent to which identified subsystems in the environment are balanced with respect to the time available for both staff and residents.

This constraint rests on the fact that the residential environment is not a holistic entity, but rather is composed of concurrently existing (and often conflicting) roles and environments, each of which must be maintained in balance with the others in order to provide an adequate service environment for both staff and students. Because residents receive behavorial programming for only a small portion of the time they spend in the institution, a question arises about what is happening to residents during the other 80% or 90% of the time when they are not involved in specific training programs. Attention to how the service environment is affecting the lives of residents during these other hours is of clear importance to program managers. At a minimum, a residential environment is a school, a hospital, a home, a work situation, a community, and a laboratory. A staff member, then, is expected to behave as teacher, nurse's aide, family member, work supervisor, friend, and researcher while the resident is expected to behave as student, patient, family member, employee, friend, and subject, depending upon the time of day and types of activities occurring in the environment.

Counter-Control

Next, we must consider the constraint of the absence counter-controls upon the individuals providing service. This issue was first raised by Skinner (1972) in a short article entitled "Compassion and Ethics in the Care of the Retarded." He pointed out that residents in orphanages, mental hospitals, nursing homes, and retardation institutions are identical with one another in their inability to control (directly or indirectly) those who provide service to them. According to Skinner, "We shall not bring about major changes in custodial management by appealing to compassion, sympathy, or ethical principles. [Rather], the contingencies affecting those who manage custodial institutions must be changed" (p. 291). This constraint has not been perceived by many persons concerned with service delivery, and has been dealt with effectively by even fewer. The problem is perhaps best summed up in the question "Quis Custodiet ipsos Custodes?" (Who will watch the guardians?). In other words, how is it possible to deliver effective service if service consumers have no choice of service or representation in the evaluation of service? This problem is particularly acute in servicing residents who are severely disturbed, non-verbal, and/or dependent upon staff for meeting a major portion of their daily needs.

The manager whose behavior is not directed to the provision of counter-controls on himself and other staff as a direct result of resident responses to the environment is likely to ensure the maintenance of a custodial environment that is aversive to all who live and work in it.

Bureaucratic Inertia

This constraint exists at all levels of bureaucratic systems and is manifested in problems like using merit system (civil service) procedures (which are oriented to Monday–Friday, 9:00–5:00 jobs) to hire persons into positions which, although having the same title, require different work behaviors on different work shifts. Other examples include: lack of direct control over budgeting; conflicting policies at federal, state, and institutional levels; organizational structures that separate the program strategy, management, and implementation process; delayed review processes for program approval; and resistance to change on the part of work groups required for support service, such as personnel, business offices, housekeeping, security, etc.

Capricious External Pressures
on the Service Delivery Environment

Other decisions of other portions of the social and political system can and do influence the service delivery groups in an unpredictable and catastrophic fashion. Typical examples would include: arbitrary "freezes" on hiring and promotion; unannounced budget reductions for ongoing programs; political pressure for admission of residents to inappropriate program environments; and uncoordinated legal pressure for the protection of ill-defined rights of selected citizens.

Staff Characteristics

There is little need to belabor the fact that service delivery personnel are usually underpaid and undertrained, and, in many instances, have a poor reinforcement history for work behavior. This is true at both the professional and the paraprofessional (direct care) staff level, and presents a major constraint for program managers who are responsible for the service environment, since effective service depends almost entirely on the behavior of those who work directly with residents.

REVIEW OF PRIOR ATTEMPTS TO
ENSURE ADEQUATE SERVICE DELIVERY

Having identified some of the constraints prevalent in the service environment, we now should review previous attempts to accommodate or deal with these constraints. It will be noted that previous efforts have frequently been conducted on a demonstration project basis, implemented by consultants, and focused on limited target behaviors, and often show little emphasis on maintenance or follow-up over time.

It has become evident that the most significant relationship that residents in institutional settings experience, both in terms of amount of contact and modeling effectiveness, is with the direct care or attendant-level staff (Gardner and Giampa, 1971; Portnoy, 1973). Thus, it has been the performance of the direct care staff that is frequently examined in evaluations of the service delivery process. Most studies have emerged from settings employing a behavioral or applied behavior analysis perspective on treatment procedures and research design (Baer, Wolf, and Risley, 1968). Most attempts at improving staff performance have generally adopted one of two strategies: 1) manipulating the consequences of staff behavior through the use of reinforcement or feedback procedures, or 2) manipulating antecedent conditions or discriminative stimuli.

Investigations that focused upon consequating staff behavior with monetary reinforcers, for example, have generally shown improvements in job performance. One researcher found that high levels of job completion were obtained when staff in a residential child facility were given tokens worth $1.00 contingent upon completion of specific assignments (Pommer and Streedbeck, 1974). In another study (Pomerleau, Bobrove, and Smith, 1973) psychiatric aides were given cash awards ranging from $20.00 to $30.00, based on the improvements of assigned patients. Appropriate behavior of patients increased when the cash incentives were present, but deteriorated when the program was terminated. Other investigators, working in settings for the severely retarded, have recognized that the performance of staff may require special reinforcers. Martin (1972) employed a group contingency to increase the number of training sessions completed. On days that 100% of the potential number of sessions were completed, five dollars were placed in a staff party fund; on days that greater than 75% of the training sessions were completed, two dollars were placed in the funds. This procedure proved effective in doubling the number of sessions run over a period of four months. The procedure was discontinued, and completion of sessions decreased "when the author ran out of money" (Martin, 1972, p. 75). As might be expected, providing monetary incentives to staff resulted in significant improvements in staff performances. Unfortunately, these techniques possess many impractical drawbacks common to institutional settings which preclude their implementation or make it difficult (Reppucci and Saunders, 1974). The use of trading stamps as reinforcers for staff has also been employed with positive results (Hollander, Plutchik, and Horner, 1973). However, using trading stamps to motivate staff can also prove to be a burdensome expense. Hollander and Plutchik (1972) employed trading stamps as reinforcers for psychiatric attendants and found significant increases in completion of assigned and "volunteer" tasks, but at a cost of $300 over a period of six weeks. In another study, the combined use of trading stamps and television feedback led to improvements in the rate and quality of staff/resident interactions (Bricker, Morgan, and Grabowski, 1972). The availability of videotaping equipment, however, would seem to make the procedures outlined in this study impractical in most residential settings.

Favorable results have also been reported with the use of posted feedback of staff performance as a reinforcer to maintain training programs. In one research study (Panyon, Boozer, and Morris, 1970) weekly feedback sheets were posted listing the total possible number of sessions for each self-help skill being trained, the number of sessions recorded and conducted, the names of the accountable staff members, and the percentage of sessions conducted. By conspicuously displaying the percentage of sessions completed data, the authors were able to produce significant improvements in the number of self-help training sessions completed by direct care staff. By using similar procedures and introducing competition between work shifts, other investigators were similarly able to increase daily performance in completing behavior modification projects (Welsh et al., 1973). The effects of posted feedback were further replicated by Quilitch (1975), who provided performance feedback to staff by publicly posting the average number of active residents in daily recreational programs. When staff were given performance feedback, the average daily number of residents engaged in activities on four wards for the retarded rose from 7 to 32.

One problem facing program administrators using such feedback procedures is that increases in desirable staff behaviors may not necessarily be related to increases in desirable resident behaviors. It is entirely conceivable, for example, that producing increases in the

number of training sessions conducted by staff may have no significant effect on the performance of the clients involved in the sessions.
This difficulty could be resolved by taking concurrent measures of
resident performance or by adopting the strategy of providing staff
with feedback on the behavioral improvement of residents (Pommer-
leau et al., 1973; Bushell, Jackson, and Weis, 1975; Jackson and
Bushell, 1975). Inclusion of resident performance feedback may not,
of course, be beneficial if residents show no change or if their rate of
progress is typically slow (Ellsworth, 1973; Loeber and Weisman,
1975). Moreover, as Martin (1972) has noted, improvement in client
behaviors may not even function as a reinforcer for some staff
members.

Other investigators, exploring the effectiveness of manipulating
antecedent conditions, have stressed the importance of providing
staff with explicit directions and discriminative stimuli for conducting their assignments. In one study, manipulation of the instructional
antecedents to staff, in the form of publicly posting itemized duties,
was shown to improve work behavior of staff and appeared to be a
necessary component in maintaining a high level of staff performance (Pommer and Streedbeck, 1974). Another investigator eliminated the pulling and tugging of retarded residents from one location to another by simply placing a poster on the wards which served
a cueing function in reminding nursing staff to employ reinforcement
techniques (Fielding, Erickson, and Bettin, 1971). Although the
provision of clear and objective discriminative stimuli is a requisite
condition for appropriate staff responding, the necessity of consequating staff behavior appears equally important. Investigations
that have allowed for an examination of the roles of instructional
antecedents have shown that unconsequated assignment sheets,
public notices, posted activity schedules, and the like have gained
additional effectiveness in motivating staff responding when carefully
consequated in some fashion. Distributing memos instructing staff to
conduct daily recreational activities, for example, was found to be
ineffective in increasing the number of retarded clients involved in
activities (Quilitch, 1975). Only when staff were scheduled to lead
activities and given performance feedback were increases observed.
Overall, it appears that incorporating a combination of both clear
instructional antecedents and systematic consequation of staff behaviors will lead to the greatest increments in staff performance. An
excellent example of consequating staff responding, in a manner that
would be expected to exert a powerful effect upon performance, is

described in a recent report by Pierce and Risley (1974). When specific job descriptions and threats to terminate the employment of Youth Corps workers in an urban recreation program proved unsuccessful, the authors attempted to make hourly wage payments contingent upon job performance. When a performance-based procedure was implemented whereby pay was proportional to the number of tasks completed, rather than number of hours present, job performance was maintained at nearly perfect levels.

Benefiting from both administrative autonomy, as well as working outside of a residential setting, one program administrator in particular (Turner, 1975) has made impressive advances toward ensuring service delivery and accountability. At the Huntsville, Alabama Community Mental Health Center (Bolin and Kivens, 1972) every service program (e.g., intake, day treatment, after-care, etc.), client, and staff member is involved in an evaluation cycle consisting of three components: 1) goal-setting, 2) data collection, and 3) evaluation. This in turn is formalized by a performance contract between each employee and his supervisor or between each client and therapist. Pay increases, promotions, demotions, or termination of staff occur solely on the basis of measurable performance. Staff performance is frequently monitored by direct observation, audio and video tapes of therapy sessions, and through the use of a "therapy evaluation data sheet," which measures the degree to which a staff member completes certain required steps involved in the course of therapy for each client. The process of frequent performance reviews may also at times lead to renegotiation of contracts, with the inclusion of new tasks or deletion of original tasks. Taken as a whole, the service delivery process at the Huntsville Clinic has provided a level of accountability that is indeed rare among human service programs.

The development of effective staff management procedures, as with any emerging area of study, is attenuated by certain conceptual and procedural difficulties. One of the most noticeable limitations of the work published thus far concerns the limited nature of the target behaviors selected for study. Measures of staff performance, for example, have typically been restricted to a single aspect of the total treatment milieu (e.g., completion of self-help training sessions or daily recreation programs) selected as a matter of convenience to the researcher and without regard to the multiple nature of the service environment. As a result, such "simplistic criteria for change" (see Willems, 1974) provide little information relating to, say, the medical, home, or community aspects of the environment. Training residents, it will be recalled, represents only one of the roles of the residential facility and its staff. It should also be noted, moreover, that most attempts to alter staff performance have been short-term endeavors with limited emphasis on maintenance or follow-up. Characteristically, measures are taken five days per week, during daytime programming hours, and for a duration of only a few months, which illustrates the discrepancy, pointed out by Reppucci and Saunders (1974), between what is "real" and what is "imagined" with respect to program implementation and maintenance in natural settings. Thompson (1975) has also provided an excellent discussion of the difficulties in maintaining "established" programs in institutional settings for the retarded. Beyond the fact that staff performance has been shown to increase along some restricted dimension, little else is known about the reactions or attitudes of staff, or about other non-technical matters, including, for example, human relations considerations (Neufeldt, 1974). In this connection, one important issue concerns the use of measures of staff behavior or monitoring procedures that are intended to be covert. Because covert measures are likely to build antagonism, it may be advisable to employ more straightforward or overt procedures. Experience suggests that, to be sure, staff do know that they are being observed. The use of covert measures seems to be a natural, yet lamentable, carry-over from laboratory settings. Overall, in most studies less attention is paid to the observation and monitoring procedures than to the intended intervention procedures, such as feedback, reinforcement, and the like. Perhaps it is merely "knowledge of being observed" or some other ignored factors of the natural setting that are responsible for the observed changes. It is also interesting to note that there are no published accounts in which the behavior of supervisory staff or others besides direct care staff was the subject under investigation. Failure to appreciate the aforementioned considerations could lead to serious difficulties for researchers and program administrators.

A final concern relates to the contribution of staff training efforts in a service implementation and maintenance process. The effects of staff training are generally shown to be only tenuously related to actual performance in a work setting (Klaber, 1970; Loeber and Weisman, 1975; Quilitch, 1975). Mager and Pipe (1970), for example, have delineated several factors, quite aside from training, that may be responsible for human performance problems. The distinction between knowledge deficiencies and environmental inadequacies (Bensberg, 1974) is important in understanding the role of staff training attempts. It is one thing to demonstrate staff training programs, but it is quite another to adopt both training and effective monitoring procedures to be maintained over extended periods of time. Increased knowledge concerning the integration of both factors may hasten the development of a more effective and efficient system of residential treatment. The next section of this chapter provides a framework for operating within the constraints previously delineated and which overcomes some of the aforementioned difficulties associated with past efforts to ensure adequate service delivery.

A METHOD FOR MANAGING SERVICE DELIVERY: A STUDENT SERVICE INDEX

Having both identified at least some of the constraints that form the operating boundaries for a front line manager and briefly reviewed limited attempts to provide service within them, let us now examine a somewhat more complex method employed to provide service in a residential unit for developmentally disabled citizens. While much of what follows is specifically related to a particular service environment, the reader should be able to identify some potential areas of application of the method in any residential human service environment.

Initial Unit Diagnosis

Unit B of the Georgia Retardation Center is a six-year-old intermediate care unit for sixty developmentally disabled ambulatory students, a majority of whom test within the "profound" range of retardation on standardized intelligence tests and have a limited repertoire of adaptive behaviors. There are 60 direct care positions associated with the unit, as well as twelve professional and seven support positions, a total of 79 in-unit staff. Architecturally, the building enforces a division of students into four separate 15-student sections (2 male, 2 female), each of which has eight bedrooms and a common bath/toilet area on the top floor, and an activity room/ dining area/office on the bottom floor (see Figure 1).

Each section is staffed by a day (7:00 a.m.–3:30 p.m.) and an evening (2:30–11:00 p.m.) shift staff, composed of six direct care positions. These positions are supervised by a Section Supervisor, who is charged with overall responsibility for the section environment. In

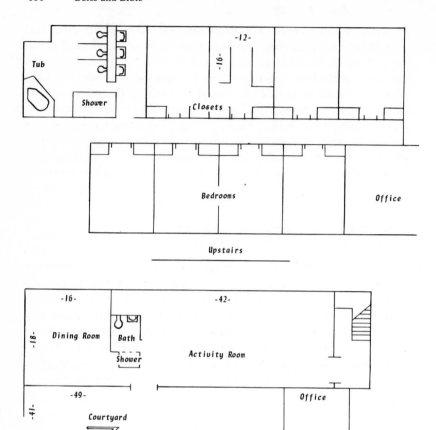

Figure 1.   Top and bottom floor plans of a section in Unit B.

addition, a night shift staff of ten direct care positions provides service between 10:45 p.m. and 7:15 a.m.

Initial observations of the environment were made in May, 1974, by Shawn M. Boles, who had assumed interim front line manager (Unit Director) responsibilities for the unit. These observations, as well as the results of individual structured interviews with each direct care staff member, revealed an environment in which direct care staff, as a consequence of lack of information, materials, and training, had developed an environment with distinct custodial characteristics. Interactions with students were highly variable in terms of consistency of form and frequency. Reinforcement was delivered noncontingently and/or in a fashion that resulted in the maintenance of maladaptive behavior in the repertoires of both staff and students. Staff members, while often acting effectively on an individual level to provide for the students, faced many difficulties in integrating their work with that performed by others who served the students in a direct (face-to-face) group or individual fashion. Student program records, where they were present, were essentially narrative in form, often identical across successive reporting periods, and provided essentially no information about student problems, specific intervention strategies, or results of service provision.[2]

Based upon these observations and interviews, a decision was made to attempt to devise a method whereby it would be possible to focus the work behavior of unit staff on the environment in which students spent most of their time—that being group contact with direct care staff. Such a method would provide one means of ensuring counter-controls for the students and would provide a means of public accountability for *all* staff with respect to the group environment for the students. It would also act as a supporting framework that would maximize the maintenance of student and staff behavior learned in individual direct contact situations. The method and the evaluation procedures associated with it that evolved as a result of this decision are what comprise the *Student Service Index*.

General Description

A service index may be conceived of as a modified changing criterion design for the repair and maintenance of the service environment to which the index is applied. There are three basic component processes related in a service index (see Figure 2).

The first process involves *establishing criteria* against which it is possible to observe the environment. Ideally, these criteria should be specified and reviewed by all providers, consumers (or their representatives), and observers of the service environment. Where this is not possible the manager may rely on representatives of these groups

---

[2] An attempted resolution of problems encountered by the lack of a meaningful records system was implemented for the total institution (including Unit B) during the time period covered in this paper. For a complete description of the revised records system and its impact on the institution, the interested reader is referred to "Development, implementation, and results of a new records system to meet ICF-MR 1977 regulations and JCAH standards" (Berkler et al., 1976), which may be obtained from Margo Berkler, Ph.D., formerly at the Georgia Retardation Center, currently at the Department of Special Education, University of Louisville, Louisville, Kentucky 40208.

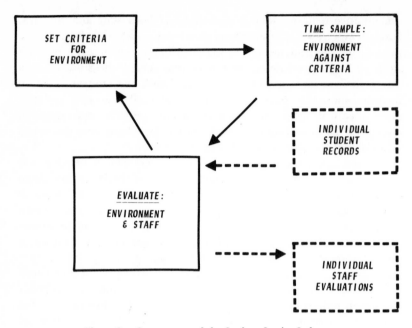

Figure 2.   Components of the Student Service Index.

as well as on federal standards for guidance in setting criteria.[3] In either case, criteria should refer to publicly observable states of the environment (products) or to social processes that are present in the environment.

The second component is the provision for *time sampling of the environment* by trained observers, the distribution and duration of time samples being specified by the times and places in which the criteria are in effect. In general, a relatively large number of randomly distributed observations of short duration have the effect of a conjunctive VR-VI reinforcement schedule (Ferster and Skinner, 1957) upon work behavior associated with meeting the criteria. Because the Student Service Index provides accountability, observations should be overt and immediately available to those using the environment.

---

[3] In many situations in which no consumer representation can be identified, the manager is forced to rely on federal or association standards for setting criteria. These standards, while giving some guidance to the manager, are often too procrustean to be applied without modification for a particular service population and environment. Even where appropriate criteria may be abstracted from the standards, the manager should still attempt to establish a more direct representation of consumer interests.

The third component of the Student Service Index is the provision for program and staff evaluation. Depending upon the criteria in effect and the measures obtained by time sampling the environment against them, it is possible to provide at least some information about how programs are being implemented and what adjustments may be required either in the physical environment, program content, or in staff behavior to achieve a continuing accomodation to changes in student behavior and the larger social system of which the indexed environment is but a small part.

The two boxes enclosed by dotted lines are included in Figure 2 as ancillary components of the Student Service Index. Information from individual student records is combined for groups of students to aid in determining the types of programs to be conducted in the environment. In addition, the results of the Student Service Index are used as one factor in conducting staff evaluations for in-unit staff in direct care, professional, and support positions.

IMPLEMENTATION OF THE STUDENT SERVICE INDEX

General Method

The Student Service Index was implemented for Unit B in June, 1974, and has provided information about the unit service environment since its inception. During the first 78 weeks of its use described in this chapter, there were four versions of the Index, reflecting the ever-increasing behavioral competency of staff and students who use the environment.

Before discussing the results of using the Student Service Index method it is necessary to provide some indication of its evolutionary nature by discussing briefly the changes that occurred in the major components (establishing criteria, observing the environment, and program/staff evaluation) across the time period for which results are reported.

Establishing Criteria Criteria for the initial Service Index were set by the Unit Director and unit education staff (Section Supervisors) using information gathered during the initial unit diagnosis. The criteria were reviewed for acceptability with the direct care staff before they were put into effect, with the latter group also determining the times and places where the criteria would be used. Although there was no viable consumer representation during the setting of the initial Student Service Index criteria, a parent group was established by week 15, and the criteria were reviewed by the group at its second monthly meeting. All subsequent revisions were made by a group composed of direct care staff representing each section/shift, all professional staff, administrative staff, and representatives of the unit parents group. (This last group of representatives were much too threatened by their natural perception of being in a situation in which, if they demanded change, they would jeopardize their child's chance to actively participate in the criteria setting process. This difficulty was overcome to a certain extent by ensuring close contact with the unit social workers, who often acted to represent parent concerns at the revision meetings.) The agenda for these meetings always included a review of the criteria, suggested additions and/or deletions, changes in times and/or places for using the Service Index, and a review of the observers and observation procedures employed to time sample the environment. Finally, no Service Index revision was used until it had been reviewed and approved by all unit staff at their regularly scheduled section/shift meetings. (The criteria for the initial Service Index are shown in Figures 4 and 5, while those associated with the third revision are shown in Figures 6 and 7. The corresponding forms for revisions 1 and 2 are found in Appendixes A-D.)

Observing the Environment   All observations throughout the four Service Index periods reported were ten minutes in length and were scheduled in a "quasi-random" fashion for the times and places to which a particular version of the Service Index applied. The term "quasi-random" for the setting described is defined as observation times that were arbitrarily chosen by the observers, subject to the following restrictions:

1. That observations occur for each section/shift at least three times each week.
2. That observations be made at all times and places where the Service Index was in effect (including weekends, evenings, and holidays) each week.
3. That at least 10% of the total observations made each week be redundant, i.e., that they sample a particular section/shift more than once during a single day.

During the initial Service Index period all observations were made by the Unit Director, the Academic Supervisor, or the Research Assistant employed by the unit. Interobserver agreement was obtained for this and all subsequent versions of the Service Index by pairing observers and requiring perfect agreement on all items for three consecutive observations. No version of the Service Index was employed until observers had met this criterion for that version. Concurrent with the first revision of the Service Index, the observer pool was expanded to include education staff who were Section Supervisors, with the proviso that no supervisor made observations on the section for which he or she was directly responsible. In conjunction with the second revision, the pool was again expanded to include all professional staff. At this time an attempt was also made to include section/shift direct care staff as observers. This was not feasible for all direct care staff because many of them did not possess the minimal compositional and computational skills required by the observation form. An approximation of this inclusion was accomplished by having each direct care staff member pair with a certified observer for at least one observation (on a section/shift other than the one on which he or she normally worked) during the time a particular version of the Service Index was being used. This enabled staff to confirm that the same procedures were used in observing all section/shifts, a matter of no little concern to most of them.

A typical observation commenced when the observer entered the area in which the observation was to take place. The observer first scanned the environment to rate those Service Index items associated with products produced by staff activities before the observation (e.g., all students engaged in program activities, clean program environment, etc.). The observer next recorded all staff/student interactions encountered in ten minutes as either appropriate or inappropriate according to the criterion applicable to the interaction pattern being used by the staff, annotating any inappropriate staff responses and/or extenuating circumstances. At the conclusion of this time period, the observer checked the status of all other items (e.g., forms filled out) and filled out the observation form by placing a " + " or "-" by each item, dividing the number of " + " items by the number of scored items, and multiplying the result by 100 to give a percentage score for the observation. This scoring method has the disadvantage of giving each item equal weight. This can be overcome by a convention that requires that certain items (e.g., all students engaged in program activities) be scored " + " if any score other than zero is to be assigned to the observation. The disadvantage of equal weighting is more than compensated for by providing a scoring system with which most of the staff are familar and which is readily interpreted in light of their own experiences with similar scoring systems used in traditional public school classrooms.

Following an observation, a copy of the observation form was immediately posted for staff to examine. The observation scores for each section/shift were averaged each week and posted publicly for each section/shift and for the unit as a whole in both the section office and the unit staff lounge area.

One final point should be made with respect to the observation procedures employed: The presence of observers may well have acted as a discriminative stimulus for appropriate work behavior, while in their absence environmental deterioration occurred. In the unit this difficulty was partially resolved by the use of redundant observations and by using criteria items that not only reflected the ongoing activities of staff-process items (e.g., the interaction pattern) but also assessed aspects of the environment that were the result of staff activities prior to the observation period–product items (e.g., materials available, students in activities, clean environment, etc.). In addition, the normal flow of all staff through the sections in the course of a work day allowed ample opportunities for identifying deviations from the environmental conditions that prevailed during an observation.

Program and Staff Evaluation Initially, the observation results were discussed by Section Supervisors and section staff from both shifts in order to rectify any factors on the section which observations identified as impediments to programming. Beginning in week 15, it was possible to hold formal weekly meetings with a group composed of the Section Supervisors, representatives of each section/shift, all other professional staff, and administrative staff (e.g., support services, budgeting, purchasing, etc.). This meeting provided a forum for reviewing the results of the Service Index at the section, section/shift, and unit levels and was held weekly from week 15 through week 78. The Service Index was reviewed by reporting the number of observations made on each section/shift, the number of perfect observations (100%) for each section/shift, the high section/shift average, the low section/shift average, and the unit average for the preceding week. This was followed by reviewing each observation that had a score of less than 100% to make sure that the discrepancies identified by the observation had been remedied. This presented an opportunity for staff to discuss any problems with the observation, to question observers, to point out needed changes in the unit, to order supplies, to request special support services (e.g., transportation, special food, etc.), and to raise any other issues they felt were important.

An evaluation system for all unit staff was installed by week 18. Although this system underwent considerable revision during the time period reported here, it always included the results of the Service Index as a component of the evaluation at all staff levels having a direct responsibility for service quality (i.e., direct care staff, Section Supervisors, Academic Supervisor, and Unit Director). For direct care staff, who were evaluated monthly, observation scores generated when the staff member was present were averaged and checked to see whether or not they were greater than 80%. This information was combined with scores from a training proficiency scale used to assess one-to-one teaching and administrative records (unauthorized absences, abuse of leave, etc.) to give an overall evaluation score upon which promotion was based. For Section Supervisors, who were evaluated quarterly, the average Service Index score for the section was calculated for the evaluation period and again checked to see whether or not it was greater than 80%. This information was combined with administrative records and other performance indicators (e.g., reports in on time, all staff training completed, etc.) in order to obtain a composite evaluation score. The Academic Supervisor evaluation was identical in format to that used for Section Supervisors, except that, because this position was responsible for service coordination across sections, the Service Index component of the evaluation was based on the total unit. The Unit Director recommended to his immediate supervisor that his evaluation also be based in part upon maintenance of the unit Service Index at greater than an 80% level. This suggestion was ignored, and, as a consequence, the Unit Director was forced to impose a weaker contingent relationship between the Service Index and his work behavior by announcing publicly to unit staff and institution administrators his intent to be responsible for maintaining the Service Index at a level greater than 80%.

Results and Discussion

Figure 3 shows the unit Service Index average as well as lowest section/shift average for each week of the 78 week reporting period. Changes in the unit average reflect the extent to which it is possible to maintain an environment that meets established criteria. The low section/shift average represents the worst observed case of performance with respect to criteria in place in a particular week. Deviations

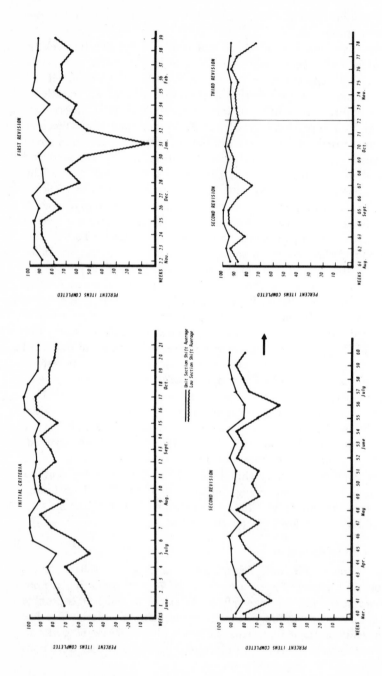

Figure 3.   Unit Service Index average and lowest section/shift average for each week of the 78-week reporting period.

of this measure from the unit average can be taken as a gross indicator of the impact of changes (both planned and unplanned) upon the unit. It is not possible to analyze the sources of this variation further because they are obviously too complex (see constraint 2 above) to yield to either the level of the data or to the analytical techniques currently available. Instead, we can examine the relationship between the two measures and note the slow convergence of the low section/shift average on the unit average across the reporting period. This convergence, coupled with the consistently high unit average across time, would appear to indicate that it is possible to develop, implement, extend, and maintain improvements in the unit environment in a fashion that is well within staff capabilities and which supports increasingly complex, consistent, and competent work behaviors on the part of all staff.

At this point a discussion of the relationships between the Service Index and some of the changes that occurred during the reporting period is appropriate. The effect of the method upon the choice of criteria employed for indexing is described first. This is followed by a description of the extension of the Service Index to a larger proportion of the residents' day and discussion of the institution of compensatory time to direct care staff contingent upon Service Index scores, a brief review of the impact of unplanned changes upon the Service Index, and an assessment of the extent to which the results of implementing the Service Index could be socially validated. Finally, some of the personnel requirements and costs of implementing the Service Index are discussed.

Criteria Changes   Table 1 summarizes the average unit Service Index value, the average low section/shift value, and the average weekly number of observations for each of the successive time periods in which increasingly more complex criteria were used as a basis for calculating the Service Index. Examination of the table reveals a generally increasing change in the average unit value and the low section/shift value between the initial Service Index (weeks 1–21) and the third revision (weeks 72–78). This is encouraging because, as we shall see, the criteria upon which the Service Index was based changed considerably across these four time periods.

Figure 4 shows the observation sheet used during the initial Service Index (weeks 1–21) and Figure 5 gives the criterion associated with each of the items. During this time period the unit was undergoing a major reorganization prior to the official imposition of a unit system on all seven residential areas at the Georgia Retardation

Table 1.   Service Index values during time periods in which criteria for indexing were changed

	Average[a] number of observations— all units per week	Average[a] unit Service Index value	Average[a] low section shift Service Index value
Initial Service Index Weeks 1–21	28	92	75
First revision Weeks 22–39	22	90	67
Second revision Weeks 40–71	38	93	88
Third revision Weeks 72–78	42	96	91

[a] Rounded down to nearest whole.

STUDENT SERVICE INDEX

    Section_____   Shift_____   Date_____   Time_____

1.   # of students participating in planned activity = _____

     # of students observed (exclusive of temps)

2.   # Appropriate staff-student interactions = _____

     # Appropriate staff-student interactions plus #
     inappropriate interactions

Quality

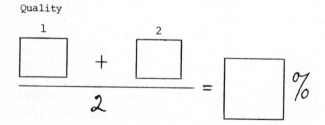

Figure 4.   Observation sheet used for Student Service Index, weeks 1–21.

CRITERIA FOR STUDENT SERVICE INDEX

1. Percentage of students participating in planned activity.   Staff
   members are engaged in activity listed on program sheet.

2. Staff/Student Interactions:
   a. instructs student
   b. if student responds or attempts to respond, guide and
       reinforce.
   c. if student does not respond within 5 seconds, guide
       student through response if possible. Do not reinforce.

Figure 5.   Criteria for observation sheet, weeks 1–21.

Center, beginning in September, 1974 (week 15). Supervisory personnel were being identified, students were being evaluated, staff
training procedures were being designed and implemented, and there
was little if any program support from professional staff outside the
unit. Given these considerations, the criteria for the initial Service
Index reflected an emphasis on moving from a custodial to an
educational model. The criterion for Item 1 on the initial Service
Index was designed to ensure that all students were engaged in
planned group activities (drawn from a file of such activities provided
by Shawn M. Boles and special educators assigned to the unit),
and that students were interacted with consistently by all staff conducting the activities. The initial interaction pattern to be used by
staff in teaching was designed to reward any attempt by students to
comply with staff requests during activities and to bring about a
decrease in *all* staff members' tendencies to attend to uncooperative
and oppositional student behavior.

The criteria during the initial Service Index period (weeks 1–21,
Figures 4 and 5) can be contrasted with those associated with the
third revision (weeks 72–78, Figures 6 and 7) in order to obtain an
idea of the increasing number of work behaviors associated with the
group environment in which the student receives service. Figure 6
shows the observation sheet associated with the third revision, while
Figure 7 gives the criterion for each item.

The first item, referring to staff/student interactions, is substantially different from the comparable item during the initial
Service Index period in that it reflects an increasing competency on
the part of students to respond to commands by staff members.
While the initial Service Index interaction pattern was intended to

---

STUDENT SERVICE INDEX   _____

Observer_____   _____

Section_____ Shift_____ Date/Day_____

                                        Time _____ AM

                                             _____ PM

1. 90% of all staff/student interactions are appropriate.
2. All students are appropriately programmed.   _____
3. Staff distribution is appropriate.   _____
4. Activity room is clean.   _____
5. Students are appropriately dressed & groomed.   _____
6. All forms are up to date.   _____
7. Off-section staff engaged in assignments.   _____

Appropriate staff/student interactions = _____
Total # staff/student interactions

Staff in Act. Room   _____

                            _____

A. Disruptive/Aggressive/Sleeping Students

B. Extenuating Circumstances

Figure 6.   Observation sheet used for Student Service Index, weeks 72-78.

increase attempts at compliance by students to instructions, the interaction pattern associated with the third revision may be conceived of as one that shapes independent behavior of the students. In this pattern of responses the student is always given the least support possible by the staff in any instructional situation. Only if the student fails to perform with minimal support (i.e., the instruction itself), are increasing amounts of support (via gesture, demonstration, and guidance) provided. The interaction pattern is designed to provide, in the environment, multiple opportunities for the student to become as independent of staff as possible.

The second item (all students appropriately programmed) should be considered in conjunction with Figure 8, which shows the daily program sheet used by a section. With adequate evaluation tools applied to the students it is possible to place them in a series of

CRITERIA FOR STUDENT SERVICE INDEX

1. Staff/student interactions:

    a. staff gives instruction in a calm & clear tone
    b. gesture
    c. demonstration (when appropriate)
    d. guidance

    Student is meaningfully reinforced at whatever stage response occurs.

2. a. Students are engaged in activities and are interacted with during observation period.
   b. Students not participating in activities are interacted with according to instructions posted in Activity Room.
   c. Students on special reinforcement schedules are interacted with according to instructions posted in Activity Room.

3. Two staff must be present for entire observation. Three staff may be present with one staff engaged in special procedures and "DRO'ing" students for appropriate attending behaviors.

4. a. no clothing on floor
   b. no towels, towel strings, paper towels, or paper wads on floor or cabinets.

5. a. students hair is combed
   b. students have on their own matched clothes and shoes which fit properly and are appropriate for the weather.

6. Forms are up to date as of previous day. Withdrawal form, release from restraint, sleep record, and program form must be up to date.

    a. Fluid intake   e. Housekeeping
    b. Menses (posted)   f. Withdrawal
    c. B.M. (Posted)   g. Sleep
    d. Meal charts   h. Program

7. Check program assignment sheet for staff activities - then check to see that all staff are engaged in assignments appropriately, i.e. self-help, or, if on break,- staff is not in Activity Room.

    a. List all students engaged in disruptive, aggressive, or sleeping behaviors. See list for examples.

    b. List any extenuating circumstances observed or told by staff members.

If no programming is available to students at beginning of observation, a zero (0) should be scored.

Figure 7.   Criteria for observation sheet, weeks 72-78.

SECTION__________

DAY__________

DATE__________

Class Format Assign.

A		
B		
C		

DAY		EVE
	CPS	
	ATT.III	
	S. KEY	
	FORMS	

TIME	PROGRAM	ASSIGN	1 to 1	OTHER	ASSIG.

A Wash/Dress/Health Ck
B Grooming
C Breakfast
D Meds
E Toothbrushing
F Handwashing
G Fountain
H Toileting
I Meds
J Lunch
K Toileting
L Rest
M Handwashing
N Toothbrushing
O Fountain
P Toileting
Q Meds
R Dinner
S Rest
T Grooming
U Toileting
V Snacks
W Undressing
X Bath/Health
Y Meds
Z Hall Duty

Figure 8. Program form.

special classes with differing formats and objectives. (The results of this placement have been reported elsewhere (Boles and Edrington, 1975).) Depending upon the time of day and staffing patterns, a student might be involved in recreational programs (swimming, trampoline, games and relays, music, dance, party, etc.), individual instruction (self-help tasks, motor imitation training, language acquisition program, etc.), maintenance activities (obtained from a card file listing over 100 recreational, social, perceptual, and leisure activities, each in a format consistent with the interaction pattern), toilet training classes, attending off-campus activities with staff or family, or going to appointments with one of the disciplines serving the entire center (dentistry, physical therapy, speech and hearing, etc.). The program format provides staff on each shift with a means of coordinating the various schedules of staff and student activities and is examined by the observer to see that activities and programs planned for all students correspond to what is actually occurring.

While the first two items on the third revision correspond rather closely with those on the initial Service Index, the remaining items reflect an expansion of the concept of service to encompass other aspects of the environment, in addition to the specific resident training programs, that affect the health and well-being of the students. This expansion occurred gradually as the Service Index underwent its first and second revisions. This expansion occurred as a result of the third constraint, cited earlier, which requires a balance of concurrently existing environments in the service setting. With continued monitoring and feedback over time, the unit began to consider the students' responses to the environment in the hospital, home, and community as well as in school.

The expansion to include hospital functions may be seen in the criteria for Item 6 on the third revision of the Service Index (all forms up-to-date). A fluid intake record (Figure 9) was devised along with a form for recording bowel movements (Figure 10) as a result of Service Index observations that revealed a failure of program occurrence attributable to multiple cases of diarrhea in sections. These "mini-epidemics" were traced to a vicious circle in which the students, who received inconsistent amounts of fluids daily, became constipated and required laxatives (often receiving multiple doses). Students (like everyone else) find it difficult to learn when they are constipated or when they have diarrhea—and staff members (again like everyone else) find it difficult to attend to anything else while attending to soiled students. The introduction of these forms made the environment somewhat better for both staff and students. Similar discoveries from Service Index observations led to the development of a form for recording menses in female students and to a sleep record (Figure 11) for monitoring student sleep patterns in attempts to achieve appropriate dosage maintenance for those who were receiving prescription medications.

The expansion to cover home functions can be seen in the criteria associated with Items 4 and 5 on the third revision of the Service Index (Figures 6 and 7). The observation that, on sections where an emphasis was placed by staff on cleanliness of both students

3/24/76 – 3/31/76		WED.	THURS.	FRI.	SAT.	SUN.	MON.	TUES.	WED.
STUDENT'S NAME	Bkfst								
	Meds								
	Lunch								
	FTW-D								
	FTN-E								
	Dinner								
	Snack								
	Meds								
	Bkfst								
	Meds								
	Lunch								
	FTW-D								
	FTN-E								
	Dinner								
	Snack								
	Meds								
	Bkfst								
	Meds								
	Lunch								
	FTW-D								
	FTN-E								
	Dinner								
	Snack								
	Meds								

1 SMALL GLASS = 4 OZ.
1 LARGE GLASS = 8 OZ.
½ PINT   = 8 OZ.

Figure 9.   Fluid intake record form.

and work environment, the Service Index was consistently higher than other sections led to including these items on the Service Index during its second revision (week 39). Other subsequent program content revisions have provided more home-like activities for the students.

The expansion to cover community functions can be seen in the presence of a form to record withdrawals from the group by individual aggressive or disruptive students (Figure 12). This form resulted

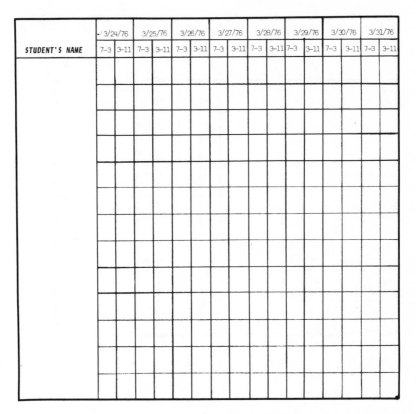

Figure 10.   Bowel movement record form.

from Service Index observations that students and staff were often subjected to unwarranted attacks by students. Rather than a straightforward time-out procedure to deal with this problem, the best compromise that could be reached, in view of the fifth constraint previsously noted (bureaucratic inertia), was one that allowed staff to withdraw students to progressively more restrictive environments, contingent upon the emission of aggressive or disruptive behaviors. Withdrawal could only occur for ten minutes, at the end of which an attempt had to be made to reintroduce the student to the group environment. This of course meant that the student would be readmitted to the group environment in a fashion that was not contingent upon both passage of time and cessation of target behavior, as in a time-out paradigm, but that was contingent upon passage of time alone.

STUDENT'S NAME															
7 AM — 8 AM															
8 AM — 9 AM															
9 AM — 10 AM															
10 AM — 11 AM															
11 AM — 12 N															
12 N — 1 PM															
1 PM — 2 PM															
2 PM — 3 PM															
3 PM — 4 PM															
4 PM — 5 PM															
5 PM — 6 PM															
6 PM — 7 PM															
7 PM — 8 PM															
8 PM — 9 PM															
9 PM — 10 PM															
10 PM — 11 PM															
11 PM — 12 M															
12 M — 1 AM															
1 AM — 2 AM															
2 AM — 3 AM															
3 AM — 4 AM															
4 AM — 5 AM															
5 AM — 6 AM															
6 AM — 7 AM															

A = AWAKE

S = SLEEPING

Figure 11.   Sleep record form.

While running the risk of intermittently reinforcing maladaptive behavior, the withdrawal form provides evidence of a process for protecting members of the community of staff and students from unprovoked assault.

Figure 13 shows a form associated with the criterion for Item 6 (d and e of Figure 7). This form resulted from observations that programs were often interrupted by housekeeping or were delayed because of food delivery problems. The form was used in an attempt to synchronize unit environmental activities with extra unit support service groups that directly effect the students' group environment. Direct care staff use this form to record the extent to which the housekeeping and food service departments are meeting time and quantity standards agreed upon with the unit. This information is provided to those departments monthly and has resulted in both groups providing service which, during weeks 70–78, was at 90% of the established criteria (e.g., housekeeping service provided within

```
a.   Corner of Activity Room
b.   Kitchen
c.   Stairwell w/ staff
d.   Courtyard-door unlocked
e.   Courtyard-door locked
```

Date	STUDENT	Staff Init.	TIME withdrawn from group	WHERE withdrawn	TIME returned to group	INAPPROPRIATE BEHAVIOR

Figure 12.   Withdrawal record form.

± 15 minutes of publicly posted schedule). While control of such support service impact upon the indexed environment may seem trivial, these services are very real in terms of their effects. In addition to assuring that these effects are beneficial, the recording forms

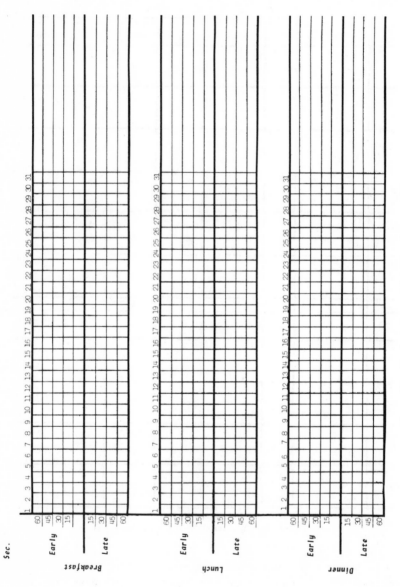

Figure 13.   Food service and housekeeping record form.

provide tangible evidence to direct care staff that aspects of the environment other than their own performance are being monitored and that their role in fact encompasses a monitoring function.

Finally, we turn to two items on the third revision that reflect an extension of the index to tie it to other aspects of the students' environment, in particular to the one-to-one direct teaching environment. Item 3 (staff distribution is appropriate) and Item 7 (off-section staff engaged in assignments) ensure that staff work time is spent in activities that are directly or indirectly related to student health and development. Among those activities that an individual staff member might conduct with students are outside walks, field trips, shopping trips, and one-to-one teaching sessions. Indirect activities might include data-recording or staff training sessions. Variations on these items were introduced as early as the first revision of the Service Index. Partially as a result of these two items, there has been a steady increase in the number of sessions conducted and tasks completed. Evidence for this may be obtained by citing data collected in conjunction with the unit's 1974-75 Annual Report, which showed a total of 19,010 twenty-minute teaching sessions devoted to 588 individual student problems during weeks 1-65 of the Service Index, which resulted in the resolution of 154 problems.

Increasing the Number of Indexed Hours   The initial Service Index (weeks 1-21) was used between 9:00-11:00 a.m., 1:00-4:30 p.m., and 6:30-8:00 p.m. for a total of 7 hours per day, 49 hours per week. In the first revision period (weeks 22-39), this was increased to 9 hours per day, 63 hours per week, by including the hours of noon-1:00 p.m., and 5:30 p.m.-6:30 p.m., using a modified version of the criteria (see Appendix A). Finally, in conjunction with the second revision of the Service Index (week 40) the indexed hours were increased to 13 hours per day (7:00 a.m.-8:00 p.m.), 91 hours per week, and this condition was maintained throughout the remainder of the 78 weeks reported. As with the effect of criteria changes, an examination of Figure 3 and Table 1 indicates that it is possible to extend the Service Index to a large portion of the students' environment at a pace that is compatible with the performance capabilities of the staff.

Introduction of Compensatory Time   Beginning in week 42 and continuing throughout the following 36 weeks, all direct care staff of any section/shift maintaining a Service Index of above 90% for four consecutive weeks were each given one hour of compensatory time. No reversal of this condition occurred, and, even if one had taken place, it would be difficult to interpret given the other changes that occurred during the time period reported. Other uses of compensatory time employed in the unit (e.g., to increase the generation of student activity cards by direct care staff) proved relatively ineffective. Although there was a substantial increase in the average low section/shift value following the implementation of compensatory time, this is probably better explained by other supporting factors (e.g., staff training programs, increasing practice in implementing and maintaining changes, feedback and evaluation) inherent in the Service Index method, rather than by this type of group contingency. The use of compensatory time to consequate productive staff behaviors, however, clearly warrants further careful study.

Unplanned Changes It is possible to demonstrate that the Service Index does in fact provide a relatively sensitive measure of the unit environment by examining some of the transient changes in the measure as a function of uncontrolled factors operating in the larger service system in which the unit was embedded (see constraints 5 and 6 above). A clear example of this sensitivity may be found by examining Figure 3 during weeks 27 through 31. This period occurred during December, 1974, when a large number of residents were scheduled by other institution staff to visit their families, and both staffing patterns and program plans were designed to reflect the expected temporary decline in resident population. The expected schedule of departure and return was seriously violated, in that many of the residents were picked up later and returned earlier than had been planned. This meant that there was a lower staff/student ratio present during these weeks, and that program plans were often inappropriate for the number of residents remaining in the unit. The Service Index appears to have reflected a sensitivity to these changing conditions. A second example of the sensitivity of the measure may be seen in Figure 3 during weeks 55 and 56. This two-week period was devoted to transporting students to a summer camp setting some 40 miles from the unit, providing a complete summer camp program, and returning to the unit each evening. Students remaining in the unit during this period tended to be those who exhibited grossly maladaptive behaviors. This fact, coupled with the demand for high staff/student ratios to implement camp programs, resulted in a natural decrease in performance with respect to criteria then in place, and this decrease was reflected in the Service Index.

Social Validation Social validation may be best conceived of as a concept that reflects the extent to which the goals, methods, and results of a particular intervention process can be evaluated at a subjective level by those who are affected by the process (Wolf, 1976). Although a universally acceptable methodology for achieving social validation has not been developed, an approximation of the concept with respect to the Service Index may be achieved by citing collateral evidence that supports its goals, methods, and results. This evidence comes from staff and parent responses to the Service Index process and from a comparison of certain administrative records kept for all units in the institution.

Staff members were initially very resistant to the idea of measuring the environment in order to ascertain whether or not established criteria were being met. Some staff agreed that public accountability for work performance was a reasonable goal, but they felt they did not need it because "anybody could see they loved the students." Others, particularly those with poor work histories before the implementation of the Service Index, were covertly resistant to the Service Index because it represented a system that would, to a certain extent, make their salaries at least indirectly contingent (see program/staff evaluation above) upon work performance rather than merely upon the passage of time. These perceptions changed slowly, but, as the Service Index involved staff in establishing criteria, provided feedback about performance, and was applied in a consistent and objective fashion, many of the staff came to support its use. Information gathered from staff in exit interviews (begun in week 42) seemed to show an increasing appreciation by staff of the Service Index as a means of providing counter-controls for the students; this appreciation was often expressed in statements like "I didn't need it, but my co-workers did." Each exiting staff member was asked whether or not the Service Index should remain in place, and, without exception, they answered "Yes." This shift in staff attitude toward the Service Index is indirectly supported by the fact that requests for transfers into the unit steadily increased. This was not true in any of the other seven residential units in the center. Finally, despite the fact that five staff members were terminated for failure to perform their jobs during the 78 weeks, only one of these terminations was appealed, although the institution as a whole was very supportive of such appeals. As one terminated staff member said, "I fired myself and you can prove it—why should I appeal?"

Comments from parents and guardians of students who were in the unit prior to implementation of the Service Index would indicate that the changes brought about by its use were perceived as beneficial. Typical comments were, "My child is finally learning," "I know what to expect when I come to the unit," "Staff aren't just babysitting," etc.

Costs and Personnel   The Service Index for the unit was designed and implemented using only those personnel and monies allotted to the unit (i.e., seventy-nine staff and an annual operating budget of $658,000 in FY '74). Total staff time allotted to the entire Service Index process (e.g., establishing criteria, observing, training, discussion of results, and analysis) was always less than 5% of any single member's time available. While the resources in the unit were high when compared to other institutional settings, this is not required for the Service Index method to be employed. (Note that during the initial Service Index period very few people were required to implement the process.) We estimate that the Service Index could be used in more impoverished environments so long as a sufficient number of observers could be identified to provide the information base required. Observers might well be drawn from those groups who are concerned with protection of residents' rights, thus giving them a useful role while allowing them to confront the realities of institutional life at a more realistic distance than that which occurs in either the courts or conference rooms where these groups normally operate.

Simple criteria in place for relatively short durations require minimal resources in terms of observers and time, an advantage that should not be overlooked in deciding whether or not the method can be extablished in other environments.

SUMMARY

The extent to which institutions are psychologically, architecturally, and culturally inappropriate for those who live and work in them cannot be overemphasized. The actions of many persons who have recognized this tragic state of affairs are slowly leading to an increasing emphasis on the identification and provision of alternative treatment environments that are more appropriate for human beings than traditional institutions. While the results of this shift in emphasis should prove most welcome to all concerned, the changes that they require are of a magnitude and a complexity that mitigate against their coming to fruition within the next five to ten years. During this time period, many of the program managers within existing institutions will still be faced with the problem of ensuring public accountability for their stewardship.

It would appear from the results obtained using the Service Index that the utilization of such a method would be helpful to front line managers responsible for addressing the question of what to do about providing service in existing residential treatment environments. Important advantages to using such a method are:

1. It provides for at least some counter-control to be exercised on staff behavior on the behalf of service consumers.
2. It allows for clear and objective specification of what constitutes service quality, such specification being made by those who deliver service, those who monitor it, and those who receive it (or their representatives).
3. The method allows for a gradual transition from a custodial environment to a true service environment by providing for a revision of the Service Index to include increasingly complex and expanded criteria across time.
4. The method, at least as it is employed in its present context, is simple enough to be understood by staff and consumer representatives, an advantage not to be under-emphasized.
5. The method allows for immediate feedback to all staff about the extent to which a quality environment is being maintained.
6. It provides at least partial information which allows for an assessment of service quality within the multiple environments inherent in an institutional setting.

ACKNOWLEDGMENTS

The authors wish to thank all those who made the work reported in this paper possible. Although they are too numerous to mention by name, each of the staff and students at the institution contributed to this work—either by providing problems for resolution or by participating in their solution.

REFERENCES

Alexander, C. The pattern language. Unpublished paper, available at the University of Oregon Planning Office, Eugene, Oregon.

Alexander, C. The timeless way of building. Unpublished paper, available at the University of Oregon Planning Office, Eugene, Oregon.

Atthowe, J. M., Jr. 1974. Behavioral innovation: An all encompassing system of intervention. In: D. Harshbarger and R. F. Maley (eds.), Behavior

Analysis and Systems Analysis: An Integrative Approach to Mental Health Programs.

Baer, D. M., Wolf, M. M., and Risley, T. R. 1968. Some current dimensions of applied behavior analysis. J. Appl. Behav. Anal. 1:90-97.

Bensberg, G. J. 1974. Administration and staff development in residential facilities. Ment. Retard. 12:29-32.

Boles, S. M. 1969. Normality—Seeking a stable label for a labile fable. Unpublished manuscript, available from the author at 3145 Whitten, Eugene, Oregon 97401.

Boles, S. M., and Edrington, M. R. 1975. Group programming with the profoundly retarded ambulatory citizen in an institutional setting. Paper presented at the Southeastern American Association on Mental Deficiency, Louisville.

Bolin, D. C., and Kivens, L. 1972. Evaluation in a community mental health center: Huntsville, Alabama. Evaluation 2:27-35.

Bricker, W. A., Morgan, D. G., and Grabowski, J. G. 1972. Development and maintenance of a behavior modification repertoire of cottage attendants through T.V. feedback. Amer. J. Ment. Defic. 77:128-136.

Bushell, D., Jackson, D. A., and Weis, L. C. 1975. Quality control in the behavior analysis approach to project follow through. In: W. S. Wood (ed.), Issues in Evaluating Behavior Modification. Research Press, Champaign.

Ellsworth, R. B. 1973. Feedback: Asset or liability in improving treatment effectiveness? J. Consult. Clin. Psychol. 40:383-393.

Ferster, C. B., and Skinner, B. F. 1957. Schedules of Reinforcement. Appleton-Century-Crofts, New York.

Fielding, L. T., Erickson, E., and Bettin, B. 1971. Modification of staff behavior: A brief note. Behav. Ther. 2:550-553.

Gardner, J. M., and Giampa, F. L. 1971. The attendant behavior checklist: Measuring on-the-ward behavior of institutional attendants. Amer. J. Ment. Defic. 75:617-622.

Hollander, M. A., and Plutchik, R. 1972. A reinforcement program for psychiatric attendants. J. Behav. Ther. Exper. Psychol. 3:297-300.

Hollander, M. A., Plutchik, R., and Horner, V. 1973. Interaction of patient and attendant reinforcement programs: The "piggyback" effect. J. Consult. Clin. Psychol. 41:43-47.

Jackson, D. A., and Bushell, D. 1975. Monitoring staff performance: a plan for quality control in project follow through. Paper presented at the Meeting of the American Psychological Association, Chicago, September.

Klaber, M. 1970. Institutional programming and research: a vital partnership in action. In: H. H. Baumister and E. C. Butterfield (eds.), Residential Facilities for the Mentally Retarded, p. 17. Aldine, Chicago.

Loeber, R., and Weisman, R. G. 1975. Contingencies of therapist and trainer performance. Psychol. Bull. 82:660-688.

Mager, R., and Pipe, P. 1970. Analyzing Performance Problems or 'You Really Oughta Wanna'. Fearon Publishers, Belmont.

Martin, G. L. 1972. Teaching operant technology to psychiatric nurses, aides, and attendants. In: F. Clark, D. R. Evans, and L. A. Hammerlynck (eds.), Implementing Behavioral Programs for Schools and Clinics. Research Press, Champaign.

Neufeldt, A. 1974. Considerations in the implementation of program evaluation. In: P.O. Davidson, F. W. Clark, and L. A. Hammerlynck (eds.), Evaluation of Behavioral Programs in Community, Residential and School Settings. Research Press, Champaign.

Panyon, M., Boozer, H., and Morris, N. 1970. Feedback to attendants as a reinforcer for applying operant techniques. J. Appl. Behav. Anal. 3:1-4.

Pierce, C. H., and Risley, T. R. 1974. Improving job performance of neighborhood youth corps aides in an urban recreation program. J. Appl. Behav. Anal. 7:207-215.

Pomerleau, O. F., Bobrove, P. H., and Smith, R. 1973. Rewarding psychiatric aides for the behavioral improvement of assigned patients. J. Appl. Behav. Anal. 6:383-390.

Pommer, D. A., and Streedbeck, D. 1974. Motivating staff performance in an operant learning program for children. J. Appl. Behav. Anal. 7: 217-221.

Portnoy, S. M. 1973. Power of child care worker and therapist figures and their effectiveness as models for emotionally disturbed children in residential treatment. J. Consult. Clin. Psychol. 40:15-19.

Quilitch, H. R. 1975. A comparison of three staff-management procedures J. Appl. Behav. Anal. 8:59-66.

Reppucci, N. D., and Saunders. 1974. Social pschology of behavior modification: problems of implementation in natural settings. Amer. Psychol. 29:649-660.

Skinner, B. F. 1972. Compassion and ethics in the care of the retarded. In: B. F. Skinner (ed.), Cumulative Record: A Selection of Papers. Appleton-Century-Crofts, New York.

Statistical Abstract of the United States. 1976. Grosset and Dunlap, New York.

Thompson, T. 1975. I'm O. K. and you are O. K. too, but the state hospital system stinks. Paper presented at the Convention of Midwestern Association of Behavior Analysis, Chicago, May.

Turner, J. 1975. Accountability in a community mental health center. Invited address, Convention of Midwestern Association of Behavior Analysis, Chicago, May.

Welsh, W. V., Ludwig, C., Radiker, J. E., and Krapfl, J. E. 1973. Effects of feedback on daily completion of behavior modification projects. Ment. Retard. 11:24-26.

Willems, E. P. 1974. Behavioral technology and behavioral ecology. J. Appl. Behav. Anal. 7:151-165.

Wolf, M. M. 1976. Social validity: the case for subjective measurement or how applied behavior analysis is finding its heart. An invited address to the Division of the Experimental Analysis of Behavior, American Psychological Association, Washington, D.C., September.

APPENDIX A: STUDENT SERVICE INDEX

Observation sheet used for first revision, weeks 22–39.

Score [ ]

Observer _____

Section_____Shift_____Date_____Time_____

1. 90% of all staff/student interactions are appropriate   _____

2. All students are appropriately programmed.   _____

3. Staff distribution is appropriate and staff are wearing   _____
    reinforcer bags.

4. Activity room is clean.   _____

5. Students are neat and clean.   _____

6. Students are completely dressed.   _____

7. All forms are up-to-date.   _____

8. Special procedures are being carried out appropriately.   _____

$$\frac{\text{\# Appro. staff/student interaction}}{\text{TOTAL \# staff/student interactions}} = \underline{\quad\quad} = \boxed{} \quad \begin{array}{c}\text{Staff}\\\text{in room}\\ \underline{\quad} + \underline{\quad}\end{array}$$

APPENDIX B: CRITERIA FOR STUDENT SERVICE INDEX

Criteria for first revision, weeks 22–39.

1. Staff/student interactions:
   a. staff given command
   b. gesture
   c. demonstration
   d. guidance

   Reinforced at whatever stage response occurs

2. a. students are sitting and are engaged in group activities
   b. students not sitting are ignored by staff
   c. see special procedures

3. Two staff members only in Activity Room, and they are wearing reinforcer bags.

4. a. No clothing on floor
   b. No towels, towel strings, paper towels, or paper wads on floor or cabinets

5. a. Students' hair combed
   b. Students have on matched clothes and matched socks.

6. a. Students have on all articles of clothing
   b. Students have shoe laces in shoes
   c. Students have socks on both feet

7. See Med forms are up-to-date.
   a. Intake—fluid
   b. Menses (posted)
   c. B.M. (posted)
   d. Meal charts
   e. Housekeeping
   f. Withdrawal forms

8. Special procedures—see back of Section Office door.

APPENDIX C: STUDENT SERVICE INDEX

Observation sheet used for second revision, weeks 40–71.

_____

Observer   _____   Score   _____

Section_____Shift_____Date_____Time_____a.m.   p.m.

1. 90% of all staff/student interactions are appropriate   _____

2. All students are appropriately programmed   _____

3. Staff distribution is appropriate   _____

4. Activity room is clean   _____

5. Students are neat and clean   _____

6. Students are completely dressed   _____

7. All forms are up-to-date   _____

8. Special Procedures are being carried out appropriately _____

9. Off-Section staff engaged in assignments   _____

$$\frac{\text{\# Appropriate staff/student interactions}}{\text{TOTAL \# staff/student interactions}} = \underline{\hspace{1.5cm}} =$$

_____

Staff in Activity Room

_____

A. Disruptive/Aggressive Students

B. Extenuating Circumstances

APPENDIX D: CRITERIA FOR STUDENT SERVICE INDEX

Criteria for second revision, weeks 40–71.

1. Staff/student interactions
   a. staff give instruction
   b. gesture
   c. demonstration
   d. guidance

   Reinforced at whatever stage response occurs

2. a. students are engaged in group activities
   b. students not sitting are ignored by staff

3. Three staff members may be in Activity Room and at transition of activities—chance for students to be involved in exercise—third staff member to be engaged in special procedures, or self-help.

4. a. no clothing on floor
   b. no towels, towel strings, paper towels, or paper wads on floor or cabinets.

5. a. students' hair combed
   b. students have on matched clothes and matched socks.

6. a. students have on all articles of clothing
   b. students have shoe laces in shoes
   c. students have socks on both feet.

7. See Med forms are up-to-date as of previous day. Withdrawal form and release from restraint and sleep records must be up-to-date.

   a. Intake—fluid
   b. Menses (posted)
   c. B.M. (posted)
   d. Meal charts
   e. Housekeeping
   f. Withdrawal forms
   g. Sleep records

8. Special Procedure—4 per section—see back of door in Section office.

9. Check program assignment sheet for staff activities, then check to see if all staff are appropriately engaged in assigned activity, i.e., self-help off Section or, if on break, staff are not in Activity Room.
   a. List all students who are engaged in disruptive or aggressive behavior. See list attached or examples.
   b. Extenuating circumstances. List any extenuating circumstances as observed or told by staff member.

MAJOR OBJECTIVES OF RESEARCH FOR THE DEVELOPMENTALLY DISABLED FOR THE NEXT TEN YEARS

William A. Bricker

The term 'research' as a descriptor of professional activity might imply the question "Is there something that you need to find?" This question constitutes the underlying theme of this chapter. The target for the question is the educational program for a group of people who are between birth and approximately 25 years of age, and who have been identified by some segment of society as handicapped. What needs to be found is a system of education that will allow these people to function in existing communities throughout the world without any *unnecessary* disruption caused by their handicapping condition. This means that the "search" of a research effort is for the most effective means to bring each person to an optimum state of normalization within the limits of the unchangeable aspects of the handicap, and to do so through the process of public instruction. A question that must be asked before embarking on a description of research efforts that might achieve this difficult goal is: Is it possible that the knowledge base for making this possible already exists and that all that needs to be done is to translate this knowledge into educational practice? The answer appears to be self-evident, although particular researchers, teachers, or therapists would answer it differently. In general, they would probably agree that there is not sufficient knowledge of human development and the educational process to maximize the normalization potentials of the majority of people whom we now label as handicapped. Consequently, there appears to be a need to continue the search for effective educational programs. Justification for this conclusion is contained in several of the following sections.

DIMENSIONS OF RESEARCH

Before launching into specific topics, one of the important pre-requisites of a discussion of research needs for the handicapped is a basic definition of research itself. In the domain of handicapped children there are at least five major dimensions by which particular forms of research can be defined. The first is the contrasting of biomedical and behavioral research. For example, in the investigation of Down's syndrome, one group of researchers may be attempting to find easier ways to establish the existence of an extra chromosome in the fetus without the dangerous use of amniocentesis, while another group of researchers attempts to determine the best method for teaching language to children who are born with the extra chromosome. The former group has training in biological analyses and medical interventions, while the latter has methods for studying the behavior-environment interaction in order to determine optimum environmental arrangements.

The second dimension is the division between basic and applied research. This dimension is not so easily defined; however, for purposes of this paper, basic research is defined as those activities that attempt to determine the effects of particular independent variables on a particular dependent variable. In biomedical research this might have to do with determining the specific metabolic effects of trisomy, while in behavioral research it might be on the effects of hypotonicity of the Down's syndrome child on the learning of a particular task, such as a two-choice discrimination problem. In applied research, the process is reversed. The dependent variable becomes critical in applied research, while it is practically irrelevant in basic research. In basic research any reasonable prototype, such as pressing a lever, touching a press-panel, or emitting the name of a particular object, can become the dependent variable against which the importance of the selected independent variable is assessed. In applied research, normal language or another human process is the goal, and the search is for the sequence of manipulable independent variables that will bring normal language into existence with a handicapped child who would probably not acquire normal language without such manipulations. This is an important distinction, in that much of the existing research literature cannot be adequately interpreted without looking at the basic or applied purpose of each investigation.

The third dimension is the distinction between descriptive and experimental research. In the former, a particular developmental process is defined according to the age of appearance of certain forms of behavior, such as the use of conjunctions in language. Children of different ages are given various tests to elicit the use of the conjunction, and the outcome of the research may indicate that children of two to three years of age do not use the conjunction, while children over four typically do. Most of the studies in developmental psychology are of this type (Bruner, 1975). Experimental research involves manipulation of the environment in some manner in order to determine the effect of particular instructional events on the acquisition of a particular form of human behavior. Much of the research in the applied analysis of behavior (Baer, Wolf, and Risley, 1968) is of this type. This is one of the more important dimensions, in that the major theoretical battles appear to be fought on the basis of the two types of data. Cognitive psychologists use descriptive and correlational data to affirm that particular types of environmental events, such as reinforcement, are not necessary for acquisition of human behavior (Brown and Hanlon, 1970), while others demonstrate experimentally how operationally defined reinforcers function in the acquisition of the same process (Guess, Sailor, and Baer, 1974). More will be said about this dimension later.

The fourth important distinction is between theory-based and non-theory-based research efforts. Many of the behaviorists (Skinner, 1959; Sidman, 1960) tend to reject premature theorizing until there is a sufficient factual basis for the inductive emergence of a set of basic principles. These experimental investigators are joined by a group of descriptive atheoretical psychologists who attempt to observe behavior in natural settings, under the heading of ecological psychology (Barker and Wright, 1955; Barker and Schoggen, 1973). On the theoretical side of this dimension, we find a number of experimental types (Baumeister, 1970; Belmont and Butterfield, 1971; Ellis, 1971; Call and Switzky, 1975) as well as some descriptive researchers (Brown, 1973; Schlesinger, 1974; Eimas, 1974). The issue of theory versus non-theory in research is sufficiently important, in the view of this writer, that a major section is devoted to it in a later portion of this chapter.

The final dimension of research is cross-sectional versus longitudinal. In cross-sectional research, a particular process, such as the relative value of specific reinforcers (Orlando and Tyler, 1966), the acquisition of the negation response (Miller, 1970), or learning the basic number concepts (Williams et al., 1970), becomes the focus of research over a relatively short period of time. In the typical cross-sectional study, children of ages near the probable age at which the concept is to be learned or tested are selected and then trained over a period of days. The targeted criterion performance usually represents only a small sample of the total concept and may often be a contrived (prototypic) form of the concept. In longitudinal research, the children who are acting as subjects will be enrolled in a program for a matter of many months, and sometimes years (Bricker and Bricker, 1973), while the effects of various instructional approaches are assessed. Because educational interventions occur over periods of months rather than days, longitudinal research may provide the better model.

As each of these dimensions is considered in relation to the educational problems of handicapped children, certain decisions can be made. First, educators are not generally trained in biomedical research, nor can they prescribe medical interventions. Consequently, the educator must trust the medical person to do what is best for the health problems of the handicapped person while focusing on how environments can be modified to improve the behavioral development of these children and young adults. Therefore, there will be no further mention made of medical research needs in this chapter. Second, while a knowledge of basic research findings is essential to applied research, the goal of educational research with the handicapped is to find ways to improve the instructional process. To do this, research must become increasingly focused on how to structure the sequence of instructional acts so that the "maximum potential" of each handicapped individual is indeed reached. Therefore, applied research is emphasized in this chapter. Third, because education is always a form of intervention, there must be more emphasis on experimental research rather than descriptive research. This is a critical decision when we deal with handicapped people because much of the existing descriptive research that forms the basis of our frequently pessimistic predictions about the futures of handicapped children has been derived from very sterile environments, such as large residential institutions (Ellis, 1971; Hobbs, 1975). Consequently, the emphasis in this chapter is on active intervention rather than on passive description. No clear conclusion can be drawn about theoretical versus non-theoretical research. The issue can only be evaluated in the application of research within specific content domains.

TRENDS IN RESEARCH DESIGN

Skinner (1959) has indicated that most research designs have tended to foster a closer relationship between a graduate student and a calculator than between a student of behavior and a behaving organism. While this may be an unfair overstatement of problems in the application of the experimental method, it does point in the direction of some needed reforms in program design that will accommodate the relationships between environmental events and the behavior of handicapped children. The ethics of research and the characteristics of the people being studied are no more strongly intertwined and in need of extreme caution than when one deals with the handicapped person. Here, as in few other domains of intervention effort, one must follow the primary ethical dictum of medical practice by agreeing that, first, one will do no harm. Children must not be deprived of food or subjected to physically aversive conditions or other forms of discomfort unless the teacher or researcher is *absolutely* certain that these procedures provide the best possible techniques for altering the behavior of the child in a positive direction. Consequently, when one is in doubt about the advantages of a specific manipulation in the environment of a child, the humanitarian considerations about the welfare of the child *must* take precedence over the possible scientific benefits of a carefully validated hypothesis. However, when one can justify the need for intervention with children, he must approach the issue being studied from within the framework of the child's construction of reality rather than from our adult and carefully trained professional perspectives. This, it seems to this writer, demands a relatively altered program design.

The design alternative that is being proposed is both novel and untested in the context in the educational domain. While one can identify the forms of behavior that typify the successive stages of human development, the prerequisites of each form of behavior or the instructional mechanisms that can be used to stimulate development in that area are usually not well specified.

The first generalization that can be applied here is that when a child knows what he is requested to do he will do it willingly and quickly unless he is asked to do it too often. Program (and motivational) problems seem to creep in when the child does not have the behavioral repertoire that is required by a given task. Program design must deal with this issue in a manner that does not oppress the child or require excessive deprivation or punishment. These considerations have led to the development of the test-teach research approach proposed in this chapter.

The test-teach approach starts with an overview of the domain being covered by the system, which can be represented as a developmental program lattice. For example, a lattice covering the sensorimotor period from birth to two years is represented in Figure 1. The lattice indicates the progressive forms of behavior that move the child from reflexive responding to preoperational and intentional behavior. A screening instrument has been developed to locate the child within this developmental structure in the various areas that appear most related to important cognitive and prelinguistic structures. This instrument was constructed from several available scales, including the Uzgiris-Hunt Provisional Instrument (Uzgiris and Hunt, 1966), the Albert Einstein Scales (Escalona and Corman, 1966), the Bayley Scales (Bayley, 1969), Gesell Developmental Scales (Gesell and Armatruda, 1949), and other items added by this writer's colleagues (Robinson, 1972) based on Piaget's description of the sensorimotor period. The child's responses to the tasks contained in the instrument provide a basis for determining the types of interaction between ongoing behavior of the infant or child and various objects or environmental events that are developmentally relevant and important. The child is then placed in contact with these objects or events over a period of a few days, and careful observations are made and recorded to determine his mode of reaction. These observations then form a basis of a specific test-teach paradigm.

The test-teach system begins with the materials and events that are immediately relevant to the development of the child. For example, the object permanence domain specifies a sequence of progressive developments from the point at which the child ignores any object that is not immediately and physically present to the point at which he wants objects that he has not seen for some period of time and initiates a search for the object in his home or in the

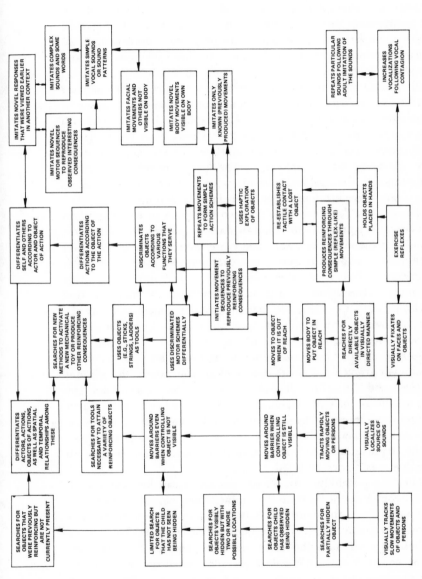

Figure 1. A developmental program lattice covering the sensorimotor period from birth to two years.

classroom. This sequence of developments has been latticed by Robinson (1972), and the lattice provides the description of what materials and manipulations can establish the perspective of the child concerning the permanence of objects, and what specific alterations in the task might stimulate progressive development. In this way, the test system leads directly into the teaching phase, and both phases may be repeated several times in a single instructional period. At this level, the system provides an instructional technology that, if it is working properly, requires no other support. However, if the system does not appear to be working (and this is quite frequently the case with developmentally delayed children), then the system is moved into the investigative domain and a strong inference approach (Platt, 1964) becomes applicable. The program research process being proposed is not related to most conventional designs, so that its mode of application requires specific detailed description.

The observable interactions between the behavior of a child and his environment provide only the raw data or phenomena that form the basis for the more important and more interesting inferences and generalizations about the child. For example, we may see a child open a cupboard door and then take out a toy and play with it. This phenomenon gives us one data point in arriving at the inference that the child "has" the structure defined as the object permanence concept. However, this is only one possible explanation of the child's behavior. The child may simply like to open doors, and when he does so he sometimes encounters interesting toys. This may have been a specifically trained act, so that toys hidden anywhere else are not discovered and the child will look in no other hiding place for any object not clearly in view. Opening the door may have been a direct imitation of an immediately antecedent model that was not observed. There may be other possibilities for the observed action of the child, and the application of a strong inference model requires that all reasonable possibilities be listed.

After the possibilities are listed, situations can be contrived in the classroom and elsewhere to determine which possibility offers the best explanation of the behavior. Platt (1964) contends that this may be most reasonably done by determining how each explanation or hypothesis about a child's behavior could be disproven. This requires that the contrived tasks not only allow for altered demands on the child's object permanence system, but also that the possible outcomes be considered in advance of the various explanations. This will tend to move the selection of the preplanned manipulation of the situation in the direction of providing the greatest amount of information about as many explanations as possible. In the case of object permanence concept, a special type of hide-and-seek could be contrived using a toy that has a high probability of use by the child. The toy is then placed in one of several cupboards in a relatively uninteresting room. The child is encouraged to find the toy, but without the observor indicating the cupboard that it is in or even that it may be in one of the cupboards. If the child moves directly to the cupboards, systematically opens one after another until the toy is found, and then takes the toy and proceeds to play with it, his behavior clearly discredits several of the previous explanations of his behavior. For example, if he moves to the cupboard closest to him and simply opens and closes the door several times without regard for what is inside, we would not be able to discredit the perference for the opening action over the search aspects; but, because the child did not repetitiously open and close the door, this is not a reasonable explanation.

Similarly, the requirement of an imitated model would also be discredited, as would be the explanation based on a single trained response chain (different rooms, different cupboard, different toy). However, there could have been many other outcomes, each having some relevance to the proposed explanations. Unexpected responses might require that additional possible explanations be added to the list. Additional manipulations could then be done with the toys in order to determine the creditability of the various explanations, and the one receiving the greatest amount of positive support with few instances of negative evidence would become the strongest explanation or inference of the child's behavior. If the most strongly supported explanation was not the one defining the terminal behavior in that area (i.e., the child "has" the object permanence concept) the information gathered to this point would provide a basis for giving the child additional experience to extend the boundaries of his behavioral repertoire.

To those who are trained as teachers, this method of working with children might be viewed as an interesting method for teaching children important concepts, but not as a scientific approach to concept formation or child development. Even those scientists who are trained in using individual subject designs might have difficulty understanding how this method leads to general insights about behavior and behavior development. The first defense of the method would be in terms of the multiple hypothesis versus the single hypothesis approach to research design, which Platt (1964) indicates is the major difference between research in microbiology and that in many other sciences. Educational research is notorious for research investigations of one hypothesis at a time. For example, in the field of mental retardation research, there are such hypotheses as stimulus trace deficit (Baumeister, 1970; Ellis, 1971), rehearsal deficit (Ellis, 1971), short-term memory deficit (Belmont and Butterfield, 1971), reinforcement history deficit (Bijou, 1963), and many others. Each has a primary sponsor, and each is tested in a variety of settings or in a very exact way by a number of different researchers. (Can the support for a hypothesis be replicated by someone other than the sponsor?) Tests of the hypothesis are made using groups of children, usually in contrived laboratory situations, and the results are frequently difficult to interpret (cf. Sidman, 1960). In this writer's experience in attempting to do research with retarded children, the outcomes of a group design are difficult to interpret because for some children the "reinforcers" do not reinforce, the manipulations are viewed in different ways by different children, entering response topographies of the children vary in substantial but unindexed ways, etc. In essence, there must be a better method for doing research on developmental processes of retarded children.

Another model that must be considered is the individual subject approach used in much of the research covered by the experimental analysis of behavior. In retardation, much of the single subject research is done in terms of a behavior modification strategy. The method used is to find a set of discriminative and reinforcing stimuli with which the behavior of the child can be brought under experimental control and then manipulated in various ways in order to clearly indicate the functional relationships between the independent variables and the selected dependent variable. The selected response may be first increased in rate of occurrence, then decreased, and finally increased to the desired level—which is called the reversal design. An alternative method, called multiple baseline, involves the selection of several response classes, which are recorded together and after sufficient baseline, one member of the set is altered (at least an attempt is made), and, if change occurs only in this one, the functional relationship is established. A second response is then selected, and attempts are made to alter its frequency, again with the remaining responses used as a control set. The procedure is repeated until all members of the selected set have been modified in the predicted direction. One of the problems often encountered in this research is that extrinsic reinforcement systems are used as part of the functional relationship, but when transfer is made to less arbitrary reinforcers, the responses extinguish (cf. Lovaas, 1968). The strong inference model would build on many of the strengths of the single subject procedures but would hopefully extend the benefits of the manipulations into more typical (less laboratory-like) environments. The need to do this has been indicated by Ferster (1972). Another problem with behavior modification procedures is that they are easily applied when the responses to be modified are in the repertoire of the child, as in the case of an undesirable form of behavior that is to be decelerated or in the case of a form of behavior, such as solving arithmetic problems, that may exist but has an extremely low rate of occurrence. When complex shaping procedures are used, any single subject design becomes extremely difficult to apply, for reasons described previously by Bricker (1970).

The strong inference approach deals with many of the problems associated with both the hypothesis-testing group design methods and the behavior modification single-subject designs. First, the screening instrument provides a general locator system for placing the child in some area of developmental progression in each of the structures involved in the system (visual tracking, object permanence, use of tools, physical causality, organization of space and time, functional use and classification of objects, seriation, and foresight). The child is then assessed in the various areas, using modification of Piaget's *methodologie clinique* (Piaget, 1967) to determine more precisely how each child functions in various alternatives of the problem domain. The recorded observations taken during this systematically varied *methodology* provide the basis for generating all possible and reasonable explanations of the child's behavior (the what, when, where, why, and how of the child's response system). As these are tested (through additional manipulations of relevant materials and events), particular explanations will become increasingly more plausable and can be even more specifically evaluated. As the procedure is repeated across domains for a given child, there may be only a very few explanations that are necessary to account for his successes and failures. These explanations will generally refer to problems in certain prerequisite behavior systems. The analysis will also provide information about the child's intrinsic reinforcement system and about the forms of environmental stimulus control that are operative in determining the specifics of the child's behavior. This information can then be used to generate instructional plans that can be used to stimulate development in the defined areas. Failures of the plan to work would generate multiple alternative explanations that would then be tested systematically. The resulting data from both the assessment phase and the instruction phase would be pooled as a systematic case study in human development.

As the system is used across children, the replications of findings in particular domains and at various levels within a domain would be analyzed and used to determine the generalization possibilities of information coming from the individual case studies. The system then combines methodologies, including observational methods, *methodologie clinique*, and experimental manipulations. Explanations must be disprovable before they can be included, and all terms used in the system to describe the child's behavior must be operational, in that they involve processes and events that are observable by two or more people. Because explanations are inferential in nature, the proof or disproof of a particular explanation must be based on logical analyses of empirically established probabilities.

If all measures were reliable, both in terms of inter-rater agreement and on a test-retest basis, then the results could be combined and analyzed using standard statistical procedures, including analysis of variance and multivariate analysis. If several of these investigations were videotaped, various types of sequential analyses could be made from the data. However, statistical evaluations of the data are secondary to the clear demonstration that the behavior of the students has changed significantly and that the change can be attributed to the activities of teachers or parents.

There is another issue here and that involves the content of research. What should be researched in the area of severe and profound handicaps? Obviously, the research should be in the basic processes of movement, initial social development, beginning language, and other processes that form the important prerequisites for subsequent complex forms of human behavior. However, much of this research can be theory-based, in that a system for training is based on a prior conception of what the child is learning and why what is learned will generalize. The present author has taken one example of an area that is in need of research and has attempted to indicate how research in concept acquisition would be based on a theoretical formulation.

RESEARCH ON THE ACQUISITION OF CONCEPTS

One of the most crucial areas of research that needs to be quickly moved forward is in the area of concept acquisition. In this area, there is a need to find a new method for defining and training concepts. This section of this chapter is used only to spell out the problems involved in concept acquisition and to structure a rather hazy picture of a workable alternative. The definition of a concept requires at least the following features: 1) only a limited number of specific exemplars of a particular concept must be explicitly taught before a child can generalize to an almost limitless number of un-trained members of the class; 2) the class must have a hierarchical relationship with both subordinate and superordinate classes when this is logically possible; 3) any class can have specific members that are simultaneously members of other classes, and they can be so assigned by the child; and, most importantly, 4) the child will respond to particulars as members of classes in the areas of phonol-ogy, objects, actions, object properties, people, and other animals, and plants, space, and time. This is no small achievement and one that is most in need of research.

The problem is so complex that more than a couple of para-graphs are used to describe it. A relatively recent article by Weimer (1973) enunciates the problem dramatically. Basing his scholarly discussion on two of Plato's paradoxes as represented in the *Meno*, Weimer concludes that knowledge of abstract entities (con-cepts) and the ability for "productive" or "creative" behavior must be innate. In reference to abstract entities, Weimer indicates the impossibility of recognizing a member of a concept class unless one has prior knowledge of the concept itself. As he states:

Factual relativity guarantees that one cannot simply go out into the world and neutrally collect facts. Without a prior conceptual framework, that is, a point of view from which to impose order upon reality, there is only the changing phenomenal flux of experience, the 'blooming, buzzing confusion' of William James. The data of sensation do not come with little tags attach-ed proclaiming their factual status. Observation is not merely focusing one's attention on the data, but rather assimilation of data into the conceptual scheme of the observer (p.20).

This leads to a restatement of Plato's paradox, namely: "We cannot learn (come to know) anything unless we already know (have learned) it." Weimer then turns to linguistic theory to supply the basis for the second paradox, which involves creative production. In Chomsky's linguistic position, a theory of language must provide a suitable explanation of the novel but appropriate use of language. This involves "... the speaker's ability to produce new sentences, sentences that are immediately understood by other speakers although they bear no physical resemblance to sentences which are 'familiar'" (Chomsky, 1966, p. 11). The second paradox derives from this point and asks the question: "... how can one exhibit knowledge for which one's prior learning history has given no preparation?" (Weimer, 1973, p. 25).

Weimer presents several attempted solutions to these paradoxes, including Aristotle's doctrines of nominalism and associationism. On the basis of his evaluation of both the data and the logic that are dependent on the principles of associationism (virtually every learning theory uses them) he feels that they are inadequate in accounting for complex human behavior. Weimer concludes the article by urging a return to the basics of Plato's thinking and proceeding from that point with clear recognition of innate abstract entities.

Before directing a response to Weimer's article, a recitation of the attempts at concept training are instructive. This training has two major paths. One approach to concept acquisition has been through the domain of receptive language training, often beginning with a two-choice paradigm initiated by Harlow (1949) under the heading of learning set. Many of the investigations were oriented toward producing a learning set among retarded children (Zeaman and House, 1963). If a child was able to discriminate on the basis of a single trial, then he was considered to "have" learning set. For example, a pair of objects was presented on a tray, and under one of the objects a small toy or piece of candy was hidden, so that if the child chose correctly he would receive the "reward," and, if not, he would receive nothing. This was repeated until the child systematically selected the rewarded item. Then he was given another problem and yet another until he was able to take the data from the first trial of a new problem and either shift the choice to other objects if he was wrong or continue to select the item if correct on the first trial. In this way, a child who had learned a learning set would always be correct on the second and all subsequent trials of a problem. Given this skill, the present writer and his colleagues (Bricker and Bricker, 1969; Bricker et al., 1969; Bricker, 1972; Bricker, Vincent-Smith, and Bricker, 1973) developed a paradigm in which the reinforced object was named just prior to the child's choice. The strategy was to shift control of the choice from the rewarding consequence to the naming antecedent event, which would mean that the child was responding to the name of the object. For reasons that will be mentioned later, none of the various procedures was successful in generating concept-like responding to object names.

Examples of stimulus control of the type described above have been demonstrated very clearly with retarded people. Sidman and Stoddard (1967) performed a classic experiment with an adult who was classified as severely retarded. Using a nine-choice system that surrounded a center panel, they taught this adult to always select an ellipse and never to select a circle. Then, through a careful sequence of fading and changing the stimuli, they taught this individual to select the circle instead. The entire procedure was done with extremely few errors on the part of the individual. Touchette (1968) followed this experiment with a clear example of how stimulus control could be demonstrated, so that, through delayed onset of the prompting stimulus, one could ascertain the point at which control shifted from the prompting stimulus to the desired stimulus. This was not a vacuous exercise, as is demonstrated subsequently, and it is an excellent example of behavioral research that is basic and experimental in design but that can be used in some important ways by the applied researcher. The clear fact is that concept training must depend on a form of stimulus control training, but in a somewhat different manner, as is indicated subsequently.

The second approach to training concepts was to use motor and then verbal imitation training until the handicapped child was able to imitate the names of various objects, actions, and people. Then name training was initiated using the echoic stimulus as a prompt in getting the correct name in the presence of the selected object (Lovaas, 1968; Guess, Sailor, and Baer, 1974; Bricker and Bricker, 1970). This approach emphasized the expressive aspect of language, although, as in the receptive mode, the investigations were examples of basic, experimental, behavioral approaches to language. However, Guess (1975) has recently reported on a two-year training program with a Down's syndrome adolescent in which he was able to take the boy from a completely mute state to one in which the boy was using conversational language.

These are a few of the pieces from which a new research direction in concept training must be constructed. The essential features of a new system would be the recognition that concepts are not mental abstractions, but rather arbitrary sets of attributes of objects and events that must become controlling stimuli for children who are learning these concepts. The child does not approach instruction in concept acquisition *de novo*; he has had at least a couple of years of sensorimotor experience that lays the groundwork for concepts (Sinclair-de-Zwart, 1969; Bricker and

Bricker, 1974). The child has preferences among objects as well as a flexible system for classifying objects according to particular functions that they serve. The child has also categorized people before the acquisition of his first formal concepts, as well as having categorized space, a rough definition of time, and a basic notion of cause and effect in a concrete sense. The term "intentional" can now be used to describe the child's behavior. The child gives definite signals of wanting particular foods, drinks, games, and events, such as going out in the car or to the park. As Premack and Premack (1974) have indicated, the child has a communication process before he has language or before he has acquired concepts, and this preverbal communication process sets the basis for concept learning. This formulation also establishes the basis for a critical research frontier that can now be broached experimentally.

The important feature is that the child attempts to communicate to a listener. The communication is probably based on some state of relative deprivation that, when analyzed, becomes the basis for defining an intention, and under which the child can clearly signal when the outcome in terms of what he gets from his attempted communication matches the source of the deprivation state. Skinner (1957) has termed this state of affairs the "mand" situation, in that the child attempts to specify his own reinforcement. Two factors come into play in this situation. The first is the feedback from the environment in terms of matching the child's communicated message. If the child stands by the kitchen counter pointing at the cookie jar and saying something equivalent to "da"..."da," then the listener could reasonably infer that the child want a cookie. Consequently, the listener could provide an echoic stimulus—"Say cookie!" —which the child would have to approximate before receiving a cookie. The second is to provide a counter-example that contrasts with the class cookie. Here, the wise parent might turn to crackers as the more healthful of the two and provide a cracker instead of a cookie to the child, which provides the starting point for a very interesting language game. Assume that the parent is consistent, in that there are some times during the day when the child signals the desire for a snack and the parent gives him a cracker. In addition, if the parent uses different verbal signals from the child as the basis of the two possible outcomes, the child will learn that salty round (or square) things are called crackers while the sweet versions are called cookies and that the use of these two terms operates successfully depending on the time of day or the time before the next meal.

With contrasts like those between coke and milk, swinging and having a book read, riding in a car and having a parent play ball, and all of the almost innumerable contrasts that we force on the child's various deprivation states, we can begin to fathom how the child begins to learn the arbitrary structure of conceptual classes of objects and events. In all of the above cases, the contrasts were drawn because parents tend to take the line of least effort in satisfying a child, but they will, on relatively fewer occasions, grant the more desirable of the options. This is a far different paradigm than one that depends on pointing to a named picture or naming an object that the parent holds in her hand. However, within this model we have the basis of successful language training because it depends on functional reinforcement that will sustain across situations (Ferster, 1972).

At this point, there is a need to return to Weimer's position as it was outlined above. An object like an apple or a cookie is something that the typical child will voluntarily select under minimal conditions of hunger. However, apples and cookies differ from instance to instance in terms of such factors as size, texture, color, degree of sweetness, temperature, and location, and in other ways that are not relevant to the concepts of either apple or cookie. How does a child come to put these items into classes when there are relatively few ways that they are the same and so many ways that particular members of a class are different? One primary hypothesis is that the parents have the concepts (which they learned from their parents, etc.) which they use to constrain the verbal requests of the child until the child comes under the control of the set of relevant properties. To speculate further, the child already classifies major object groups, such as animals, fruit, juices, pops, candy, and vehicles, as well as object properties, such as colors, sizes, and textures, and such actions as walking, running, climbing, riding, and throwing, before he learns the names for any of these. The classifications are functional, rather than linguistic, in terms of what the child likes to do and what he needs in order to do it. Consequently, he has already formed groupments, which are not true concepts (Piaget, 1970). When the child is required to name objects, he is under the control of the larger, rather than the smaller, groupments, in that all forms of fruit might be called apple, just as all animals might be called doggie. Here is where the parents function in terms of constraining the behavior of the child in order to differentiate the various types of fruit or the various types of animals. Through various forms of corrections, imitated responses, and differential consequation, the parents help the child form subcategories. Within this form of learning, the child has no prior knowledge of the classes but rather learns them from the parents.

This is only the beginning of a relatively complex set of assumptions concerning the acquisition of concepts by children and how such concepts can be taught to handicapped children. However, some of the important points within this system that apply to education of the handicapped have been made, although each needs subsequent research confirmation. The first point is that particular forms of training, such as self-help, language, or functional arithmetic, do not begin in a vacuum. Each has prerequisite forms of behavior. In concept acquisition, the child needs prior exposure to a range of different environments and different members of various groupments in order to have the basis for using verbal concepts. This exposure is more readily available at home than in an institution, especially with parents who understand the acquisition process as well as the prerequisites. Concepts are more easily understood when they are defined in terms of stimulus control—for example, the concept "cup" is controlled by opaque cylinders that hold fluids and generally (but not always) have handles. Cups tend to be used with hot fluid, while glasses tend to be used with cold ones. By operationalizing stimulus control in this way, a teacher or parent can determine if the child is under the control of relevant properties of an object class or remains somewhat under the control of irrelevant properties. Determining this is simply an extension of Piaget's notion of the *methodologie clinique* described above. A second important point is that each instance of concept training should be adapted to the child's current motivational system (deprivation states) so that each child learns functions without the use of contrived systems of reinforcement. Finally, as Brown has indicated, the concepts to be emphasized should be those that best fulfill the criteria of ultimate function.

REFERENCES

Baer, D. M., Wolf, M. M., and Risley, T. R. 1968. Some current dimensions of applied behavior analysis. J. Appl. Behav. Anal. 1:91–97.

Barker, R. G., and Schoggen, P. 1973. Qualities of Community Life. Jossey-Bass, Inc., San Francisco.

Barker, R. G., and Wright, H. F. 1955. Midwest and Its Children. Harper and Row, New York. (Reprinted by Archon Books, Hamden, Conn., 1971.)

Baumeister, A. A. 1970. The American residential institution: Its history and character. In: A. A. Baumeister and E. Butterfield (eds.), Residential Facilities for the Mentally Retarded. Aldine Publishing Co., Chicago.

Bayley, N. 1969. Bayley Scales of Infant Development. Psychological Corporation, New York.

Belmont, J. M., and Butterfield, E. C. 1971. What the development of short-term memory is. Hum. Dev. 14:236–248.

Bijou, S. W. 1963. Theory and research in mental (developmental) retardation. Psychol. Record 13:95–110.

Bricker, D. D., and Bricker, W. A. 1969. A programmed approach to operant audiometry for low-functioning children. J. Speech Hear. Disord. 34:312–320.

Bricker, D. D., and Bricker, W. A. 1973. Infant toddler and preschool research and intervention project report: Year III. IMRID Behavioral Science Monograph No. 23. Institute on Mental Retardation and Intellectual Development, George Peabody College, Nashville, Tenn.

Bricker, D. D., Vincent-Smith, L., and Bricker, W. A. 1973. Receptive vocabulary: Performances and selection strategies of delayed and nondelayed toddlers. Amer. J. Ment. Defic. 77:579–584.

Bricker, W. A. 1970. Identifying and modifying behavioral deficits. Amer. J. Ment. Defic. 75:16–21.

Bricker, W. A. 1972. A systematic approach to language training. In: R. L. Schiefelbusch (ed.), Language of the Mentally Retarded. University Park Press, Baltimore.

Bricker, W. A., and Bricker, D. D. 1970. A program of language training for the severely language handicapped child. Except. Child. 37:101–111.

Bricker, W. A., and Bricker, D. D. 1974. An early language training strategy. In: R. L. Schiefelbusch and L. L. Lloyd (eds.), Language Perspectives—Acquisition, Retardation, and Intervention. University Park Press, Baltimore.

Bricker, W. A., Heal, L. W., Bricker, D. D., Hayes, W. A., and Larsen, L. A. 1969. Discrimination learning and learning set with institutionalized retarded children. Amer. J. Ment. Defic. 74:242–248.

Brown, Roger. 1973. A First Language: The Early Stages. Harvard University Press, Cambridge, Mass.

Brown, R., and Hanlon, C. 1970. Derivational complexity and order of acquisition in child speech. In: J. R. Hayes (ed.), Cognition and the Development of Language. John Wiley, New York.

Bruner, J. S. 1975. The objectives of developmental psychology. Paper delivered during acceptance of G. Stanley Hall Medal to American Psychological Association, Sept. 2.

Call, R. J., and Switzky, H. N. 1975. Effects of auditory and pictorial-auditory stimulus enrichment on the verbal abstracting abilities of low-SES children. Amer. J. Ment. Defic. 80:256–265.

Chomsky, N. 1966. Cartesian Linguistics. Harper & Row, New York.

Eimas, P. D. 1974. Linguistic processing of speech by young infants. In: R. L. Schiefelbusch and L. L. Lloyd (eds.), Language Perspectives—Acquisition, Retardation, and Intervention, pp. 55–73. University Park Press, Baltimore.

Ellis, N. R. 1971. International Review of Research in Mental Retardation, Vol. 5. Academic Press, New York.

Escalona, S. K., and Corman, H. H. 1966. Albert Einstein Scales of Sensorimotor Development. Unpublished manuscript, Albert Einstein College of Medicine.

Ferster, C. B. 1972. Clinical reinforcement. Seminars in Psychiatry, 4:101–111.

Gesell, A., and Amatruda, C. S. 1949. Gesell Developmental Schedules. Psychological Corporation, New York.

Guess, D. 1975. Current dimensions in the development of communication skills in the severely handicapped. Paper delivered to American Association for the Education of the Severely/Profoundly Handicapped, Kansas City, Missouri.

Guess, D., Sailor, W., and Baer, D. 1974. To teach language to retarded children. In: R. L. Schiefelbusch and L. L. Lloyd (eds.), Language Perspectives—Acquisition, Retardation, and Intervention. University Park Press, Baltimore.

Harlow, H. F. 1949. The formation of learning sets. Psychol. Rev. 56:51–65.

Hobbs, N. 1975. The Futures of Children. Jossey-Bass, Inc., San Francisco.

Lovaas, O. I. 1968. A program for the establishment of speech in psychotic children. In: H. Sloane and B. MacAulay (eds.), Operant Procedures in Remedial Speech and Language Training. Houghton Mifflin, Boston.

Miller, J. O. 1970. Cultural deprivation and its modification: effect of intervention. In: H. C. Haywood (ed.). Social-Cultural Aspects of Mental Retardation. Appleton-Century-Crofts, New York.

Orlando, R., and Tyler, R. M. 1966. Experimental analysis of reinforcer hierarchies in developmental retardates: baseline stabilization. Institute on Mental Retardation and Intellectual Development. Papers and Reports 3:3.

Piaget, J. 1967. Six Psychological Studies. Random House, New York.

Piaget, J. 1970. Piaget's theory. In: P. H. Mussen (ed.), Carmichael's Manual of Child Psychology, Vol. 1. John Wiley & Sons, Inc., New York.

Platt, J. R. 1964. Strong inference. Science 146:3642.

Premack, D., and Premack, A. J. 1974. Teaching visual language to apes and language-deficient people. In: R. L. Schiefelbusch and L. L. Lloyd (eds.), Language Perspectives—Acquisition, Retardation, and Intervention. University Park Press, Baltimore.

Robinson, C. C. 1972. Analysis of stage four and five object permanence concept as a discriminated operant. Unpublished doctoral dissertation, George Peabody College, Nashville.

Robinson, C. C., and Filler, J. W., Jr. 1972. A parent teaching style assessment scale. Paper presented at the American Association on Mental Deficiency, Minneapolis, May.

Schlesinger, I. M. 1974. Relational concepts underlying language. In: R. L. Schiefelbusch and L. L. Lloyd (eds.), Language Perspectives—Acquisition, Retardation, and Intervention. University Park Press, Baltimore.

Sidman, M. 1960. Tactics of Scientific Research. Basic Books, New York.

Sidman, M., and Stoddard, L. 1967. The effectiveness of fading in programming a simultaneous form discrimination for retarded children. J. Exper. Anal. Behav. 10:3–15.

Sinclair-de-zwart, H. 1969. Developmental psycholinguistics. In: D. Elkind and J. Flavell (eds.), Studies in Cognitive Development. Oxford University Press, New York.

Skinner, B. F. 1957. Verbal Behavior. Appleton-Century-Crofts, New York.

Skinner, B. F. 1959. Cumulative Record. Appleton-Century-Crofts, New York.

Touchette, P. E. 1968. The effects of a graduated stimulus change on the acquisition of a simple discrimination in severely retarded boys. J. Exper. Anal. Behav. 11:39–48.

Uzgiris, I. C., and Hunt, J. McV. 1966. An instrument for assessing infant psychological development. Unpublished manuscript, University of Illinois.

Weimer, W. B. 1973. Psycholinguistics and Plato's paradoxes of the *Meno*. Amer. Psychol. 28:15–33.

Williams, W., and Coyne, P., et. al. 1970. A rudimentary developmental math skill sequence for "severely handicapped" students. A privately published paper. Madison, Wisconsin.

Zeaman, D., and House, B. J. 1963. The role of attention in retardate discrimination learning. In: N. R. Ellis (ed.), Handbook of Mental Deficiency, pp. 159–223. McGraw-Hill, New York.

FIRST LANGUAGE ACQUISITION PROGRAMMING FOR THE DEVELOPMENTALLY DISABLED

Louise R. Kent

The major emerging trend in language training for developmentally disabled children is the increase in the utilization of paraprofessional language trainers. Although the primary language assessment and prescriptive programming usually is done by a language professional, the actual day-to-day training is more and more likely to be entrusted to a parent, teacher aide, or other paraprofessional, with the language professional acting as a consultant. Such a strategy necessitates the availability of clear, simple, effective language training programs that are adaptable to individual needs and that possess built-in accountability.

The following comments describe some factors to be considered in the construction of language programs and propose some safeguards designed to ensure their effective execution. From the many factors that might be considered in the construction of language programs, the following have been chosen for comment: 1) the population to be served, 2) the skills to be taught, 3) the procedures to be used, and 4) the data to be collected.

SOME PROCEDURAL SAFEGUARDS

*The population to be served by the program must be clearly de-
scribed in terms of the entry-level skills that the children are expected to have.* In other words, what are the program's prerequisites?
What are the sensory prerequisites with respect to the vision and
hearing of the population to be served? What are the motoric
prerequisites with respect to balance and coordination? What are the
social prerequisites with respect to attending and affective responses
to other persons? And, what are the prerequisite language skills,
receptive and expressive?

*The skills to be taught by the program must be specified, and
the order in which they are to be taught must be specified.* The
specification of the behaviors to be learned is usually not as difficult
as the specification of the order in which the behaviors to be learned
are to be taught. There are multiple problems in sequencing the
content of a language program. First to be faced is the basic issue of
whether or not training in receptive skills should precede training in
expressive skills. The next dilemma is the apparent non-linearity of
the course of language acquisition. The literature that exists on
normal children acquiring language suggests that some skills are
acquired concurrently with others, although their prerequisites may
be different! Such a situation indicates the need for a complexly
branched program. The problem is in finding the desired information that is available with respect to sequencing and, when lacking,
how to obtain it or to proceed without it. There is a literature from
which quantities of information may be extracted with respect to the
issues of sequencing; however, this literature is spread across multiple
journals and texts of developmental psycholinguistics, psychology,
special education, and speech pathology, and it is expanding rapidly.
Even if one were knowledgeable about all that this literature contains
and were capable of synthesizing it, there would still remain gaps
and areas of controversy leaving the programmer without the answers
to certain questions of sequencing. The programmer is forced to
make some decisions about sequencing that are based only on inferences that he draws from the available information. After these
decisions have been operationalized into sequences of behaviors to be
learned and after data are available from the children subjected to
these decisions of sequencing, the sequences can be revised; however,
in the beginning the programmer must be willing to make some
decisions that are based only on inferences. Nevertheless, the process
of program construction is self-correcting. New findings reported in

the literature and results of analysis of data obtained from execution can be used to revise, refine, improve, and extend the sequencing of the content of language acquisition programs.

The programmer should be aware of each sequential decision that he makes, and he should be able to defend each decision on some identifiable basis. To fail to recognize that a decision has been made is a serious error because the basis for an unrecognized decision will remain unquestioned, untested, and unsupported. Decisions made on the basis of authoritarianism are particularly difficult to recognize; therefore, the programmer should be especially alert to the possible influence of authoritarianism on his decisions. One example of authoritarianism is the notion that training on specific receptive language skills should always precede training on their expressive counterparts.

Developmental data suggest that specific receptive skills *are* learned before their expressive counterparts. Some programmers conclude from these data that receptive skills should be taught *before* their expressive counterparts. This conclusion may or may not be valid. The programmer should recognize that the order of language acquisition reflected by the normal child as he learns the language on his own in a haphazard manner may not be the most efficient order. Attempts to accelerate language acquisition by sequencing content on bases other than developmental order alone have been made in the past and continue to be made. If research supports a teaching order that is different from the order that is viewed as the correct developmental one, the programmer should consider the indicated sequential revisions, even though the resulting sequence would be at variance with developmental order. It is possible that a programmer might design a sequence that would be more efficient than the developmental sequence. The ultimate measures of the merit of the sequence are the extent to which learning is errorless, the extent to which retention is errorless, and the extent to which spontaneous functional language behavior, receptive and expressive, becomes an integrated part of the child's behavioral repertoire.

Time constraints may require that the programmer selectively exclude some content that is learned by the normal child. These sorts of programmatic decisions should be defensible on the basis of the relevancy of the content to the needs of the child. When programming for a population who have severe and multiple deficits, the programmer does not deliberately include training on a task of low functional utility unless that task is considered to be a necessary prerequisite for a task of high functional utility.

The procedures to be used in teaching the behaviors to be learned must be effective and clearly stated. The person charged with the responsibility of executing the program must be told exactly how to do it. This person has a right to expect the procedures to be understandable and possible, and he has a right to expect to be reasonably successful in teaching the behaviors to be learned, provided he faithfully executes the procedures. Ideally, procedures should be utterly unambiguous; they should be possible to perform with the population to be served; and they should be effective. Again, one source of procedures is the literature, and, again, this literature is ever-expanding. Through the literature, then, the programmer attempts to keep abreast of effective new strategies for training the population of interest, and he attempts to be alert to strategies that might be effective if adapted to his population. Other sources of procedures are his own experience with procedures that he has already operationalized and his intelligence and imagination in combination with the experience, intelligence, and imagination of his associates. When *designing* new procedures, the programmer attempts to base them on established principles of vigilance, discrimination learning, schedules of reinforcement, density of reinforcement, etc. In much the same manner as for sequencing content, procedures in programming are self-corrective, provided the programmer is responsive to the relevant literature and to the data obtained from actual use of the program.

The consequences of the misuse of the procedures must be considered. The programmer should be wary of punishment, over-correction, reversal, response-cost, and time-out. These procedures are often misused and misunderstood. Because the least damage probably is done by the misuse of positive reinforcement procedures, procedures based on positive reinforcement are preferred.

Once designed, the procedures must be edited for simplicity and clarity. The programmer should favor simple procedures over those that are more complex. The programmer should be skeptical of complex procedures because they sometimes conceal unrecognized weaknesses in the sequencing of the content; provided that the prerequisites have been correctly identified and mastered, new behaviors to be learned tend to be acquired with an ease that does not necessitate elaborate procedures. Clarity is an ideal—something to reach for. Although its attainment may be impossible, there are degrees of approximation. Only those who strive to attain clarity in writing their procedures have even the slightest chance of being understood.

Finally, the data to be collected must be defined. Requirements for data collection differ as a function of the *reason* that the data are being collected. In a clinical setting, data are required for periodic reassessments in order to demonstrate that the child is or is not receiving training appropriate to his needs and for various other ongoing accountability purposes. The periodic reassessments should demonstrate the child's mastery of the prerequisites of the program and the prerequisites of any part of the program on which he currently might be receiving training; furthermore, the assessment procedure should measure change or progress since the last assessment. On the other hand, if data are to be collected for research purposes or for the purpose of detecting weaknesses in the program, data must be taken that will allow the investigator to test statistical hypotheses, to make inferences, and to make programmatic decisions.

ADDITIONAL PRECAUTIONS

Assuming that one has a clear simple effective language training program that is adaptable to individual needs and that possesses built-in accountability, there are several precautions that, if taken, will increase the likelihood of effective execution of the program.

The training and supervision of the individuals who deliver the training directly to the child should be the responsibility of a language professional. The magnitude of this responsibility cannot be over-stated. The trainer is an extension of the professional, and the extent to which the professional is effective is largely a function of his ability and willingness to train and to supervise the trainer.

The assignment of the child to a particular program should be the responsibility of a language professional. This person should be accountable for the appropriateness of the match between the program and the child. Achievement will be enhanced to the extent that the child is clearly a member of the population that the program is designed to serve. Therefore, the professional should assess each child with respect to whether or not he meets the minimum entry prerequisites of the program: i.e., the sensory, motor, social, and linguistic prerequisites. Without adequate assessment geared to the entry-level requirements and to the range of the language skills to be taught in the program, the child may unneccessarily experience failure or fail to achieve maximally, and the child's and the trainer's time will have been abused.

After the most appropriate program has been selected for the child, *the specification of the child's entry-point into the program should be the responsibility of a language professional.* After training has been initiated, the professional should observe the trainer at work with the child at least once a month, and he should meet with the trainer at least once every two weeks to discuss problems, to review the data that he has asked the trainer to collect, to assess the child's response to programming, and to direct the trainer with respect to the training to be done for the next two weeks. The professional should not assume that the trainer is executing the program as intended. If the professional has doubts about what the trainer is doing, he should observe the trainer at work with the child more frequently and for longer periods of time, request more data from the trainer, demonstrate what should be done with the child, and/or otherwise provide additional training to the trainer. Many errors in execution can quickly be detected and corrected through direct observation and demonstration.

A language professional should be accountable *for the selection of the language mode* to be used with a particular child: oral, manual, total, Blissymbols, or whatever. Similarly, the specification of the type and amount of *amplification* to be used by the child should be the responsibility of the professional. Further, *the assignment of the child to a diad or group,* if training is to be done on other than an individual basis, should be the responsibility of the professional. And, if the program to be used has inadequate, or no, procedures for group administration, the language professional is responsible for their development.

Specification of the type of reinforcement procedures to be used with a particular child should be the responsibility of a professional. Also, the professional should be accountable for teaching the trainer how to identify the child's preferences among reinforcers. The professional should demonstrate how to deliver correctly whatever reinforcers are used. It should be made clear that reinforcers are selected on the basis of the child's preferences and not the trainer's. In addition, it should be made clear that preferences may change, even within a single training session!

The language professional should be accountable for the *record-keeping* and for the *specification of the data to be collected.* The professional may request that the trainer collect certain minimal data required for accountability and for tracking the child's response to programming; nevertheless, it is the professional who is accountable for seeing that appropriate records are being kept. The language professional himself should be responsible personally for recording the child's response to programming at least once a month, for routinely reassessing the appropriateness of his treatment plan every six months, and for revising his treatment plan whenever needed to be consistent with his current needs and response to programming.

If the professional asks the trainer to collect data for the purpose of detecting weaknesses in the program, he should avoid the tendency to over-collect this type of data. The over-collection practice can be minimized by adherance to the following rules:

1. Only experienced trainers who have demonstrated that they execute the program as written should be asked to collect this type of data.
2. Only data that are addressed to some specific question should be collected.
3. Only data that, once collected, can be analyzed promptly should be collected.

SOME PREVIOUS MISTAKES

A few personal examples of situations that have led to these comments and words of caution and advice may be helpful. These examples are actually anecdotes of mistakes that this writer has made. The errors have been illuminated both through the self-correcting process described above and through the process of discovering bits of relevant information in the literature.

When first beginning to teach a receptive naming vocabulary for common objects, it is counter-productive to attempt to build a vocabulary of more than seven or eight items in a category. With even such a small number of object names it is possible to teach quite a lot of language. What happens if you try to continue to expand the object name vocabulary? In my experience, what happens is that, after mastering seven or eight items, the child will begin to confuse any new items introduced with items in the corpus of old ones. This confusion can expand until it includes most of the old items. In other words, the error rate increases as too many new items are introduced. The child reacts emotionally; he may cry, object to the training session in various ways, refuse to respond to requests, etc. The combination of the increase in error rate and the emotional behavior of the child suggests that the trainer has induced some kind of clinical neurosis by attempting to teach the child to make discriminations that the child is unable, at that point, to learn to make given the procedures that the trainer has been using. The solution is to teach small clusters of vocabulary items, five or six in a category, and to allow these items to be over-learned by using the same items in a variety of language contexts. For example, once the object names are learned, the child can be taught to respond appropriately to commands that include the object names but occasion the child's placing the objects in different locations, such as "in the box" or "on the floor." Happily, as language training progresses this problem seems to disappear, so that large numbers of naming items are eventually mastered, without an inordinate increase in error rate on other items, and without emotionality.

Another error that I made at one time was to assume that, once I had taught a child to correctly point to several objects when named, I could expect to teach the child to deny incorrect object names. Let's say that the child has learned to give me a shoe when I say, "Give me the shoe," when the shoe is visible along with, perhaps, a hat and a key. Having accomplished this, I thought I could easily teach the child to say, "No," or to shake his head when I picked up the shoe and said, "Is this a key?" No such luck. Typically, the child just sits there at first; then, he is apt to offer you the shoe. This procedure was such a disastrous failure that it was quickly abandoned without replacement. It was quite a few months later that I read for the first time Ursulla Bellugi's (1967) doctoral dissertation on the acquisition of negation. Here she points out, among other things, that the denial form of negation is the last of the three elementary forms of negation to be learned. First the child learns to recognize the absence of previously present items; this usually takes the form of "All gone" or "All gone + Noun." Next the child learns to reject items or events; this may take the form of throwing the rejected item, shoving it away, or by physically resisting participation in rejected events, such as baths or bedtimes, or by coming indoors or relinquishing a toy. Much later, the child learns the denial form of negation. The solution to this problem is to defer efforts to teach denial until the two less advanced forms of negation have been taught. This is not to say that denial cannot be taught. There may be a procedure that will teach it flawlessly. What I am saying is that: 1) there is no crucial need to teach negation in an order that violates developmental sequencing, and 2) perhaps the training time can be better spent teaching the child language forms for which he already possesses the linguistic and cognitive prerequisites. This is a pretty good example of the sort of situation that can lead the programmer to develop elaborate procedures and instrumentation to teach a bit of language for which the child simply has not been taught the prerequisites.

At some undetermined time, exactly when I've not had the leisure or thought it important enough to discover, some authority of tremendous influence put forth the notion that something akin to the acquisition of a generalized motor imitative repertoire is a prerequisite for language learning. When I first heard of this idea, I did briefly consider the obvious contradiction that there are a lot of severely motorically handicapped individuals who experience little if any delay in language learning. Casting logic to the wind, however, I began to program as though the authority were unquestionably correct. Further inspiration was obtained from the efficient teaching procedures that had been described by Baer and Sherman (1964). Later, it occurred to me, and I think to William Bricker at about the same time, that we weren't having such an easy time teaching generalized motor imitation, and we both were somewhat seduced by this problem. Now we had two independent language workers attempting to sequence the acquisition of generalized motor imitation. A lot of time and data and students went into this effort before I decided that I didn't need a generalized motor imitative repertoire. I just needed a few basic motor responses which usually weren't that difficult to teach to the degree of precision that was needed to differentiate them from random motor activity! The point is that this is an example of how the forces of authoritarianism wield their influences.

One final example of the failure of "arm chairing" to predict the sequence of language learning: Once again, imagine having taught a child to correctly give you, upon request, several objects in the presence of other "known" objects; i.e., in the presence of the key, hat, and shoe, the child will offer you the shoe when you say "Give me the shoe." Now, searching for a language activity that would extend this skill just a bit further, I conceived of the idea of asking the child to give me *two* objects: "Give me the shoe and the key." Simple. No. Some children were able to respond correctly to this command; they apparently had mastered or possessed some as yet unrecognized prerequisite. Other children were unable to respond correctly. Typically, in the presence of only three objects, they would fail to achieve a better than chance correct performance. Usually, they would offer me two items—first one and then the other. Differential reinforcement for two correct objects has not proved to be sufficient to teach this task, which would appear to be so simple. Many hours of pondering the work of Estes (1970) and three M.A. theses later, I remain fascinated by this problem. The solution, so far as programming language acquisition goes, is 1) to defer this type of training activity until the child has acquired some type of expressive repertoire that would avail him of a rehearsal strategy, and 2) to increase the amount of training devoted to teaching the child to discriminate among the relevant stimulus dimensions of the objects and to attend to the discrimination task, without prompts, for two to three minutes.

These examples, while not endless, could go on for quite a while. Perhaps they will serve to exemplify some of the fascination of unraveling the sequencing of language acquisition and some of the challenges of trying to work scientifically in an applied arena.

REFERENCES

Baer, D. M., and Sherman, J. A. 1964. Reinforcement control of generalized imitation in young children. J. Exp. Child Psychol. 1:37–49.

Bellugi, U. 1967. The acquisition of negation in children's speech. Doctoral dissertation, Harvard University.

Estes, W. K. 1970. Learning Theory and Mental Development. Academic Press, New York.

INDEX